# FAMILY
## LITERACY
### Connections in Schools and Communities

**Lesley Mandel Morrow**

*Rutgers University*

New Brunswick, New Jersey

Editor

The International Reading Association attempts, through its publications, to provide a forum for a wide spectrum of opinions on reading. This policy permits divergent viewpoints without assuming the endorsement of the Association.

**Director of Publications**   Joan M. Irwin
**Managing Editor**   Anne Fullerton
**Associate Editor**   Christian A. Kempers
**Assistant Editor**   Amy L. Trefsger Miles
**Editorial Assistant**   Janet Parrack
**Production Department Manager**   Iona Sauscermen
**Graphic Design Coordinator**   Boni Nash
**Design Consultant**   Larry Husfelt
**Desktop Publishing Supervisor**   Wendy Mazur
**Desktop Publishing**   Anette Schütz-Ruff
                          Cheryl Strum
**Proofing**   David Roberts

### Library of Congress Cataloging in Publication Data

Family literacy connections in schools and communities/Lesley Mandel Morrow, editor.
    p.    cm.
    Includes bibliographical references and indexes.
    1. Literacy—United States.    2. Family literacy programs—United States.
3. Reading—Parent participation—United States.    I. Morrow, Lesley Mandel.
LC151.L525    1995    94-43139
302.2'244—dc20    CIP
ISBN 0-87207-127-8

Photo credits: CLEO Freelance Photo, cover, p. 218; The Barbara Bush Foundation for Family Literacy, pp. viii, 190; Skjold Photographs, p. 28; Boston University Photo Services, p. 40; Cynthia Lake, p. 93; Lou Coopey, p. 117; Craig Blankenhorn (courtesy Children's Television Workshop), p. 202; Laima Druskis, pp. 2, 215; Rick Reinhard (©Reading Is Fundamental, Inc. Used with permission), pp. 137, 148, 229.

# Contents

## Organization-Sponsored Programs

*This book is dedicated to my family, Stephanie and Frank;
to the families of the authors; and to the families of the International
Reading Association community.*

# Foreword by Barbara Bush

## former First Lady of the United States

Ever since the creation of The Barbara Bush Foundation for Family Literacy in 1989, people have been asking me questions about the focus we chose: What *is* family literacy? How does it work? What can we do to support it? And why is it different from just plain *literacy*? So, I was delighted to learn that the International Reading Association would be publishing this comprehensive volume of family literacy programs and practices, put together by Lesley Mandel Morrow and IRA's Family Literacy Commission and written by other experts, to answer the questions and spread the word about the truly exciting developments in family literacy.

Literacy has been my number one "cause" for quite a while now. Back in 1978, I had put some hard thought into what my focus as first lady might be and realized that many of the problems I worried about—crime, homelessness, teenage pregnancy, hunger, and disease—would certainly be diminished if people had the literacy skills they need to help them accomplish their goals and realize their dreams. Unfortunately, there are currently far too many adults (tens of millions according to the National Adult Literacy Survey released by the U.S. Department of Education in September 1993) who do not read, write, and comprehend well enough to participate fully in our wonderful democracy. I believe that these disturbing statistics are directly linked to the fact that there are also far too many children who do not start school "ready to learn," as the first of U.S. National Education Goals recommends. After all, the adults in this survey are the parents of our nation's children.

Also, as someone for whom reading has always been a tremendous source of joy, entertainment, information, and sometimes just plain escape, I agree wholeheartedly with Benjamin Franklin who was once asked what condition of man he thought deserved the most pity. He answered almost immediately: "A lonesome man on a rainy day who does not know how to read." The joy and all the economic and spiritual benefits of reading should be part of everyone's life, and the family is the place it all begins!

Common sense tells us and the experts agree: the home is the child's first school and the parent (or adult who fills the role of primary caregiver) is the child's first and most important teacher. That is one of the main reasons that improving the literacy skills of adults is so critical to our future. Children who are read to and who grow up in print-rich environments learn to read more easily than those who do not.

This link between the literacy level and practices of the parent and a child's success in school seems clear; however, we all know the success stories of children whose parents lack formal literacy skills. Often literacy is *valued* in those homes, and the parent finds ways to *support* the child's educational development. Where literacy is valued, it is nurtured. That's why an important part of our mission at the Foundation is to help make literacy a value in every home. This, by the way, includes encouraging parents who can read but don't read to their children or grandchildren to start doing it—early and often!

To paraphrase one of my favorite songs, it's clear to me that family literacy is here to stay. The number of programs, the amount of legislation, and even the money available to fund family literacy programs have all increased dramatically in the past six years or so. *Family Literacy Connections in Schools and Communities* gives us all an opportunity to reflect on what we've been doing and to think about what we need to be doing in the years ahead. My congratulations to the International Reading Association, Lesley Mandel Morrow, and the Family Literacy Commission on the publication of this timely and much-needed book.

# Part One

# Perspectives on Family Literacy

Part One deals with perspectives on the varying definitions of family literacy in the United States. A lead piece by Lesley Mandel Morrow describes the origins of the Family Literacy Commission, offers a definition of the concept, and explains the types of initiatives that exist in the broad field of family literacy. Finally, Morrow outlines the organization of the book for readers.

In the next chapter, Elsa Roberts Auerbach invites teachers to explore the ideologies implicit in various approaches to family literacy. Focusing primarily on immigrant and refugee families, she examines the underlying assumptions of predominant programs that are structured to intervene in language-minority family literacy interactions and transmit school-based, mainstream literacy practices. These practices are often grounded in a deficit perspective of language-minority families. Auerbach suggests that we study the families and then prepare a model that will enable immigrant and refugee parents or other caregivers to enhance their literacy by addressing problems that arise from the social conditions they confront daily. In this model, community concerns and cultural practices inform curriculum development: family and community strengths are uncovered and built on as the basis for an empowering approach to family literacy.

# Chapter 1

# Family Literacy: New Perspectives, New Practices

### Lesley Mandel Morrow
*Rutgers University, New Brunswick, New Jersey*

In 1991 the Board of Directors of the International Reading Association formed a Family Literacy Commission to study issues and initiatives in family literacy from a broad perspective. Earlier approaches to family literacy centered primarily on parents as partners with schools in helping their children learn to read. That perspective is important, but, with vast changes in the demographics of schools and communities, family literacy needs to be approached in a comprehensive context. Specifically, the Commission was asked not only to maintain the earlier perspective, but also to focus on issues related to "environments which enable adult learners to enhance their own literacies, and at the same time provide environments which promote the literacies of their children" (Braun, 1991, p. 1).

A major goal of the Family Literacy Commission is to disseminate information that defines family literacy, explains existing programs, and describes relevant work of organizations and professional associations. The scope of that information includes both school and community programs serving infants to adults. It is hoped that such dissemination will increase general recognition of the significance of the family's crucial role in the development of literacy.

It is clear that by attending to the home when we discuss literacy development, whatever strategies we carry out in school or the community will be more successful. Family literacy should be viewed by schools and community agencies as one of *the* most important elements in literacy development. Family literacy concerns need to be treated with the same importance given to other issues such as whole language, assessment, and reading and writing connections. Schools need to view family literacy as part of the curriculum with a coordinator in charge of initiating and supervising programs. Community organizations need to exert energy in this direction as well (Morrow et al., 1993).

## Family Literacy: A Broad Perspective

As early as 1908, Huey wrote of children's learning in school: "It all begins with parents reading to children" (p. 103). Parents are the first teachers their children have, and they are the teachers that children have for the longest time. Parents or other caregivers are potentially the most important people in the education of their children. Research supports a strong link between the home environment and children's

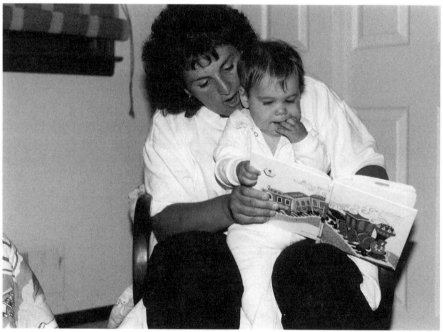

*Parents are potentially the most important people in the education of their children.*

acquisition of school-based literacy. Such practices as shared reading, reading aloud, making print materials available, and promoting positive attitudes toward literacy in the home have been found to have a significant effect on children's literacy learning (Clark, 1984; Cochran-Smith, 1984; Morrow, 1993; Teale, 1984).

However, research points out that the types and forms of literacy practiced in some homes are largely incongruent with those that children encounter in school (Auerbach, 1989; Heath, 1983; Taylor & Dorsey-Gaines, 1988). Despite the fact that literacy activity is present in one form or another in most homes, the particular kinds of events that some parents or other caregivers share with their children may have little influence on school success. Conversely, the kinds of literacy practiced in classrooms may have little meaning for those children outside school walls. It has also been suggested that there is a correlation between poverty and illiteracy. However, it is important to review all the literature thoroughly because there is evidence that many low-income, minority, and immigrant families cultivate rich (though perhaps not school-like) contexts for literacy development and that they support family literacy with exceptional effort and imagination (Auerbach, 1989).

Because of all the information available, it is essential to adopt an eclectic approach in surveying family literacy and to accept that what is to be learned will come from family members and children as well as from scholarly publications, agencies, and professionals. Family literacy must be studied from the widest possible perspective—by respecting cultures in which no books exist but storytelling, for example, is a strong part of the cultural environment, as well as reporting on cultures within which print is a dominant medium.

## Defining Family Literacy

The term "family literacy" does not have a clear definition. The complexity of the concept may keep it from ever having one definition that is embraced by all, but there are some basic tenets that can probably be agreed on. The Family Literacy Commission has published a brochure that offers these ideas as a definition.

> Family literacy encompasses the ways parents, children, and extended family members use literacy at home and in their community. Sometimes, family literacy occurs naturally during the routines of daily living and helps adults and children "get things done." These events might include using drawings or writings to share ideas; composing notes or letters to communicate messages; making lists; reading and following directions; or sharing stories and ideas through conversation, reading, and writing. Family literacy may be initiated purposefully by a parent or may occur spontaneously as parents and children

go about the business of their daily lives. Family literacy activities may also reflect the ethnic, racial, or cultural heritage of the families involved (Morrow, Paratore, & Tracey, 1994).

Family literacy activities are also initiated in response to suggestions or requests from outside institutions or organizations. These are often intended to support the acquisition and development of school-like literacy behaviors of either parents, children, or both. Tasks may include family storybook reading or the completion of specific homework assignments.

Educators have become increasingly convinced of the promise of family literacy programs in promoting successful learning experiences for children and their families. Policy makers at all levels and from various agencies have been requested to join in the effort to create and support effective family literacy programs. The emphasis placed on collaboration and partnerships in support of family literacy is evident in the number and diversity of organizations involved in implementing or investigating programs. They include adolescent, adult, and alternative education centers; churches and clergy; corporations and industries; daycare centers; public and private preschools and elementary and secondary schools; federal, state/provincial, and local governments; hospitals and health care centers; human resource agencies; immigrant and refugee agencies; libraries; migrant education programs; professional associations; prisons; private foundations; universities and colleges; and welfare agencies.

The efforts of such a variety of organizations and their potential for collaboration represent an invaluable strength in the continued study of family literacy. Only by examining many viewpoints in a field so complex and broad will we come to understand it fully.

## Goals for the Book

One of the goals of this volume is to present multiple perspectives of the varied definitions of family literacy. In addition, we hope to provide ideas for schools, community agencies, and families by presenting different types of programs to put into practice. It is not our purpose to advocate one perspective over another; rather, we are interested in disseminating information.

The book is intended for practitioners such as teachers and supervisors and administrators from preschool to college whose major interest is literacy development. It is also designed for parents, policy makers, clergy, associations, industry, and government agencies that deal with family literacy.

## Organization of the Book

As discussed in the section introduction, Part One of this volume is intended to give readers more in-depth explanation of the concept of family literacy. The wide range of perspectives on this issue is evident in the types of programs and initiatives that have been labeled or described in professional literature as "family literacy." In Part Two the authors discuss some of these practices and initiatives. Many of them have similar goals; some will appeal to teachers, and some to agencies. We have grouped the chapters to reflect programs operating in the schools and organization-sponsored programs such as those funded by The Barbara Bush Foundation for Family Literacy and Reading Is Fundamental. Within this section, the programs described can be categorized as either parent involvement or intergenerational initiatives.

The remaining chapters in Part Three, "Developing New Practices: Research and Perspectives," explain the meaning of family literacy in the United Kingdom—giving an international perspective—and explore the uses of literacy in families. After reading in Part Two about the wide variety of established programs in the field, readers should gain valuable research information from Part Three to enable them to develop better and new programs. These chapters serve also as a reminder that when implementing any type of family literacy program, practitioners must focus on how literacy naturally occurs within family environments.

## Family Literacy: Issues and Questions

There is widespread agreement on the importance of family literacy but substantially less agreement on the goals of family literacy programs and on how families, schools, and community agencies can collaborate to learn from one another. As interest in and commitment to family literacy continues to grow, how can educators be confident that they are providing families beneficial, rather than intrusive, experiences? How should schools adjust to what they learn about families? How can program effectiveness best be assessed? How can documentation best be collected and shared? What kinds of outcomes should we expect? Throughout this volume, initiatives will be presented that address some of these issues.

*Family Literacy Connections in Schools and Communities* emphasizes the importance of collaborations by presenting programs including home and school partnerships, community and school collaborations, and government and business organizations that have come together to promote family literacy. The authors were selected for their diverse viewpoints; they are representative of various cultural backgrounds and present perspectives from education, sociology, and anthropology. We hope that this volume provides detailed information to help increase awareness of family literacy and promote the need for greater involvement.

## References

Auerbach, E.R. (1989). Toward a socio-contextual approach to family literacy. *Harvard Educational Review, 59,* 165–181.

Braun, C. (1991). *Commission on Family Literacy: Proposal to the International Reading Association Board of Directors.* Newark, DE: International Reading Association.

Clark, M.M. (1984). Literacy at home and at school: Insights from a study of young fluent readers. In H. Goelman, A. Oberg, & F. Smith (Eds.), *Awakening to literacy* (pp. 122–130). Portsmouth, NH: Heinemann.

Cochran-Smith, M. (1984). *The making of a reader.* Norwood, NJ: Ablex.

Heath, S.B. (1983). *Ways with words.* Cambridge, UK: Cambridge University Press.

Huey, E.B. (1908). *The psychology and pedagogy of reading.* New York: Macmillan.

Morrow, L.M. (1993). *Literacy development in the early years: Helping children read and write.* Boston, MA: Allyn & Bacon.

Morrow, L.M., Paratore, J., with Gaber, D., Harrison, C., & Tracey, D. (1993). Family literacy: Perspectives and practices. *The Reading Teacher, 47,* 194–201.

Morrow, L.M., Paratore, J., & Tracey, D. (1994). *Family literacy: New perspectives, new opportunities.* (Available from the International Reading Association, Newark, DE)

Taylor, D., & Dorsey-Gaines, C. (1988). *Growing up literate: Learning from inner-city families.* Portsmouth, NH: Heinemann.

Teale, W.H. (1984). Reading to young children: Its significance for literacy development. In H. Goelman, A. Oberg, & F. Smith (Eds.), *Awakening to literacy* (pp. 110–121). Portsmouth, NH: Heinemann.

# Chapter 2

# Which Way for Family Literacy: Intervention or Empowerment?

**Elsa Roberts Auerbach**
*University of Massachusetts at Boston*

Before you read further, please consider the following statements and decide whether you agree or disagree with each; make a note of your responses so that you can look back at them after reading the chapter.

1. School success begins in the home. Family literacy programs are important because parental support is the key to children's success in school.

2. Parents or other caregivers should support their children's literacy development by helping with homework and making special time in the day to focus on reading and writing. Family literacy programs should provide parents with concrete training for home tutoring.

3. The most important way that parents can support their children's literacy development is by reading to them.

4. Family literacy programs should include the teaching of positive parenting skills.

5. Family literacy programs should encourage parents to value literacy and promote positive attitudes toward it.

6. Family literacy program staff should start by learning about participants' own literacy practices and beliefs.

7. One of the most important ways that parents can support their children's literacy development is by integrating literacy into the daily life of the family and using it to accomplish their own tasks.

8. Family literacy programs should focus on parents' concerns, whether or not those concerns are directly related to children's schooling or literacy development.

At first glance many of these statements may seem to be common sense and to represent aspects of the same perspective. However, I believe that they embody a range of views about the rationale for family literacy programs and are based on quite different assumptions about the relationship between literacy in families and schools. Clearly "family literacy" has become a new buzzword in the last 10 years, and it is receiving enormous attention from policy makers, researchers, and practitioners. Increasingly, in the United States private and public funding is earmarked for family literacy through, for example, The Barbara Bush Family Literacy Foundation, the Keenan Family Trust, and the Coors Family Literacy Foundation—to name only a few. Family literacy is being touted as a new solution to the problems of schooling. Who would argue against helping parents help their children acquire literacy?

There is a danger of jumping on the family literacy bandwagon without having a clear conceptual framework or critical understanding of the implications of this movement. As Edelsky (1991) says, "Buzzwords and movements not only can promote change; they can prevent it" (p. 161). Unless the differing ideological perspectives implicit in the earlier statements are examined, this may be the fate of family literacy. I want to examine these perspectives in part by describing a family literacy project in which I was involved and explaining how the staff of that project arrived at the understanding put forward in this chapter. In 1986 the University of Massachusetts at Boston received a three-year grant from the U.S. Office of Bilingual Education and Minority Language Affairs to develop a family literacy project entitled the English Family Literacy Project. Through the grant, my colleagues and I were funded to work with parents of bilingual children in English as a second language classes based at adult literacy centers. Our students represented up to 25 nationalities at any given time and came from a wide range of schooling and literacy backgrounds. While this project focused specifically on work with immigrant and refugee families, the analysis and pedagogical implications may well be valid for other populations because they are informed by a broad base of research in various cultural and economic contexts (Chall & Snow, 1982; Goldenberg, 1984; Heath, 1983; Taylor, 1983; Taylor & Dorsey-Gaines, 1988; Tizard, Schofield, & Hewison, 1982).

When we received the grant, we knew little about family literacy. We began by trying to find out as much as we could about what the term meant and how it was being put into practice. We examined existing family literacy programs, ethnographic research on family contributions to literacy development, and the evidence provided by our own students (Nash, 1987). In gathering this evidence, the project staff did not go into students' homes or communities to examine literacy uses and practices or to collect data; instead, we listened, read, and talked with students about literacy in their lives as a regular part of classroom interaction. What we found was that there is a gap between research and implementation: the predominant existing models for family literacy programs seemed not to be informed by either research or what we learned from the students.

## Examining Existing Program Models

What struck us first as we looked at the family literacy programs in existence at that time (particularly those for language-minority parents) was that they seemed to focus on giving parents or other caregivers specific guidelines, materials, and training to carry out school-like activities in the home. Simich-Dudgeon (1987) argues that parents with limited English proficiency must become their children's tutors, performing "structured academic activities that reinforce schoolwork" (p. 3). Programs for these parents often focus on such practices as the following:

- ◆ teaching parents about the U.S. educational system and philosophy of schooling;
- ◆ providing parents with concrete methods and materials to use at home with children;
- ◆ assisting parents to promote "good reading habits";
- ◆ working with parents on the development of their own basic literacy skills;
- ◆ giving parents guidelines and techniques for helping with homework;
- ◆ training parents in how to read to children or listen to children read;
- ◆ providing training in "effective parenting";
- ◆ giving parents a calendar or recipe book of ideas for shared literacy activities;

- ◆ teaching parents to make and play games to reinforce skills; and
- ◆ teaching parents how to communicate with school authorities.

Although the programs we studied took many forms (including competency-based, behavior modification, and, in some cases, whole language approaches), they seemed to have a shared goal: to strengthen the ties between the home and the school by transmitting the culture of school literacy to the family. In such programs, parents are taught about mainstream ways of relating to print and about specific school literacy tasks that they can engage in with their children. I call this a "transmission of school practices model" (Auerbach, 1989). This model starts with the needs, problems, and practices that educators identify, and then transfers skills or practices to parents in order to shape their interactions with children; its direction moves from the school or educator to the parents, and then to the children.

Together with these programs there has been growing media attention to family literacy, which is largely framed in terms of a comparison to congenital illness. For example, an advertisement for the Coors Family Literacy Foundation states, "The problem with illiteracy is that it is so contagious." This quote appears beside a picture of a parent and two children with no faces—just hollow heads. The contention is that illiteracy breeds illiteracy: the "disease" passes from one generation to the next in an intergenerational cycle of illiteracy and creates a permanent, self-perpetuating underclass.

## Examining the Ethnographic Research

After looking at existing programs, our project staff again looked at the origins of the term "family literacy" and at the ethnographic research about literacy in families to get a sense of what is known about family contributions to literacy acquisition. It became clear that the "transmission of school practices model" and the discourse about the disease of intergenerational illiteracy were based on many assumptions not supported by this research or from what we were learning from our students. These assumptions included the following:

1. Language-minority students come from literacy-impoverished homes where education is not valued or supported.
2. Family literacy involves a one-way transfer of skills from parents to children.
3. Children become literate to the extent that their parents extend school-like activities in the home.

4. Existing school practices are adequate, and it is home factors that will determine who succeeds.

5. Parents' own problems get in the way of creating positive family literacy contexts.

*Assumption 1.* The first assumption of the transmission model is that the homes of low-income, minority, and ESL students are literacy impoverished, that there are limited reading materials in their homes, and that the parents neither read themselves nor read to their children. The claim is that these parents do not provide adequate models of literacy use and do not value or support literacy development. As we began to look at research about what actually happens in the homes of language-minority children, however, we found counterevidence to this picture. Study after study (for example, Chall & Snow, 1982; Delgado-Gaitan, 1987; Diaz, Moll, & Mehan, 1986; Goldenberg, 1984) refutes the notion that poor, minority, and immigrant families do not value or support literacy development. In fact, often the opposite seems to be the case for immigrants: those families most marginalized frequently see literacy and schooling as the key to mobility, to changing their status and preventing their children from suffering as they have. For some, the desire to get a better education for their children may even be the central reason for coming to the United States (Delgado-Gaitan, 1987).

Taylor and Dorsey-Gaines (1988) studied the literacy contexts of families living below the poverty level in conditions where neither housing nor food could be taken for granted, where the parents often had not completed high school, and where families had been separated. They found that even in these homes where daily survival was a struggle, "families use literacy for a wide variety of purposes (social, technical, and aesthetic purposes), for a wide variety of audiences, and in a wide variety of situations" (p. 202). Homes were filled with print, and literacy was an integral part of daily life. *Taylor and Dorsey-Gaines argue that it is the lack of social, political, and economic support for parents in dealing with housing, health, and other social problems that puts children at risk—as opposed to lack of parental support for children's literacy development.*

The Harvard Families and Literacy Study (Chall & Snow, 1982; Snow, 1987) investigated the home literacy practices of successful and unsuccessful low-income elementary school students to identify those factors and patterns of interaction that contributed to the acquisition of literacy. This study also found a range of literacy practices and materials in the homes of working-class, minority, and ESL students.

Perhaps the most surprising finding was the generally high level of literacy skill and literacy use among the parents of the children. For example, only 20 percent of the parents said they did not like to read and never read books. Thirty percent read factual books...and could name at least one favorite author. Fifty percent read a major newspaper on a regular basis, and 30 percent could remember books from their childhoods. These low-income children also demonstrated considerable familiarity with literacy. The vast majority owned some books of their own and half owned more than 20 books.... *It seems then that explanations implicating the absence of literacy in low-income homes as the source of children's reading failure are simply wrong* (Snow, 1987, p. 127, emphasis added).

In a study of the functions and meaning of literacy for Mexican immigrants, Delgado-Gaitan (1987) also found that each of the four families she investigated used a range of text types in various ways that went beyond school-related reading. Despite the fact that parents had little prior schooling and did not perceive themselves as readers, they regularly used texts in English and Spanish (including letters from family members, newspapers, and their children's schoolbooks) as an integral part of daily life. Each family in this study, for example, systematically rewarded children for work well done, completed homework, and good grades. Moreover, these parents recognized that their support could extend beyond helping with skills:

Some parents assisted their children in schoolwork by sitting with them to do homework and working out the problem, showing them examples for solving their problems, encouraging them to do their homework before playing, reading to them, taking them to the community library, and providing them with a space at the kitchen table to do their homework (p. 28).

Further, parents in each of these studies wanted to develop their own English literacy as a way to support their children. They understood that supporting children academically went beyond helping them with skills to include emotional and physical support. Our students in the English Family Literacy Project repeatedly confirmed these findings. One student, for example, wrote:

I help my kids by staying together with them, by talking to them. I help them by confronting them and telling them what's wrong or right just as they do me. I help them when they need a favor or money, just as they do me. It's just like you scratch my back, I scratch your back in my family (Auerbach, 1992, p. 7).

*Assumption 2.* A second false assumption of the predominant model is that the "natural" direction of literacy learning is from parent to child and, more narrowly, that the parent's role is to transmit literacy skills to the child. The excerpt just cited was written through a collaborative mother-daughter writing process. The woman who wrote it was at a beginning literacy level and could only produce this text with the help of her daughter—it became a language-experience exercise for them. This two-way support system characterizes the literacy interactions of many immigrant families.

Tizard, Schofield, and Hewison (1982) found that children who read to their parents on a regular basis made significant gains—in fact, greater gains than did children receiving an equivalent amount of extra reading instruction by school specialists. Particularly interesting is their finding that low parental English literacy skills did not detract from the results. This study suggests that a supportive context provided by parents may be more important than any transfer of skills.

Diaz, Moll, and Mehan (1986) found that when children's English and literacy proficiency is more developed than parents' in immigrant families, there may be highly charged, emotionally loaded family dynamics. This uneven distribution of language and literacy skills can lead to complicated role reversals in which parents feel that respect for them is undermined and children feel burdened by having to negotiate with the outside world for their parents. Diaz, Moll, and Mehan found that because children often take responsibility for conducting transactions with important social institutions (banks, schools, and so forth), "they assume control and power usually reserved for adults" (p. 210).

Work with students in our English Family Literacy Project indicated that the distribution and sharing of language and literacy practices in immigrant and refugee families is complex and by no means unidirectional from parents to children. Family members each contribute in the areas where they are strongest: instead of parents assisting children with literacy tasks, children help their parents with homework, act as interpreters for them, and deal with the outside world for them. Parents, in turn, often foster their children's first-language development and help in areas where they feel competent.

What emerges from the composite of these studies is not at all a picture of deficit or literacy impoverishment but instead a picture of mutual support—family members working together to help one another in various ways. A model that rests on the assumption of unilateral parent-to-child literacy assistance, with a neutral transfer of skills, misses important aspects of this dynamic and may in fact exacerbate already stressful family interactions. *These studies suggest that rather than telling parents to spend more time working on literacy with their kids, separate time for parental learning may be beneficial because it re-*

*duces parent-child literacy dependency and frees the children to attend to their own development (including schoolwork).*

*Assumption 3.* A third assumption concerns the nature of family contributions to literacy development. The recognition that certain ways of using literacy in the home may better prepare students for success in school (see Heath, 1983) is often accompanied by the assumption that children succeed because their families do specific school-like tasks with them, that structured home learning activities are the key to success for literate children, and that literacy programs must provide support for this kind of interaction. However, an examination of the actual family contexts for the acquisition of literacy provides compelling counterevidence; studies that examine the home literacy environments of successful readers (both low- and middle-class) reveal that a wide range of experiences (rather than narrow, school-like reading and writing activities) contribute to literacy development. Taylor's (1981, 1983) classic three-year study of six families of proficient readers, which introduced the term "family literacy," found that parents of successful readers often intentionally avoided "doing literacy" with their children in the ways they had been taught in school to avoid replicating what they remembered as negative experiences. Interactions around print varied from family to family and were, within each family, "situationally diffuse, occurring at the very margins of awareness" (1981, p. 100). Taylor found that these interactions were not activities that "were added to the family agendas, but that they had evolved as part of everyday life" (1981, p. 100). She concluded:

> The approach that has been taken in recent years had been to develop parent education programs, which very often provide parents with a battery of specific activities that are designed to teach reading, and yet *very little available information suggests that parents with children who read without difficulty actually undertake such "teaching" on any kind of regular basis* (emphasis added). The present study suggests that there are great variations in approaches the parents have evolved in working with their children and that the thread that unites the families is the recognition that learning to read takes place on a daily basis as part of everyday life (1981, p. 101).

Another study by Taylor and Dorsey-Gaines (1988) among poor urban families confirms these findings and suggests that similar dynamics are at work across social classes. These studies show that successful readers' homes provide many contexts for using literacy, that literacy is integrated in socially significant ways into many segments of family life, and that it is not isolated as an autonomous, add-on instructional activity. The more diverse the contexts for using literacy, the wider the range of literacy achievement factors affected.

The Harvard study (Chall & Snow, 1982) found no simple correlation between parents' literacy level, educational background, or time spent on literacy work with children, and children's overall achievement. Rather, the acquisition of literacy was found to be affected differentially by such factors. Indirect factors including frequency of children's outings with adults, number of maternal outings, emotional climate of the home, time spent interacting with adults, level of parental financial stress, enrichment activities, and parental advocacy at the schools had a stronger effect on many aspects of reading and writing than did direct literacy activities such as help with homework.

*Together, these studies suggest that the extent to which parents use literacy in socially significant ways as an integral part of family life (rather than the extent to which they do intentional, add-on literacy tasks with children) is key in shaping children's literacy acquisition.*

*Assumption 4.* The fourth assumption concerns the relative importance of home and school factors in literacy acquisition. In the transmission of school practices model, what happens at home is seen as the key to school success, often with the assumption of a direct correlation, even a cause-and-effect relationship, between home factors and school achievement. Former Secretary of Education Terrell Bell (1988) characterized this position with the comment: "Not even the best classroom can make up for failure in the family." Again, there is counterevidence from various sources.

In a study that examined both home and school contexts of Southeast Asian children in the United States, Urzua (1986) contends that it is school rather than home factors that shape differences in attitudes and abilities relating to literacy. She reports that two refugee children who had homes that appeared not to be conducive to literacy acquisition were successful in school. Although their mothers were illiterate in their first language, did not speak or read English, and provided no reading materials in the home, these children made great progress in reading and writing. In contrast, another child whose home was filled with reading materials (books, maps, newspapers, dictionaries, and so forth), who had his own study space and school supplies, and whose parents overtly supported his literacy development had enormous difficulties with reading and writing. Urzua asks, "What makes children like Vuong, loved and encouraged by parents who have offered many possibilities for literacy events in their home, face school with rigidity and approach literacy with fear?" (p. 108). She suggests that the answer to this question may be found in the children's classroom experiences. Both of the children who came from less literate home environments were in classes where the teacher valued writing: writing took place nearly every day, different writing genres (such as autobiographies, fables, and journals) were offered, and subskills work (spelling and phonics) emphasized the expression of meaning rather than form. In the class of the child who came from a home where more support for literacy acquisition was provided, however, students never wrote more than one sentence at a time, filled in the blanks in workbooks, copied dictionary definitions, and so forth. Urzua then asks, "How powerful are the influences of curriculum and instructional techniques...which either teach children to find their own voices or discourage them from doing so?" (p. 108).

The Harvard study offers further support for the view that school factors, including the availability of a wide variety of reading materials, the amount and nature of writing, the use of the library, and the quality of instruction, account for the acquisition of literacy as much as home factors. The researchers found that in the early grades, "either literate, stimulating homes or demanding, enriching classrooms can make good readers" (Snow, 1987, p. 128). However, while strong parental factors could compensate for weak schooling up to grade three, even those children with nurturing home literacy environments did poorly in reading after this point if school practices were inadequate; both positive home and school factors are necessary in the upper grades. One significant finding of this study is that parental involvement in an advocacy role is key because it shapes teachers' perceptions, which in turn influence student achievement.

Heath's (1983) ethnographic investigations of three rural communities in the Piedmont Carolinas in the United States found not a lack of literacy practices in the two poorer, working-class communities, but a difference in the ways that literacy is used and perceived. In each community, there is a wide and different range of uses of literacy at home. The relationship between home and school literacy practices is significant: the ways of using print in middle-class homes are similar to those of the school, while those in nonmainstream homes are not. Heath's analysis suggests that the problem is not one of deficit in the nonmainstream family environments, but one of differential usage and power. Because authority is vested in those belonging to the mainstream culture, the literacy practices of the mainstream become the norm and have higher status in school contexts. Thus, Heath posits that *it is the schools that need to change to accommodate family and community literacy practices rather than the homes that need to change to support schooling.*

*Assumption 5.* The final assumption that bears reexamination is the view that parents' problems and cultural values are obstacles to their children's development. The social context of parents' lives is often ignored or seen as a detrimental factor that ultimately undermines the possibilities for learning. This social context may include family obligations, as well as housing, health care, and employment needs. Cultural differences may also be perceived as impediments to parental participation in children's schooling or literacy acquisition. The solution is then framed in terms of *overcoming* obstacles and cultural differences. Parents are expected to reorder their priorities so that they can become involved in school-determined activities; they are often trained in "positive parenting practices" according to mainstream expectations.

Counterevidence to this assumption comes from studies that show that if the family and community social context is seen not as a negative external force but as a central resource for learning, literacy work can become more relevant for parents. Many programs are beginning to acknowledge housing, education, work, and health as issues to be explored as part of the curriculum. In this model, literacy becomes a tool for addressing these issues, and cultural differences are viewed as strengths that can bridge home and school learning. A study of Mexican families in San Diego, California (Diaz, Moll, & Mehan, 1986), confirms the importance of situating literacy in its social context. Rather than starting with mainstream ways of using literacy and transmitting them to families, researchers looked at community practices as the basis for informing and modifying school practices. Local residents were trained as ethnographers to collect data on community writing practices; they then worked with teachers to use this data in developing classroom instructional modules. The function of writing to address community issues proved to be important:

> Parents, students, and others all impressed us with their concern for social issues that permeate community life. Virtually every conversation that began as a discussion of writing eventually turned to the problems of youth gangs, unemployment, immigration, the need to learn English, and the like. It became clear to us that writing, schooling, and social issues are complexly related phenomena in the community (p. 211).

Thus, by investigating community uses of writing, the researchers discovered critical social issues, which, when introduced into the classroom, became a vehicle for improving writing instruction. Student writing focused on family life histories, community conditions, and educational values. The underlying direction of curriculum development was *from the community to the classroom,* rather than from the classroom to the community.

In Pajaro Valley, California, parents and children have been involved in a project in which they read, discuss, and write children's stories together (Ada, 1988). Critical for this project is the positive value placed on the use of the home language both as a vehicle for communication within the family and as the foundation for children's academic success. Also important is the linking of readings to students' lives through dialogue: readers share personal reactions and feelings, relate the stories to their own experiences, critically analyze the events and ideas in the stories, and discuss real-life applications of this understanding. The process of sharing Spanish children's literature becomes the foundation for then asking children and parents to write their own stories about significant events in their lives. This kind of family literacy work draws on parents' cultural strengths and encourages critical thinking about key issues in family life.

Work with parents in the English Family Literacy Project confirmed the power of instruction centered around community and family issues. Through a process of collaborative teacher-learner investigation, concerns about issues such as housing, AIDS, language use at work, and bilingualism were identified as relevant for the adult students. Parents developed their own language and literacy proficiency in the process of exploring these concerns through the use of student-generated texts, thematic readings, language-experience stories, dialogue journals, process writing, and photo stories. They wrote letters to the editor about community problems, presented testimony for state-funding hearings, and wrote about their children's schooling as well as their own language and literacy use in the community. *Not surprisingly, the teachers found that the quality of students' work improved dramatically when the content was most closely linked with their real concerns.*

## Why Is Family Literacy So Popular Now?

The danger of the assumptions just explained is that together they contribute to a new version of the deficit hypothesis, which places the responsibility for literacy problems with families and ignores the social conditions in which the problems may be embedded. They paint a picture of family inadequacy and promote the view that only intervention by mainstream professionals will prevent an unending downward spiral of intergenerational illiteracy. Yet, when the counterevidence in the research is considered, why is it that we continue to be immersed in this discourse of family inadequacy? Why do we continue to be bombarded by media images of ignorant and diseased parents?

This discourse can only be understood within the context of the overall alarmist concern with the crisis in American education: declining skills of college students are blamed on inadequate high school preparation, which is blamed on inadequate preparation in elementary school, which in turn is blamed on inadequate preschools. The buck stops with the family. Problems of schooling are seen to originate with family inadequacies and thus, the argument goes, need to be "fixed" within families. In the meantime, public education continues to suffer cutbacks, and the social conditions in which families must live continue to deteriorate. Thus, the "blame the families" hypothesis may serve the important ideological function of deflecting attention away from the very conditions that give rise to literacy problems—poverty, unemployment, and inadequate health care and housing. Suggesting that enhanced family literacy interactions will break the cycle of poverty or compensate for problems facing the educational system only reinforces the ideology that blames poor people for their own problems and leaves social inequities intact.

## Alternatives to the Predominant Model

In challenging this version of the deficit hypothesis, however, we need to be careful not to abandon the potential of family literacy. The experience of the English Family Literacy Project suggests revisiting Taylor's original findings: we need to look for ways that literacy and literacy learning can become socially significant in family life as it was in the families she studied. This may be done best by designing programs in which parents can use literacy acquisition as a context to address critical social problems in their lives. For schools, this may mean asking, "How can we support parents in accomplishing their own aims and learn from their cultural experience to inform instruction?" (rather than, "How can we encourage parents to help with homework, read to children, and become involved in schools on our terms?"). It may turn out that parents' aims include helping with homework or reading to children; however, when these practices are imposed as social intervention, the danger is that they will turn away the people they are designed to assist. Thus, research suggests that we need to reverse the "from the school to the family" model and allow what happens in families and communities to inform schooling.

For family literacy programs, research suggests a model that incorporates community cultural forms, literacy practices, and social issues into the curriculum content. This view recognizes that the conditions that shape family literacy are integral to learning; it brings the conditions that give rise to literacy problems into the curriculum rather than shifting the focus away from them. As participants' concerns become central to their own learning and literacy becomes a means for challenging oppressive conditions in their lives, literacy will become more socially significant for families, which, as Taylor and others remind us, is what characterizes the families of successful readers.

In this alternative model, inspired by the work of Freire (1970), instruction starts with each group of participants and their communities. Because the curriculum is context specific and not a predetermined set of practices or activities, the curriculum development process is participatory and is based on a collaborative investigation of critical issues in family or community life. As these issues emerge, they are explored and transformed into content-based literacy work, so that literacy can become a tool for shaping this social context (see Auerbach, 1992, for a guide to this kind of participatory curriculum development and documentation of its application in the English Family Literacy Project). The focus of the curriculum is on empowering participants to direct their own learning and use it for their own purposes.

This approach creates a new definition of what counts as family literacy, which may include, but is not limited to, direct parent-child interactions around literacy tasks (for example, reading with or listening to children; talking about and giving and receiving support for homework and school concerns; or engaging in other activities with children that involve literacy—cooking, going on outings, and so on). Equally important, however, are the following, often neglected, aspects of family literacy work.

1. *Parents or other caregivers working independently on reading and writing.* On the most basic level, just by developing their own literacy, parents contribute to family literacy. As parents become less dependent on children, the burden shifts, and children are freer to develop in their own ways.

2. *Parents using literacy to address family and community problems.* Dealing with issues such as immigration, employment, or housing through literacy work makes it possible for parents to make reading, writing, and other related activities socially significant in their lives. It models the use of literacy as an integral part of daily life for children.

3. *Parents addressing child-rearing concerns through family literacy class.* By providing support and a safe forum for dialogue, family literacy programs can help parents share and develop strate-

gies for dealing with issues such as lack of adequate play space, safety, drugs, discipline, and intergenerational cultural conflicts.

4. *Parents supporting the development of their home language and culture.* As parents contribute to the development of their home language and culture, they build the foundation for their children's academic achievement, positive self-concept, and appreciation for their multicultural heritage.

5. *Parents interacting with the school system.* The classroom becomes a place where parents can bring school-related issues and develop the ability to understand and respond to them. They can explore their attitudes toward their own and their children's school experiences. They can assess what they see and determine their responses, rehearse interactions with school personnel, and develop support networks for individual and group advocacy.

Our attempts to implement this approach in the English Family Literacy Project took a variety of forms, including the following:

◆ investigating home language use (for example, documenting who uses what language, to whom, and when);

◆ exploring family literacy practices (for example, evaluating critically a "how to help your children with homework" guide sent home by the school, which includes questions such as, "Which of these things do you already do?" "Which would you like to do?" "Which do you think are not possible?" and "What do you do that's not already included here?");

◆ exploring cultural issues (for instance, writing about children's positive and negative attitudes toward their home language, participating in a community Spanish literacy day, and writing about faith healing);

◆ modeling whole language activities that parents might do with children (for example, telling stories or making books);

◆ validating culture-specific literacy forms (for example, reading, writing, and telling folktales and proverbs);

◆ exploring parenting issues (for example, exchanging letters with other parents in an adult basic education program or writing letters of advice to pregnant teenagers in a high school program);

◆ exploring issues of learning and teaching (responding to pictures of different educational settings in terms of their own educational experiences and expectations for children's education, for instance);

- addressing community, workplace, and health care issues (for example, writing a class letter about police discrimination to a local newspaper or writing testimony for funding hearings on adult education and community services);
- practicing advocacy in dealing with schools (for example, writing letters about concerns to children's teachers);
- exploring political issues (for example, writing language-experience stories about elections in their home countries; see Auerbach, 1992, and Nash et al., 1992 for full descriptions of these activities).

## Rethinking Definitions of Family Literacy

You began reading this article by responding to some statements about family literacy. As you finish, look back at the statements and your responses to see if you have any further observations about various conceptions of family literacy. I have tried to show that many ideological orientations are implicit in these common-sense statements. I have highlighted two approaches, one that defines family literacy narrowly to mean reinforcing school-like literacy activities within the family setting and one that defines it more broadly to include a range of practices that are integrated into daily life in a socially significant way. In the former approach, successful literacy and language acquisition are closely linked to the culture of schooling and to mainstream literacy practices. Experts from mainstream institutions intervene in families to prescribe specific ways of interacting around literacy. Life demands are seen as taking parents away from their literacy development and that of their children. In the latter approach, the social context is seen as a rich resource that can inform rather than impede learning. As such, learning becomes a context for participants to develop strategies for addressing problems that they have identified. The teacher's role is to connect what happens inside the classroom to what happens outside so that literacy can become a meaningful tool for addressing critical issues in families and communities.

Of course, the polarity between these views is an artificial one: in reality, most programs, including some described in this volume, fall somewhere along a continuum between a prescriptive, interventionist model and a participatory, empowering one. As educators, we need to reflect on where our own practice puts us on this continuum and how the family literacy movement can become a vehicle for promoting change, rather than a bandwagon that impedes it.

# References

Ada, A.F. (1988). The Pajaro Valley experience: Working with Spanish-speaking parents to develop children's reading and writing skills in the home through the use of children's literature. In T. Skutnabb-Kangas & J. Cummins (Eds.), *Minority education: From shame to struggle* (pp. 224–238). Philadelphia, PA: Multilingual Matters.

Auerbach, E.R. (1989). Toward a socio-contextual approach to family literacy. *Harvard Educational Review, 59,* 165–181.

Auerbach, E.R. (1992). *Making meaning, making change: Participatory curriculum development for adult ESL literacy.* Washington, DC: The Center for Applied Linguistics; and McHenry, IL: Delta Systems.

Bell, T.M. (1988, October). Keynote address at Adult Learners, Arizona's Future Conference, Phoenix, AZ.

Chall, J.S., & Snow, C. (1982). *Families and literacy: The contributions of out of school experiences to children's acquisition of literacy.* A final report to the National Institute of Education, Washington, DC.

Delgado-Gaitan, C. (1987). Mexican adult literacy: New directions for immigrants. In S.R. Goldman & K. Trueba (Eds.), *Becoming literate in English as a second language* (pp. 9–32). Norwood, NJ: Ablex.

Diaz, S., Moll, L., & Mehan, K. (1986). Socio-cultural resources in instruction: A context-specific approach. In *Beyond language: Social and cultural factors in schooling language minority children* (pp. 87–229). Los Angeles, CA: California State Department of Education and California State University.

Edelsky, C. (1991). *With literacy and justice for all: Rethinking the social in language and education.* London: Falmer.

Freire, P. (1970). *Pedagogy of the oppressed.* New York: Seabury.

Goldenberg, C.N. (1984, October 10–13). *Low-income parents' contributions to the reading achievement of their first-grade children.* Paper presented at the meeting of the Evaluation Network/Evaluation Research Society, San Francisco, CA.

Heath, S.B. (1983). *Ways with words.* Cambridge, UK: Cambridge University Press.

Nash, A. (1987). *English family literacy: An annotated bibliography.* Boston, MA: University of Massachusetts at Boston, English Family Literacy Project.

Nash, A., Cason, A., Gomez-Sanford, R., McGrail, L., & Rhum, M. (1992). *Talking Shop: A curriculum resource for participatory ESL.* Washington, DC: The Center for Applied Linguistics; and McHenry, IL: Delta Systems.

Simich-Dudgeon, C. (1987, March). Involving limited English proficient parents as tutors in their children's education. *ERIC/CLL News Bulletin, 10*(2), 3–7.

Snow, C. (1987). Factors influencing vocabulary and reading achievement in low income children. In R. Apple (Ed.), *Toegepaste Taalwetenschap in Artikeken, Special 2* (pp. 124–128). Amsterdam: ANELA.

Taylor, D. (1981). The family and the development of literacy skills and values. *Journal of Research in Reading, 4*(2), 92–103.

Taylor, D. (1983). *Family literacy: Young children learning to read and write.* Portsmouth, NH: Heinemann.

Taylor, D., & Dorsey-Gaines, C. (1988). *Growing up literate: Learning from inner-city families.* Portsmouth, NH: Heinemann.

Tizard, J., Schofield, W.N., & Hewison, J. (1982). Symposium: Reading collaboration between teachers and parents in assisting children's reading. *British Journal of Educational Psychology, 52,* 1–15.

Urzua, C. (1986). A children's story. In P. Rigg & D.S. Enright (Eds.), *Children and ESL: Integrating perspectives* (pp. 93–112). Washington, DC: Teachers of English to Speakers of Other Languages.

# Part Two

# Family Literacy Practices

## Programs in the Schools
## Organization-Sponsored Programs

Part Two describes a wide range of family literacy practices, which include both *intergenerational programs* and *parent involvement programs*. Intergenerational initiatives are designed to improve the literacy development of both adults and children. Because parents or other caregivers and children are viewed as co-learners, such efforts are generally characterized by planned instructional events for parents and children working either collaboratively or separately in parallel settings. Parent involvement programs include initiatives designed to involve parents in literacy activities and events that support school-like goals or other community agency goals. Such efforts focus on parents as agents or intervenors in support of their children's literacy learning in school. They often reflect the emphasis a particular school places on strategies for literacy development. The programs change as schools and other agencies change their ideas about how literacy develops.

### Programs in the School

Jeanne R. Paratore's chapter discusses an intergenerational literacy program in Chelsea, Massachusetts. Now in its fifth year, it has served more than 400 families, who are mostly new immigrants from Central American and Southeast Asian countries. Project events and experiences caused those involved to rethink many widely held assumptions about parents and their partnerships with schools and about the ways families use literacy at home, which led to the formation of some general principles about intergenerational literacy programs. This chapter presents a detailed description of the interactions that occur when adults in this program join together each day to study English literacy and language learning and to explore how to support their children's literacy learning in U.S. schools. Paratore uses her experiences to suggest several lessons about implementing family literacy programs.

In her chapter, Patricia A. Edwards relays parents' and teachers' thoughts and concerns about storybook reading. In response she developed the Parents as Partners Reading Program to help parents learn how to share books with their children. The author also describes a course she designed for primary teachers to broaden their understanding of multiple literacy environments. The knowledge gained by both parents and teachers as a result of participating in the two programs is explained.

Lesley Mandel Morrow with Jody L. Scoblionko and Dixie Shafer describe a family literacy initiative that was in its early stages at the time the chapter was written, called the Family Writing and Reading Appreciation Program (WRAP). It was designed to foster an interest and appreciation for reading and writing for parents and children as they work together at home and was modeled from a school initiative called the WRAP program. The authors discuss material preparation, project design, and coordination with administrators and teachers in getting such a home-school program underway as well as the problems involved in such an endeavor and the gratification from success stories. Brief case studies of parents and children are presented with their reactions to the program thus far.

Patricia S. Koskinen, Irene H. Blum, Nancy Tennant, E. Marie Parker, Mary W. Straub, and Christine Curry outline their program that provides elementary school teachers with a structured home-school reading program with books and audiotapes. The gradually increasing level of language difficulty makes these books particularly appropriate for second-language learners and beginning readers who are native English speakers. The accompanying audiotapes provide a form of scaffolding to support and extend language learning. Parents are informed about the program, and they are requested to help ensure that children use the audiotapes and return them to school and asked to discuss progress. The results of the program indicate that children benefit from the opportunity to practice rereading, at home, books that are introduced in school.

Susan B. Neuman's chapter begins with a discussion of how adolescent parents' lack of information concerning child growth and development can result in inappropriate interactions and unrealistic expectations of their children's abilities and behaviors. Adolescent mothers' beliefs about children's language and literacy development are examined. Neuman then describes an intervention program for adolescent mothers designed to enhance their literacy and their understanding of developmentally appropriate literacy behaviors for early readers and writers.

In the next chapter Billie J. Enz and Lyndon W. Searfoss discuss the significant numbers of teenagers who are becoming mothers and fathers while attending U.S. public high schools. Many of them have difficulty reading and writing, yet, at the same time, they are expected to be parents and assume the traditional role of being their children's first teachers. Enz and Searfoss suggest, as does Neuman in the previous chapter, that as educators we have the responsibility of offering family literacy programs that meet two urgent needs of teenage parents: (1) improving their own literacy levels and (2) preparing them to be effective models of literacy for their children. This chapter presents another successful program designed for high school students who become parents. The program serves students from a wide range of socioeconomic levels and cultural and linguistic backgrounds.

## Organization-Sponsored Programs

The remaining chapters in this section outline select government-, community-, and media-sponsored programs. Most of these initiatives take place in schools, but they originate from organizations outside schools that support family literacy. In Chapter 9 Ruth Graves and James H. Wendorf note the research that supports the Reading Is Fundamental approach to family literacy and describe the history of the organization's outreach services to parents. The chapter focuses on two recent initiatives: (1) Shared Beginnings, an activity program for parents of very young children, with special emphasis on teen parents and their children, and (2) the companion programs Family of Readers and RIF for Families, which provide guidance to parents who are enrolled in adult education classes or whose children are enrolled in a Head Start program, and which enlist them in planning and implementing a book activity program for their children. Both initiatives reflect RIF's motivational approach: the emphasis is on encouraging children to read for pleasure and make books part of their everyday lives.

In their chapter, Linda B. Gambrell, Janice F. Almasi, Qing Xie, and Victoria J. Heland describe a home-school family literacy program called RUNNING START, created by Reading Is Fundamental for first grade children. The purpose of this program is (1) to create a book-rich classroom environment; (2) to create a book-rich home environment; (3) to increase book reading experiences at school and at home; (4) to foster reading success; and (5) to provide home, school, and community support for literacy development. The authors also outline evaluation results of this literacy program, which reveal that children in RUNNING START were more motivated to read and exhibited more reading behaviors than those in the control group and that parents in the program read to their children and talked about books more than those in the control group.

"The Even Start Family Literacy Program" written by Patricia A. McKee and Nancy Rhett explains the Even Start model, which serves to help parents become full partners in the education of their children; assist children in reaching their full potential as learners; and provide literacy training for parents in need. McKee and Rhett also discuss elements of the program such as eligibility, services provided, and home instruction. Evaluation of Even Start is a focus as well.

Chapter 12 by Meta W. Potts and Susan Paull begins with a brief history of the family literacy movement and the work of the National Center for Family Literacy. The authors then describe the four-component program model of the Center: adult basic skills and literacy education; early childhood education; parent and child interaction; and parent education and support group activities. Potts and Paull discuss the importance of integrating these components and give examples of how integration works in the classroom to create a comprehensive, family-focused approach to learning. Findings from ongoing program evaluation and follow-up studies of former program participants are summarized as well as administrative issues in implementing programs and knowledge gained from early experiences.

Benita Somerfield discusses the launching of The Barbara Bush Foundation for Family Literacy and its mission. According to Somerfield the Foundation has become part of the U.S. education agenda—both rhetorically and in practice. This chapter explains lessons learned in the policy and program arenas; profiles some of the more successful strategies, programs, and initiatives; and then discusses family literacy as a key element of the solution to larger social problems.

The following chapter by Iris Sroka, Jeanette Betancourt, and Myra Ozaeta begins by describing the mission of Children's Television Workshop, the producers of *Sesame Street* and other educational shows for children. This mission is to help educate children and young people through high-quality and entertaining media and outreach efforts, with a special commitment to affect minority and economically disadvantaged children. It is with this component in mind that the Community Education Services division of CTW developed a project called the *Sesame Street* Preschool Educational Program—an educational enrichment program for three- to five-year-olds. *Sesame Street* PEP's primary goal is to encourage children's natural curiosity and love of learning and to foster an enthusiasm for reading by forging links between home and childcare through its materials for families. These materials, prepared in English and Spanish, are designed to provide adult family members with suggestions for becoming involved in the education and early literacy of their young children.

Twila C. Liggett has written about an exciting project that is reaching many at-risk families by bringing them together with stories and books—using television stories to lead the way. This chapter describes the Family Literacy Alliance, a unique collaboration among the producers of three award-winning Public Broadcasting Service series: *Reading Rainbow, Long Ago & Far Away,* and *Wonderworks Family Movie.* These literature-based TV series have combined with community outreach programs to provide book discussions and activities that encourage parent and child involvement. The FLA has established reading programs in a shelter for homeless families in Massachusetts, in a Native American wellness center in Nebraska, and with an Even Start Program in New Mexico, among others.

# Chapter 3

# Implementing an Intergenerational Literacy Project: Lessons Learned

**Jeanne R. Paratore**
*Boston University, Boston, Massachusetts*

In the Intergenerational Literacy Project in the Chelsea, Massachusetts, Public Schools, parents, grandparents, aunts, and uncles join together in daily classes to practice reading, writing, and speaking in English and to learn about U.S. education and ways they can support their children's literacy learning. One morning a grandmother named Innocencia, who had for several months quietly but consistently participated in the project, entered the classroom and shyly handed her teacher a note that read:

Mi Sueño Realizado
My Dream Realized

| | |
|---|---|
| Cuando yo era pequeña | When I was small |
| Mi padre no pensó | my father didn't think |
| ponerme en la escuela | to put me in school. |
| No me educó. | He didn't educate me. |
| Cuánto diera yo | How much I would have given |
| por haber aprendido | to have learned |
| a leer un libro | to read a book! |
| de letras menores | And with printed letters |
| y escribir mi nombre | to have written my first name |
| tambien mi apellido | and then to have written my last. |

Innocencia's words reinforced what we had begun to learn during the months of the program: although intergenerational literacy programs are often designed and evaluated on the basis of the needs of children, the success of our program seemed to be clearly attributable to the extent to which we were being responsive to the needs of the adults as well. Adults were by no means disinterested in their children's literacy and indeed practiced shared literacy daily and kept journals of their literacy interactions with their children. But what seemed to keep them coming to class was not only what they were learning about supporting their children's literacy, but also what they were learning about their own literacy. Their motivation was made explicit in a coauthored statement that was prepared for presentation at a recent award ceremony by one group of parents:

> This program is important because we learn English. The teachers come every day to help us with pronunciation, writing, reading, and everything in English. When we learn English we can find better work and we can study a career. We can read a newspaper, a magazine, and a letter. We can also help our children with their homework. We find more opportunities to communicate about our culture, our feelings, and ideas with the people. In this project, everybody is important.

Now in its fifth year, the project has taught us many lessons about families and literacy. It has caused us to rethink many widely held assumptions about parents and their partnerships with schools and about the ways families use literacy at home, and it has helped us formulate some general principles about intergenerational programs.

## Description of the Program

Funded through various grants from both public and private sources,[1] intergenerational literacy classes are held at an elementary school where free childcare is provided for preschool-aged children. During the first four years of the project, 464 adults and their children completed at least one 15-week instructional cycle. Although our initial expectation was that we would serve mothers of young children, our actual enrollment has included 311 mothers, 88 fathers, 36 grandparents, 14 aunts, 9 uncles, 2 siblings, and 4 adult caregivers. Within the families, there were 291 preschool and 786 school-aged children. Ethnicity included 311 Latino, 117 Southeast Asian, 20 Caucasian, 14 African American, and 2 Arabian families. Of the 464 adults, 446 spoke English as a second language. Families represented 28 different countries of origin and 14 different first languages. For second-language learners, the range of English proficiency levels generally varied from limited to fair, and the range of literacy in the first language varied from limited to high.

There are two criteria for parents' or other caregivers' enrollment in the classes: a desire to improve their own literacy and a commitment to engage in shared literacy events with their children on a daily basis. The enrollment history of the project is interesting to note. On the first day of the project, only two families attended, which left us bewildered and discouraged because we had conducted an extensive recruiting effort through teachers, clergy, and community leaders. During subsequent days and weeks recruitment efforts continued, and participation gradually increased. By the end of the first instructional cycle, however, only 16 families participated, despite space and funding for a total of 40. Over time and through continued efforts to share information about the program through a broad community network, enrollment grew. By the third year of the project, we were fully enrolled with 75 families participating during each instructional cycle and a waiting list occasionally of as many as 60 families.

Adults attend literacy classes 4 days per week, 2 hours per day, for an instructional cycle of 15 weeks. When planning the program, we reviewed the research on bilingual education, second-language learning, and multicultural education (Genesee, 1985; Nieto, 1992; Sleeter & Grant, 1987; Weinstein, 1984) and concluded that classes composed of multicultural and multilingual learners would enrich the learning climate. Therefore, classes are deliberately formed to reflect the demographics of the community, with each class comprising approximately 70 percent Latinos, 20 percent Southeast Asians, and 10 percent other ethnic groups.

In multilingual groups of 25 or fewer, instruction is planned to achieve three goals: (1) offer opportunities for adults to read and respond to literacy materials of personal interest; (2) provide a selection of books, strategies, and ideas for adults to share with their children to support their literacy learning; and (3) organize a forum through which adults can share their family literacy experiences with their friends and teachers, which enables us all to learn more about the uses of literacy in diverse families. Heeding the cautions of researchers such as Auerbach (1989) (the author of Chapter 2 in this work) and Taylor (1993), we placed emphasis on situating literacy experiences within the routines of daily life, rather than on creating school-like contexts in the home. Parents are encouraged to use literacy in multiple ways with their children, including reading and writing oral histories, composing letters to friends and relatives or notes to family members, journal keeping, story writing, and publishing. Adults are also taught how to help children with homework, what types of questions they might ask the classroom teacher to find out about their children's progress, and how to ask their children questions about the school day.

Classes are taught by a team of five people, including two certified and experienced literacy teachers and three tutors. The teachers are graduate students at Boston University in Massachusetts; the tutors are undergraduate students who, in addition to tutoring a minimum of six hours each week, attend a two-hour literacy tutoring seminar once a week throughout the academic year. Each teaching team has at least one member who is fluent in Spanish and Vietnamese, the primary languages of many of the families in the project, and two teams have tutors who speak Khmer. This staffing framework allows us to flexibly group learners to meet individual needs at different times during the instructional period, and still maintain large, multicultural, and multilingual groups for discussion and response.

Instructional reading and writing strategies used in these classes have received support in professional literature related to adult literacy edu-

*Leonsa and her son, Pedro, read together.*

Paratore

cation (Thistlethwaite, 1983) and include assisted reading and writing, paired rereadings, cooperative learning, and metacognitive training. Although experiences in each classroom vary daily, a typical instructional period looks like this. At the beginning of each class, parents or other caregivers make an entry in a literacy log. Here, they record a literacy event that they shared with their child the day before and comment on their reactions to it. Who initiated the event? Why? Did it connect to something else? Did the child like it? How did they know? Did they like it? Why or why not? After writing, parents share their log entries with a small group or a partner. Often, this includes sharing and exchanging favorite children's storybooks. Usually a teacher or tutor joins the group to participate in this discussion. Figures 1, 2, and 3 represent the different ways parents may choose to share their literacy interactions. We have found that the two open-ended response forms have provided much richer information for us and are generally preferred by parents.

Following the small group interaction, the class convenes. Sometimes questions raised in the small groups become the focus of a large group discussion. For example, what should parents do if their child does not seem to be interested in a book? Is it good for a child to ask "so many questions"? Should parents ask their children questions? How can parents help their children write? What can they do if they do not understand their children's homework? How can they talk to the child's teacher about a school problem? Other times, the large group lessons grow out of a more formal plan designed to introduce parents to ways of supporting their children's literacy learning. For example, during the first week of classes, emphasis is placed on sharing storybooks with children. Teachers explain how storybooks can be shared with or without the author's language and demonstrate how parents can rely on book illustrations to tell stories. Teachers encourage parents to select storybooks in their first languages to share with their children or wordless picture books to tell the story in their first language. Throughout the week, teachers demonstrate how to interact with children using books, the kinds of questions that might be asked, and the ways that children might be invited to participate. During the early days of the instructional cycle, teachers and tutors also encourage parents to consider the ways literacy is used routinely in their daily interactions with children. Literacy is broadly defined to include activities involving reading, writing, and language, and these ideas are listed on charts and displayed in the classrooms for parents to comment on and discuss. In later lessons, teachers, tutors, and parents talk about storytelling and about how they each share their memories and experiences with their children through stories. Such discussions lead to activities in which parents write and publish books to read with children. Other lessons include conversations about television viewing, parent and child play, talking to children about school, and helping with homework.

Afterward, one of the teachers introduces a topic or an article that will be the focus of the day's lesson. Topics for reading and writing are deliberately chosen to stimulate a discussion of ethnicity and culture, as

**Figure 1**
**Literacy Log**

Name _Salvadora_

Month _4-15-92_

| Date | Reading, Writing, Viewing, and Talking Activities I Shared with My Child or Children | Child's Name and Age |
|------|-----------------------------------------------------------|--------|
| 4-15-92 | I read with my child a book about of animal and he review every colors Also we were watched TV cartoons and a program for children to Sesame Street | |
| 4-21-92 | Last week end I went with My child to visited her friend and him play too much time Last Saturday I read a book Called the Seven Kids and Wolf Also I teach the alphabet at him | |
| 4-22-92 | Yesterday I played with my child with toy or the floor and also we counted numbers from 1 to 10 in English After we reviewed all parts of body | |
| 4-23-92 | I read with my child a book called "GoldiLoc and the three bears. Then we watched cartoons and after we reviewed some words which saw in the program | |
| 4-27-92 | I read with my child a book called The dog and the cat and after I sang a song a my children five Little Monkeys jumped on the bed | |

Paratore

**Figure 2**
**Reading Log**

Name _Salvadora_

Date _3-17-92_

| What books did you read with your child last week? | How did your child respond or react? | What did you think of this book? |
|---|---|---|
| 1- With My Brother | With This book he enjoyed | I think which this book |
| 2- Toot-A-Toot-Toot | it more because the pictures | is interesant because it explained |
| 3- Los cinco Sentidos | is relation with the family | which the big brother could |
| in Special The tact. | He liked the book | care for the baby. |
| 4- I like Me | because it's about the animals | Also the other books I |
| By Nancy Carlson | in the farm. | learned more information and |
| 5- Good Night Moon | He liked very much because | The good function of tact. |
| | the pictures are interesting. | the vocabulary is easy |
| | interesting. | and I understan/it very much |

From the Intergenerational Literacy Project, Boston University/Chelsea Public Schools, Massachusetts. Copyright 1991. Reprinted with permission.

## Figure 3
## Parent-Child Weekly Activities

Name_____

Week_____

| Activity | Weekend | Monday | Tuesday | Wednesday |
|---|---|---|---|---|
| Recited or sang a nursery rhyme to child | _____ | _____ | _____ | _____ |
| Shared a fingerplay or song | _____ | _____ | _____ | _____ |
| Labeled or named items in child's room or other rooms in a house | _____ | _____ | _____ | _____ |
| Played with child | _____ | _____ | _____ | _____ |
| Talked about child's play or activities | _____ | _____ | _____ | _____ |
| Visited a park or museum | _____ | _____ | _____ | _____ |
| Read to child | _____ | _____ | _____ | _____ |
| Listened to child read a book | _____ | _____ | _____ | _____ |
| Helped with or looked at homework | _____ | _____ | _____ | _____ |
| Asked about homework | _____ | _____ | _____ | _____ |
| Wrote note or message to child | _____ | _____ | _____ | _____ |
| Visited a library | _____ | _____ | _____ | _____ |
| Borrowed or bought a book | _____ | _____ | _____ | _____ |
| Played a game with child involving words or reading | _____ | _____ | _____ | _____ |
| Helped child write a letter or greeting card | _____ | _____ | _____ | _____ |
| Viewed television together | _____ | _____ | _____ | _____ |
| Discussed program viewed | _____ | _____ | _____ | _____ |
| Asked child questions about school or reading | _____ | _____ | _____ | _____ |
| Attended a school activity or visited with child's teacher | _____ | _____ | _____ | _____ |

Other shared activities:

| _____ | _____ | _____ | _____ | _____ |
|---|---|---|---|---|
| _____ | _____ | _____ | _____ | _____ |
| _____ | _____ | _____ | _____ | _____ |

Please list children's books read:

_____    _____

_____    _____

_____    _____

a way to "discover and explore ethnic connections" (Ferdman, 1990). Reading selections come from many different sources, but all are considered to be materials that participants encounter in their daily lives. Local and U.S. national newspaper articles, news magazines, school newsletters, short stories, and informational brochures are often used. Sometimes parents bring in articles or topics that they would like to have the class explore. As one example, a recent increase in gang activity in the community caused parents to have significant concerns about their children's safety. Several days were spent reading and discussing newspaper reports and editorials about this particular gang, and a police lieutenant was asked to come to class to answer parents' questions.

Because the adults speak many different languages, no attempt is made to provide texts for in-class reading in different languages. All written text is in English, although some of the children's books from the library are written in Spanish and Vietnamese. Before reading, however, the class often forms into small groups of learners who share the same language. A teacher or tutor discusses the topic with each group first by introducing key concepts or vocabulary in the first language or by asking learners to connect settings, situations, or experiences in their reading to those in their countries of origin or their own cultures. This practice consistently leads to a large group discussion of multiple perspectives on a particular idea or concept, which serves as a bridge to the reading of the text in English.

After reading, parents again form small groups to discuss their understanding in their first language before reconvening as a large group to share their general impressions, questions, and comments in English. Then, some learners might form pairs to talk about a part of the reading that was particularly interesting to them; others might work individually or in a small group with a teacher or tutor to receive extra help on a particular reading or writing strategy. Finally, learners end each day by making an entry in a personal journal to respond to the selection or the day's discussion. Parents choose whether to compose this entry in their first language or in English.

Throughout the instructional cycle, attention is given not only to the acquisition of literacy skills and strategies, but also to developing skill in exploring the relationship of literacy to the learners and their families. Adults are encouraged to reflect on the ways that they use literacy to get things done and to consider what they already know about literacy, as well as what they want to learn.

At the end of each cycle, an award ceremony is held to honor participants with a certificate of completion and an opportunity to share their accomplishments with friends and family. At the ceremony, adults present a group composition that describes their thoughts about the project and their own literacy. At a recent ceremony, some parents elected to create a display of the literacy artifacts from their own countries, which included labeled photographs, envelopes and letters received, articles about their countries, and objects accompanied by explanations about the importance of the items in their country. Other parents chose to create a display of their children's uses of literacy at home: posterboard exhibits were filled with children's stories, drawings, and letters, and old tape and torn corners suggested that items were taken off home walls to create the display.

## Lessons Learned

Formal investigations of this project document that it has been effective at recruiting and maintaining participation, supporting acquisition and development of English literacy by adults, and encouraging parent and child literacy interaction (Paratore, 1993, 1994). In addition, there is extensive anecdotal evidence that has led us to important understandings about families and literacy and about home and school partnerships. These understandings are described following.

*Recruitment must be community based, collaborative, and long term.* Our experiences during recruitment document two important elements of the process. First, the inclusion of many community agencies is necessary to achieve widespread interest and participation. Although elementary and secondary teachers were supportive in distributing program information, it was the community leaders who helped us reach parents during the first weeks of the project. Project staff visit and call community agencies frequently; they brought program information to meetings with staff and parents at various agencies. Of particular help in recruiting families were clergy, leaders of bilingual and cultural organizations, and health professionals. Announcements were made at church services and community center meetings. Community leaders reviewed written notices and helped develop accurate translations for bilingual parents. They also distributed information by including notices in church bulletins and posting them in community centers and neighborhood stores. Many community leaders contacted parents directly to describe the project and ask if they would like to participate. Since the first instructional cycle, our best recruiters have been the parents who are participating. We have found that classes grow as parents bring their friends and family members. In several cases, we have enrolled the mother, father, and grandmother or grand-father from a single family.

Second, we learned that building a stable attendance rate takes time. It took several weeks and a great deal of networking to recruit the initial 16 families, and then several more weeks and meetings with community leaders to build beyond that initial enrollment. Program administrators who expect or demand quick enrollment may be disappointed in the results.

*Elementary and secondary schools are appropriate and effective settings for adult literacy classes.* There is a widely held assumption that adults are intimidated by the elementary and secondary school setting, and therefore programs that focus on adult learning are more appropriately located in the community or home. During the first three years of this project, our classes were offered in a community setting, but we found that despite the fact that the classes were well attended and valued by the adults, we were unable to establish a strong connection with the elementary and secondary schools. At the beginning of the fourth year, we relocated to an elementary school, and parents and caregivers began participating in classes in the same building attended by many of their children. Although parents were undeniably intimidated by the school setting, and both enrollment and attendance dropped during this transitional period, by the second cycle we had reestablished the initial trust that had been built, and attendance is again at the very high levels (an average rate of 74 percent) that it had been during the first three years (Paratore, 1993).

The elementary school location is significant because it has enabled us to do many important, collaborative projects. Several of the parents in the project participate in elementary classrooms as storybook readers and share favorite selections or books they write themselves or with their children. Others have been invited to serve as literacy tutors, particularly in bilingual classrooms. In this role, they are primarily read-aloud partners for young children. Some of the parents have chosen to become library aides in the school: they help children select and check out books and conduct story hours during library visits. These experiences not only permit parents to become important members of the school's literacy community, but they also provide them with valuable circumstances for practicing their own literacy.

*Parents and caregivers engage in a wide range of literacy activities with their children.* Although shared storybook reading has been identified as "the single most important activity" in preparing children for success in school (Anderson et al., 1985, p. 23), homes where children do not engage in shared storybook reading are not devoid of literacy. As reported by Heath (1983), Taylor and Dorsey-Gaines (1988), and Teale (1984) and mentioned earlier by Morrow and Auerbach, families use literacy in many different ways. In the homes of the families with whom we work, parents report telling stories, playing word games, discussing TV programs, and reading the Bible as routine ways of using literacy with their children. We have learned that affirming and valuing the many ways in which families share literacy are just as important as introducing new uses of literacy. We have tried to accomplish that by asking parents to keep journals about any shared literacy events, not just storybook reading. We have found that creating a school-based forum through which parents and caregivers can routinely tell about home-based literacy practices has helped to bridge the gap between home and school.

In addition, however, it is clearly the case that storybook reading provides a context through which children can learn a great deal about print and particularly about school-based literacy and is therefore valuable as a way to prepare children for success in school. As reported by Delgado-Gaitan (1992), Eldridge-Hunter (1992), and Goldenberg, Reese, and Gallimore (1992), all of whom examined the storybook reading behaviors of Latino parents, parents often ask few questions and engage in minimal interactions when reading to their children. The interactive storybook reading behaviors that are familiar to classroom teachers and to mainstream parents who have been educated in U.S. schools may be unfamiliar to other parents. We have learned that it is not sufficient to provide parents with access to good storybooks, nor is it enough to give them a suggested read-aloud routine and an occasional demonstration. Rather, they need repeated opportunities to observe and practice interactive storybook reading, and they need opportunities to discuss their children's responses to the shared event.

*The types of literacy activities that parents and caregivers choose to practice are largely dictated by the circumstances within their lives, with literacy events emerging from both their children's school-based assignments and activities and their own interests and needs.* As mentioned earlier, researchers have found that in virtually all homes, some type of literacy is practiced. However, in some homes incidences of print literacy, particularly writing, are sparse. In a study designed to examine what types of interventions are most beneficial in working with Mexican American secondary students, Moll and Diaz (1987) reported that homework plays an important role in creating opportunities for family literacy. They suggested that homework "more than any other factor, set the occasion for literacy to occur" (p. 202). This finding, of interest to teachers of both children and adults, was confirmed by the experiences with the families in our project, in which we found that even after intensive demonstration and modeling, few incidences of parents writing with their children occurred. Because homework assignments have been found to influence the types of literacy that parents and children practice, assignments that can be integrated in the routines of family life have potential for providing parents and children with opportunities to engage in literacy activities and with a model for self-initiating such practices. For example, elementary school children may be asked to interview their parents or other community members about a particular topic and record their responses in a journal. Television viewing might become the basis for shared literacy if parents and children coauthor a review of a favorite program for a school newspaper. Meal preparation might provide a context for recording a family recipe for inclusion in a school collection. Collaborative letter writing may be a way for parents and children to tell family and friends about recent experiences and events. Dialogue journals might be suggested as a way for parents and children to say things that are difficult to voice aloud.

Finally, after trying checklists and open-ended journal formats, we learned that asking parents to keep a journal of shared literacy events provides a natural context for beginning each class, as parents reflect on their children's responses to various literacy activities. The journal has the added benefit of giving parents a reason to practice their own writing.

*Although parents are interested in supporting their children's literacy learning, there is a consistent focus on and desire for self-enhancement.* The promise of helping their children succeed in school may be the initial reason parents inquire about and enroll in intergenerational literacy programs, but our experience suggests that it is this interest in combination with a feeling of personal success and accomplishment that promotes continued participation. Opportunities to build friendships, learn about cultures and traditions different from their own, and extend their knowledge of English language and literacy all contribute to parents' and caregivers' sense of accomplishment. Texts that challenge them, inform them about community issues, and help them confront parenting dilemmas are welcomed by the participants. Creating small, cooperative groups provides contexts where they can share personal experiences, take risks, and express diverse opinions. Keeping written response journals allows opportunities for adults to reflect on the thinking of the group and self-reflect. We make no attempt to sort out the relative influence of each of these factors, but we suspect that they combine to create a context in which adults feel intellectually challenged and emotionally supported in their own learning and in understanding how to give their children academic support.

*Parents seize opportunities to use literacy in practical ways.* Often, learners who have limited English proficiency or who are novice readers and writers are assumed to benefit from short, easy tasks. As a result, adult learning centers often abound with specially designed materials that may be costly and ineffective. We have found that parents want to use literacy in practical ways: for example, when a tutor suggested that the parents create a newsletter, they leaped at the suggestion, titled it themselves, and submitted and edited their own writing and that of their children to publish.

In another example, when parents learned of an opportunity for them to submit grant applications for special school projects, they worked cooperatively to write a grant to purchase multicultural and bilingual books. As in any cooperative group activity, parents offered different types and levels of skills: some served as group leaders who monitored group process and organized people; others suggested ideas; others had the English language proficiency necessary to articulate the ideas in writing. The grant was funded for US$250. Parents and caregivers then visited a bookstore to select the books they had requested.

Finally, the adults frequently choose to compose stories that they can read to their children. Sometimes they use these opportunities to amuse or entertain their children and at other times to share an important experience or lesson, as in the following example:

Story to Tell My Kid
by Tuoi Nguyen

Children are living in the United States who are happier than the other children who are living in a poor country. So I tell my daughter a story that will make her understand something about where her family came from and how much she is luckier than her mother.

When I was a little girl, I lived in South Vietnam with my grandmother. My mother went to work in another town; she came home to visit me a gave Grandmother money a few times a year. Then she got married and left the country and came to America when I was nine years old. At that time, my grandmother and I moved to live with my uncle's family. I had to work hard like and adult person: I cleaned the house, washed clothes, cooked and did everything they ordered me to do for them.

I went to private school, but they didn't pay money for school. I saved money which they gave me every morning for breakfast to pay for school and clothes, too. I had to take care of myself. I walked home from school alone when my friends had their parents come to pick them up after school.

During Christmas and New Year I felt lonely when I saw my uncle's children who were happy together to celebrate the party. It's a nice family which

I wish I had. I hoped someday I would have a family. I don't want my children to live like my childhood.

As years passed by, I learned a lot of lessons from my own experiences of how to act with other people in life and other people's experiences of how to act with other people.

Now I have a daughter. She will be four years old next March. I don't care about myself, but I care everything about her, and she is a very happy girl. I teach her wrong from right, how to be a good girl and she makes me proud of her. I'm very happy when she hugs, kisses me and says, "I love you, Mom." How do you feel when you hear your kid say that? You know the answer, right! Thanks to God who always helps me to make a better like for my kid to live in America.

*Intergenerational literacy programs provide a valuable opportunity for parents to learn about schools and classrooms and for teachers to learn about parents and family literacies.* Family literacy programs are often viewed solely as opportunities for parents to learn about schools and classrooms. Parents are seldom viewed as contributors of information, but rather are cast in the role of recipients who acquire knowledge that they will need if their children are to compete effectively with their mainstream peers. White, Taylor, and Moss (1992) analyzed six widely cited reviews of parent involvement in early intervention programs and concluded that in 80 percent of the programs studied, the parent-school partnership focused primarily on parents' roles and responsibilities in preparing children for success in school. More recently, studies have begun to investigate the reciprocal nature of parent-school relationships and, particularly, what teachers can learn from parents. Studies by Hartle-Schutte (1993), Taylor (1991), and Voss (1993) highlight the importance of considering families as a rich source of information both for understanding individual children and also for planning the general school curriculum. Our experiences support that conclusion: we have learned that teachers continue to hold many false assumptions about the literacy experiences and attitudes toward learning in nonmainstream families, as Auerbach argued. In response to the need to establish routine ways for parents to share information with teachers about children's literacy experiences at home, we have recently asked parents in our project to serve as ethnographers and keep a portfolio of their children's home literacy. We have also asked teachers to invite parents to share the portfolios during parent-teacher conferences and combine the information with the children's classroom portfolios. While it is too early to draw any conclusions about the outcomes of this particular effort, we are convinced that exploring paths for parents and teachers to join their knowledge about children's literacy experiences is important in today's changing schools.

## Reflections

Intergenerational literacy programs represent many different purposes in every community. In our case, we have sought to create a program that is responsive to the diverse and often complex needs of parents and other caregivers, children, and schools and to provide a context where all community members can learn from one another. Our efforts are affirmed by the positive responses we receive from family members, such as the comment from one father who told us that "if this program ended I would lose my eyes and my ears." And yet, such programs carry very serious risks and pose important moral dilemmas. As noted by Martin (1992), "The line between basic socialization and middle-class veneer, between being a contributing member of a culture and acquiring the manners of a cultural elite, is not easily drawn" (p. 34). Those who are often referred to as "learners" in intergenerational literacy projects—that is, parents and caregivers—must be permitted and encouraged to assume the role of teachers, so they can help those of us who are formal educators discover where to draw the line.

## Note

[1] During the first three years, the project was funded by a grant from the U.S. Department of Education, FIRST office, a grant from the Massachusetts Department of Education, and a gift from the Xerox Corporation. During the fourth year, the project was supported by the Chelsea public school budget. At the present time, the project is funded by a three-year grant from the Annenberg Foundation, a one-year grant from The Barbara Bush Foundation, and a one-year grant from the Massachusetts Department of Education. In addition, the project is supported by several small grants from various sources.

## References

Anderson, R.C., Hiebert, E.H., Scott, J.A., & Wilkinson, I.A.G. (1985). *Becoming a nation of readers: The report of the Commission on Reading.* Washington, DC: The National Institute of Education.

Auerbach, E.R. (1989). Toward a social-contextual approach to family literacy. *Harvard Educational Review, 59,* 165–181.

Delgado-Gaitan, C. (1992). School matters in the Mexican-American home: Socializing children to education. *American Educational Research Journal, 29,* 495–516.

Eldridge-Hunter, D. (1992). Intergenerational literacy: Impact on the development of the storybook reading behaviors of Hispanic mothers. In C.K. Kinzer & D.J. Leu (Eds.), *Literacy research, theory and practice: Views from many perspectives* (Forty-first Yearbook of the National Reading Conference, pp. 101–110). Chicago, IL: National Reading Conference.

Ferdman, B.M. (1990). Literacy and cultural identity. *Harvard Educational Review, 60,* 181–204.

Genesee, F. (1985). Second language learning through immersion: A review of U.S. programs. *Review of Educational Research, 55,* 541–561.

Goldenberg, C., Reese, L., & Gallimore, R. (1992). Effects of literacy materials from school on Latino children's home experiences and early reading achievement. *American Journal of Education, 100,* 497–536.

Hartle-Schutte, D. (1993). Literacy development in Navajo homes: Does it lead to success in school? *Language Arts, 70,* 642–654.

Heath, S.B. (1983). *Ways with words.* Cambridge, UK: Cambridge University Press.

Martin, J.R. (1992). *The schoolhome: Rethinking schools for changing families.* Cambridge, MA: Harvard University Press.

Moll, L., & Diaz, R. (1987). Teaching writing as communication: The use of ethnographic findings as classroom practice. In D. Bloome (Ed.), *Literacy and schooling* (pp. 193–222). Norwood, NJ: Ablex.

Nieto, S. (1992). *Affirming diversity: The sociopolitical context of multicultural education.* White Plains, NY: Longman.

Paratore, J.R. (1993). An intergenerational approach to literacy: Effects on the literacy learning of adults and on the practice of family literacy. In D.J. Leu & C.K. Kinzer (Eds.), *Examining central issues in literacy research, theory, and practice* (Forty-second Yearbook of the National Reading Conference, pp. 83–92). Chicago, IL: National Reading Conference.

Paratore, J.R. (1994). Parents and children sharing literacy. In D. Lancy (Ed.), *Emergent literacy: From research to practice* (pp. 193–215). New York: Praegar.

Sleeter, C.E., & Grant, C.A. (1987). An analysis of multicultural education in the United States. *Harvard Educational Review, 57,* 421–444.

Taylor, D. (1991). *Learning denied.* Portsmouth, NH: Heinemann.

Taylor, D. (1993). Family literacy: Resisting deficit models. *TESOL Quarterly, 27,* 550–553.

Taylor, D., & Dorsey-Gaines, C. (1988). *Growing up literate: Learning from inner-city families.* Portsmouth, NH: Heinemann.

Teale, W.H. (1984). Reading to young children: Its significance for literacy development. In H. Goelman, A. Oberg, & F. Smith (Eds.), *Awakening to literacy* (pp. 110–121). Portsmouth, NH: Heinemann.

Thistlethwaite, L. (1983). Teaching reading to the ABE student who cannot read. *Lifelong Learning, 1,* 5–7, 28.

Voss, M.M. (1993). "I just watched": Family influences on one child's learning. *Language Arts, 70,* 632–642.

Weinstein, G. (1984). Literacy and second language acquisition: Issues and perspective. *TESOL Quarterly, 18,* 471–484.

White, K.R., Taylor, M.J., & Moss, V.D. (1992). Does research support claims about the benefits of involving parents in early intervention programs? *Review of Educational Research, 62,* 91–126.

# Chapter 4

# Combining Parents' and Teachers' Thoughts About Storybook Reading at Home and School

### Patricia A. Edwards
*Michigan State University, East Lansing, Michigan*

A ngela, a 32-year-old African American mother with 5 children ranging in ages from 22 months to 16 years old, becomes fearful and sometimes defensive when her child's teacher requests that she read to her child. The mother quietly admitted to me something that mirrors the reality of some parents:

> I'm embarrassed, scared, angry, and feel completely helpless because I can't read. I do care 'bout my children and I want them to do well in school. Why don't them teachers believe me when I say I want the best for my children? I know that my children ain't done well in kindergarten and first grade and had to repeat them grades. My older children are in the lowest sections, in Chapter 1, and are struggling in their subjects. My children are frustrated, and I am frustrated, too. I don't know how to help them especially when the teacher wants me to read to them. These teachers think that reading to children is so easy and simple, but it is very difficult if you don't know how to read.

Mrs. Colvin, a first grade teacher at Donaldsonville Elementary School, expressed her frustration with parents or other caregivers like Angela:

Year in and year out these parents who are mostly low-income African American and white send their children to school with serious literacy problems. It seems as if the children have no chance of passing. They don't recognize letters of the alphabet, numbers, and they can't even recognize the letters in their own name. Consequently, it is not surprising that most of them have had to repeat kindergarten and first grade. All of the kindergarten and first grade teachers have seen similar behaviors in these children. These behaviors include limited language skills and the inability to interact with adults. We feel that these children have not been read to and have rarely engaged in adult-child conversations. Each year when we see parents at the beginning of the school year we tell them the same old thing, "Please read to your child at least two to three times per week. It will make a world of difference in how well your child does in school." We know the parents hear what we are saying, but we don't think they have read or plan to read one *single* book to their children. We, as kindergarten and first grade teachers, cannot solve all of these children's literacy problems by ourselves. The parents must help us.

The statements made by Angela and Mrs. Colvin (both pseudonyms) prompted me to ask myself, "Are these statements representative of a larger number of kindergarten and first grade parents' and teachers' thoughts about storybook reading at Donaldsonville Elementary School?" To answer this question, I talked separately with parents and teachers to determine whether this was indeed the case. This chapter highlights the conversations I had with more than 80 percent of the kindergarten and first grade parents and the 11 kindergarten and first grade teachers in this rural Louisiana community about their thoughts and concerns related to storybook reading. In response, I developed the Parents as Partners in Reading Program to assist parents in understanding how to share books with their children. I also designed a course to broaden teachers' understanding of multiple literacy environments and African American children's learning styles.

## Parents' Response to the Teacher's Directive, "Read to Your Child"

In October 1987 I met in the Donaldsonville school library to talk with kindergarten and first grade parents about a series of questions, which are listed here along with their responses.

1. What does reading to your child mean?

> "I think it means helping your children sound out words."

> "Reading means opening the book and reading to the end, just try to get the job done. My problem is my children won't sit still."

"Could it mean selecting fun books for your child?"

"I really don't know what teachers mean when they say, 'Read to your child.'"

"I don't read that well myself, so I don't read to my child. I don't know how to get started."

2. Why do you think your child's teacher often requests that you read to your child?

"Because it is good for them, I think."

"That's something teachers tell me every year, but they don't tell me what they mean."

"Maybe it is something that kindergarten and first grade teachers just say to parents, I don't know. I get so tired of them saying the same old thing every year. I don't even know what they mean, anyway."

"Books can help our children learn to speak better."

3. Do you understand what the teacher means when he or she asks you to read to your child?

"No, I don't know what the teacher means."

"No, I don't know the correct way to begin reading to my child."

"I don't know what to do when I open the book. I mean I don't know what to do first, second, third, and so on."

"I wish somebody would tell me what to do, because I am fed up with teachers saying, 'Read to your child.'"

"I am tired of teachers saying, 'Your child would do so much better in school if you read to them and talked to them.' I do talk to my children. Maybe I don't read to them 'cause I have difficulty reading myself."

4. What difficulties have you encountered when you have attempted to read to your child?

"I guess my answer to this question is if you can't read or don't feel comfortable reading, you ain't gonna want to read to your children."

"I try to read, but I guess I am not doing it right. My child becomes bored, not interested in the book, so I quit trying to read."

"I don't know what books to read to my child."

"Because I don't read well, I don't make time in my schedule. I just pray that they will learn to read in school."

5. Is storybook reading an important part of your daily interactions with your child?

"No, storybook reading is not an important part of my daily interactions with my child." (This comment was made unanimously by the parents.)

## Learning from the Conversation with Parents

My conversation with the parents led me to conclude that they wanted their children to succeed in school, but they did not have a plan for helping them succeed. Perhaps one of the reasons storybook reading was not an important part of the parents' daily interactions with their children is that many of them were unable to assume the responsibility of being their child's first tutor in "unraveling the fascinating puzzle of written language" (Anderson et al., 1985, p. 57). As a result, the "global statements teachers [made] to parents about book reading interactions 'sail[ed] right over their heads,' making it difficult for parents to translate into practice the much requested teacher directive, 'Read to your child'" (Edwards, 1994a, p. 269).

Storybook reading meant, as one parent explained, "opening the book and reading to the end, just to get the job done." Most of the parents appeared not to know that they could stop before finishing the book. When parents were asked what they would do if their children did not cooperate, they responded that they would either verbally or physically reprimand them, which was discouraged.

The parents were unsure about what to do once they "got into the book." Directing children's attention to the story, asking questions, and permitting them to explore the text were storybook reading behaviors unknown to these parents. Not surprisingly, the parents were unsure how to involve their children in the story. "Do I point to the pictures? Do I say the title of the book?" asked one father. Other caregivers asked, "What do I do while I'm holding the book?" I also discovered in my conversation with the parents that they did not know how to label or describe the pictures or to connect items in a book to their child's life, which implied that these parents could not provide the necessary scaffolding for their children. The teachers had assumed that these parents had this knowledge.

Perhaps the most revealing insight I gained from my conversation with the parents was that many of these parents were not competent readers, which supports France and Meeks's (1987) contention:

> Parents who do not have basic literacy skills are greatly handicapped in meeting the challenge of creating a "curriculum of the home" to prepare their children to succeed in school. Furthermore, they can't help their children build a foundation for literacy because they are unable to read to them (p. 222).

Darling (1988) iterates this point by stating, "Parents who lack basic literacy skills cannot know the joy of reading a story to their children, and these children cannot reap the documented educational benefits of being read to" (p. 2).

These comments regarding caregivers who lack basic literacy skills characterized the Donaldsonville Elementary School parents. Also, the comments made by Angela (the African American mother of five children) about storybook reading represented a majority of the parents' thoughts and concerns. The parents felt as Angela did—"embarrassed, scared, angry, and…helpless because [they] could not read."

## Teachers' Reactions to Parents' Lack of Response

Following my conversation with the parents, I used a similar format to initiate a conversation with teachers. In my first meeting with the teachers, they wasted little time informing me that most of the children in their classes were having difficulty and probably would repeat the grade. I found such statements unsettling because school had only been in session for two months. From this initial dialogue, I began to ask them questions that centered around exploring why these students seemed so destined to fail. The primary teachers' responses were insightful and reflected their frustration and anxiety with teaching children who entered school with what they called "limited literacy skills." The teachers' comments also mirrored Mrs. Colvin's feelings (the first grade teacher who was highlighted at the beginning of the chapter). The four questions along with teacher responses are listed here.

1. Why do you think the children in your classroom are having difficulty emerging as readers and writers?

   "Their parents have not done anything to prepare them for school."

   "The parents have not read to their children or talked to them."

   "The children have had very limited opportunities to engage in literacy interactions before school."

   "Sometimes I don't think their parents care whether their children read or not. Every year I tell them what to do, but nothing happens. It seems as if the parents don't hear you, or if they hear you they just don't plan to do anything."

2. Do you think parents understand the directive, "Read to your child"?

   "Yes, but they just don't care."

   "I guess they do understand because they never ask any questions."

   "Maybe they understand but don't know what to do."

   "Perhaps some of the parents don't have time and think their children will learn to read in school without them having to help them at home."

3. Why do you suspect parents aren't reading to their children?

"It has puzzled me for years that we tell parents to help their children, but nothing happens. It makes me wonder if they really understand what we are really saying when we say, 'Read to your child.'"

"We have a high dropout rate in this community, and I suspect that many of our parents are illiterate and semiliterate. However, we don't have time to teach parents how to read. It takes so much time to teach their children how to read."

4. What are some past parental responses to your requests for them to read to their children?

"As I said before, every year since I have been at Donaldsonville Elementary School, I have told parents to read to their children. However, I don't think they have."

"I think we have a group of parents who think that it is not their job to read to their children. Their attitude is 'You are the teacher, so you teach them how to read. That is your job not ours.' They simply don't get it. It is both our jobs!"

## Learning from the Conversation with Teachers

The teachers at Donaldsonville felt that they were doing all they could to help these children. Without parental assistance at home, the children were going to fail. Teachers expected and demanded that parents be involved in their children's education by reading to them at home, which, to the teachers, was not an unreasonable request. They were indeed "telling" and "giving" parents the right advice. However, the teachers assumed that the parents knew how to read to their children and had a clear understanding of what to do while reading. Edwards's (1989) study of five low-socioeconomic households showed that four of the five mothers did not share books successfully with their children, and they needed assistance with their own literacy skills. This study suggests an urgent need for ongoing intervention in low-SES homes and continued, expanded literacy training for parents, both for themselves and their interactions with their children.

Even though the teachers suspected that the parents were unable to read, they still expected them to read to their children. The teachers did not seem to take into account that 40 percent of the parents at Donaldsonville were illiterate or semiliterate. Teachers mistook parents' unfamiliarity with the task being asked of them and their low literacy skills as disinterest in their children's education. The continued demand that caregivers read to their children at home sparked hostility and racial tension between teachers and parents. Each group blamed the other for the children's failures; each felt victimized by the interaction. Children were caught between their two most important educators—their teacher and their parent.

## The Need to Develop Programs for Parents and Teachers

After the conversations with parents and teachers, it became increasingly clear to me that something needed to be done to help parents understand school-based literacy practices and teachers understand home-based literacy practices. As a result, I decided to develop the Parents as Partners in Reading Program as well as a course in literacy learning for primary teachers.

One reason I created a storybook reading program for parents is that other researchers have highlighted low-SES parents' inability to participate successfully during storybook reading, but did not go on to the next step of recommending strategies for improving parental participation (Farron, 1982; Heath, 1982a, 1983; Snow & Ninio, 1986). Researchers have also stressed the importance of parent-child book reading. As Morrow mentioned in Chapter 1, more than 80 years ago Huey (1908) advised parents to read to their children: "The secret of it all lies in the parents reading aloud to and with the child" (p. 332). More recently, Teale (1981) found that "virtually every reading methods book or early childhood education book written and dozens of articles recommend that families read to young children in order to provide a sound foundation for learning to read and write in later years" (p. 902). And in 1984, Vukelich surveyed more than 40 sources and found that reading to children was the parent involvement activity that teachers requested most frequently.

Another reason I decided to develop the storybook reading program for caregivers was that a number of researchers have supported the notion that parents could profit from receiving assistance in how to read effectively to their children (Pflaum, 1986; Spewock, 1988; Swift, 1970). By showing the parents how to read to their children I could help them fulfill an important personal expectation, which is for their children to have a successful school experience. They could also learn to identify pedagogical techniques, reading strategies, text factors, and familial factors that are central to literacy acquisition. I thought the storybook reading program could also help the parents help their children acquire the rituals, verbal interaction patterns, and language forms preferred in schools as well as prompt the parents to examine and improve their own personal reading skills.

My conversation with the primary teachers confirmed the need for all teachers to increase their awareness and understanding of multiple literacy environments. Taylor (1983) proposed ten years ago:

> We [as researchers] need [to help teachers] know more of the learning styles, coping strategies, and social systems of the children [they] teach if instruction

in reading and writing is to be a meaningful complement to…[the] lives [of their students] (p. 93).

Talking with teachers made me realize that people can live in close proximity to one another and know very little about other ways of becoming literate. This was the case at Donaldsonville Elementary School. Consequently, the course I developed provided a forum for the teachers and me to discuss issues related to multiple literacy environments and African American children's learning styles.

## Parents as Partners in Reading Program

*Program goals.* In my conversation with the parents, they explicitly stated that book reading was not a part of their daily lives. My goals were to "introduce these parents to book reading techniques that could help them help the teacher build their children's background in reading instruction" and to "correlate the book reading program to goals and objectives of the kindergarten and first grade reading curriculum" (Edwards, 1992, p. 354). Showing these low-income parents how to share books with their children was not to justify a "transmission of school practices" model, in which the only solution, as Auerbach (1989) states, is for nonmainstream families to become acculturated. Instead, I informed the parents of the following:

> Ideally, schools should recognize and incorporate the different interaction patterns and literacy events that characterize nonmainstream communities. For this to happen, however, we need considerably more research—documenting the different types of interaction patterns and literacy events common in nonmainstream communities—and more teacher training (Edwards & Garcia, 1991, p. 183).

*A meeting place and a change in school policy.* The parents met in the Donaldsonville school library, which became a place for gathering socially to talk about literacy and to exchange ideas. The library atmosphere helped the caregivers relax and enjoy learning how to help their children; they came to know about books, learned how to share books with their children, and developed a love of books. For the first time, the parents became aware of what Pflaum (1986) calls "[their] impact on their child's reading" (p. 10).

For this program, the school's librarian agreed to allow parents to check out up to five books each week. She designed a computer program that listed the names of each child whose parents were participating in the book reading program to enable the parents to check out books under their child's name. The librarian also kept a computerized

*Parents and children read together in school and use the library as a family room.*

list of the types of books the parents were borrowing, which was shared with me and the child's teacher. This was the first time in the school's history that parents were allowed to borrow books, which changed the school's policy but also changed the lives and experiences of parents and children. (For a fuller description of how caregivers were recruited for the program and how the Donaldsonville community participated in this process, see Edwards, 1991, 1992, 1994a)

*Program structure.* The book reading program operated from October 1987 to May 1988 in the Donaldsonville School and consisted of 23 two-hour sessions divided into three phases: coaching, peer modeling, and parent-child interactions. Each phase lasted for approximately six to seven weeks. During phase one I met with the parents as a group. I modeled effective book reading behaviors and introduced various teacher tapes, which highlighted specific reading techniques. The tapes often began with the teacher providing a rationale for why a book was appropriate for accomplishing a particular objective. The objective could be pointing to pictures, labeling and describing pictures, or making real-life connections. The teacher would then model book reading with a child, highlighting the particular objective they had selected. Af-

Edwards

ter parents viewed the tape, I involved them in a guided discussion of the applications of the strategy modeled by the teacher. The parents could stay after the sessions to review tapes and speak with me.

During the peer modeling phase, I helped the caregivers manage the book reading sessions and strategies. This phase was specifically based on Vygotsky's (1978) work, which states, "The zone of proximal development defines those functions that have not yet matured but are in the process of maturation" (p. 86). I assisted the parents by (1) guiding their participation in book reading interactions with one another, (2) finding connections between what they already knew and what they needed to know, (3) modeling effective reading behaviors for them when such assistance was needed (encouraging them to review teacher tapes), and (4) providing praise and support for their attempts.

During the last phase, parent-child interactions, I relinquished control to the parents and functioned primarily as a supportive and sympathetic audience. I offered suggestions to the caregivers as to what books to use during reading interactions with their children, evaluated the parent-child book reading interactions, and provided feedback or modeling. In this phase, the parents shared books with their own children and implemented strategies they learned in the previous two phases. From these interactions, they learned the importance of involving their children in a book reading interaction and recognized that "the parent holds the key to unlocking the meaning represented by the text" (Chapman, 1986, p. 12). (For more details about the three phases of the book reading program, see Edwards, 1990a, 1990b, 1991, 1994b.)

## Literacy Learning Course for Primary Teachers

*Course goals.* I wanted to increase the teachers' knowledge and understanding of multiple literacy environments and African American children's learning styles. In the course, I included readings that would help teachers begin to think more critically and reflectively about these issues (see Edwards, 1994b, for a complete listing of these readings and Edwards, 1994a, for a listing of the topics covered in the course).

*Course structure.* During the fall of 1987, we met once a week for the entire semester in the school's library to discuss readings related to parental involvement and family literacy. Each week two teachers and I assumed the primary responsibility for leading class discussions around two to three readings. We spent at least two class sessions on the topic "cultural differences in families." In the first class discussion, we read the work of Anderson and Stokes (1984), Au (1980), Gee (1987), Michaels (1981), and Schieffelin and Cochran-Smith (1984). In the second class discussion, we read the work of Heath (1982a, 1982b, 1983). An excerpt from the first class discussion on cultural differences in families is described following in which I refer to myself as the leader and the two teachers that assisted me as teacher leaders (TL).

> Leader: Children from some families may differ in their values, their orientation toward school, and their speech patterns from those in the American mainstream. Most of the children from Donaldsonville are from homes that differ economically, socially, and culturally from your middle-class backgrounds. (The teachers nodded their heads in agreement.) Although these children's cultural environments may be full and rich, they differ markedly from the school setting. Most teachers come from middle-class families and as a result have middle-class expectations regarding goals, behaviors, and academic achievement. Instructional materials often deal with experiences unfamiliar to culturally different children. Therefore, a considerable gap exists between the environment of the culturally different children and the middle-class school situation. Because of this discontinuity, many of these children have difficulty learning in school. (The teachers agreed.)
>
> Am I correct in saying that many of the children in the Donaldsonville community live in poverty, and some of their parents may be illiterate? (The teachers nodded their heads in agreement.) In my study of low-SES mothers in northern Louisiana, I found four of the five mothers did not share books successfully with their children. That is, they did not engage their children in the reading events. Additionally, they needed assistance with their own personal literacy skills.

> Teacher: We believe that's accurate.

> Leader: As many of you have already noted, the children who enter your kindergarten and first grade classes are not ready for traditional reading readiness programs; they do not know how to control their behavior and interact socially with other children, and their oral language is inadequate for communication. (The teachers overwhelmingly agreed with this statement.) Lastly, many of the children you teach may be unfamiliar with pencils, scissors, paints, and books, and they may never have heard a story read to them.

> Teacher: What you are saying is so true, and it represents the parents and children we deal with here at Donaldsonville Elementary School.

> Teacher: What can we do?

> Leader: We can start by learning something about how different families prepare their children for school. All children come to school with some experiences with reading and writing. However, the nature of the experiences varies from child to child and community to community. One of the goals of this class is to help you learn about multiple literacy environments.

Teacher: That's good.

TL: I found after reading the Anderson and Stokes article it made me recognize these children participated in or witnessed a range of reading and writing experiences. For example, literacy events for daily livings needs (paying bills or obtaining welfare assistance), entertainment (solving a crossword puzzle or reading a television guide), and religion (Bible-reading sessions with children). After reading the article by Schieffelin and Cochran-Smith about the experiences of a Sino-Vietnamese family, in which the son had entered school in Philadelphia in second grade and was successful in learning to read and write at nine years of age, it is so interesting for me to learn that a prominent feature of this home was its lack of reading materials or an abundance of print. Instead literacy was functional, meaningful, and relevant in the lives of this family and other Asian refugees studied.

Teacher: Both of these articles were interesting and gave me a lot to think about.

TL: Gee's discussion of primary discourse and secondary institutions really made a lot of sense when I read Michaels's work on "sharing time" and Au's work on "talk story." In Michaels's 1981 article, she stated, "Sharing time could either provide or deny access to key literacy-related experiences, depending, ironically, on the degree to which teacher and child start out 'sharing' a set of discourse conventions and interpretive strategies" (p. 423). That is a powerful statement. What was also powerful for me was Au's observation that teachers who insisted that Hawaiian children speak one at a time in answering their questions had great difficulty in conducting effective reading lessons. On the other hand, teachers who allowed the children to cooperate or speak together in answering questions could conduct highly effective lessons. Teachers who used this second style of interaction were teaching in a manner consistent with the rules for talk story, an important nonschool speech event for Hawaiian children. In talk story, speakers cooperate with one another in telling stories. Rather than one person telling the whole story, two or more speakers take turns, each narrating just a small part. Again, I found it so interesting to read real accounts of how other cultures interact outside of school.

Leader: I'm looking forward to our discussion of Heath's work, especially her article on bedtime stories in three different communities.

## Lessons Learned by Parents and Teachers

The parents realized that the teachers did not want to assume full responsibility for educating their children. Instead they wanted them to become partners in their children's education. They came to recognize that the ways in which they interacted with their children affected how well their children performed in school. The parents learned how to share books with their children. They also learned that storybook reading is the cornerstone of reading instruction in the early grades (Edwards & Garcia, 1991), which is evident in the comments of one parent:

> I had a lot of doubts about myself, and it was hard for me to make up my mind about coming. With some encouragement from another mother who was attending the program, I decided to come. She told me that the program would help me help my kids in school. I said to her, "Okay, I'll come one time," but I ended up coming all year. By coming to this program, I found out that there was a lot that I didn't know and a lot of things that I wasn't doing, but I didn't know what to do. I really didn't know book reading was so important. I wish I had known that sooner, because I would have been able to help my other children in school.

The course on literacy learning acquainted teachers with the literacy environments of children outside of school. It made them pause and begin to look critically at the ways in which their classroom environments were incongruent with their students' out of school learning experiences. The course also enabled teachers to recognize that all literacy environments should be acknowledged and not ignored or dismantled. Although these teachers were able to take the first important step of exploring the different ways in which parents prepare their children for school, this newly created dialogue did not necessarily translate into different classroom practices. More important, the course made teachers stop and think more seriously about the directives they gave parents. The teachers came to understand that "read to your child" is a simple teacher directive, but it is a very difficult and complex task for parents who are unable to read.

## Implications and Recommendations

If parents' ways of preparing their children for school are significantly inconsistent with school-based literacy practices, it can create problems for children when they enter the school's environment. I believe we should ask ourselves two questions if and when this situation occurs: (1) Do we as educators simply acknowledge that an inconsistency between home and school exists? or (2) Should we attempt to develop programs to bridge the gap between home- and school-based literacy practices? I suggest the latter approach. More than 20 years ago, Leichter (1973) supported this approach when she argued:

> Cultural distance in education values between parents and teachers should be examined in two directions, asking by what processes the school reinforces, complements, contradicts, or inhibits the efforts of the family and com-

munity and by what processes the family and community reinforce, contradict, or inhibit the efforts of the school (p. 73).

I also believe that we should not spend time blaming either parents or teachers for failure in students' literacy achievement. Snow and colleagues (1991) point out:

> Studies of failure in literacy achievement have tended to shift the blame back and forth between home and school.... Those who look to the home as the main cause of poor literacy skills tend to cite as factors leading to poor achievement a low level of parental literacy, a low level of parental education, instability of the home, absence of books in the home, and low parental aspirations for children's achievement. Those who look to the school as the main cause point to such facts as limited school resources, ...inadequate or inappropriate teacher preparation, low expectations for the children's achievement, ...a mismatch in discourse patterns and behavioral expectations between home and school, and the use of inadequate teaching methods (p. 7).

Blaming the parent or the school for failure in students' literacy achievement is a waste of time and energy: we should support parents and teachers by helping them become border crossers. By doing this, we will provide them with "the opportunity to engage the multiple references that construct different cultural codes, experiences, and histories...to cross over into diverse cultural zones that offer a critical resource for rethinking how the relations between dominant and subordinate groups are organized" (Giroux, 1991, p. xiv).

## References

Anderson, A.B., & Stokes, S.J. (1984). Social and institutional influences on the development and practice of literacy. In H. Goelman, A. Oberg, & F. Smith (Eds.), *Awakening to literacy* (pp. 24–37). Portsmouth, NH: Heinemann.

Anderson, R.C., Hiebert, E.H., Scott, J.A., & Wilkinson, I.A.G. (1985). *Becoming a nation of readers: The report of the Commission on Reading.* Washington, DC: The National Institute of Education.

Au, K. (1980). Participation structures in a reading lesson with Hawaiian children: Analysis of a culturally appropriate instructional event. *Anthropology and Education Quarterly, 11*(2), pp. 91–115.

Auerbach, E.R. (1989). Toward a social-contextual approach to family literacy. *Harvard Educational Review, 59*, 165–181.

Chapman, D.L. (1986). Let's read another one. In D.R. Tovey & J.E. Kerber (Eds.), *Roles in literacy learning: A new perspective* (pp. 10–25). Newark, DE: International Reading Association.

Darling, S. (1988). *Family literacy education: Replacing the cycle of failure with the legacy of success.* Washington, DC: Office of Educational Research and Improvement (ED 332 749).

Edwards, P.A. (1989). Supporting lower SES mothers' attempts to provide scaffolding for bookreading. In J. Allen & J. Mason (Eds.), *Risk makers, risk takers, risk breakers: Reducing the risks for young literacy learners* (pp. 222–250). Portsmouth, NH: Heinemann.

Edwards, P.A. (1990a). *Parents as partners in reading: A family literacy training program*. Chicago, IL: Childrens Press.

Edwards, P.A. (1990b). *Talking your way to literacy: A program to help nonreading parents prepare their children for reading*. Chicago, IL: Childrens Press.

Edwards, P.A. (1991). Fostering early literacy through parent coaching. In E. Hiebert (Ed.), *Literacy for a diverse society: Perspectives, programs, and policies* (pp. 199–213). New York: Teachers College Press.

Edwards, P.A. (1992, Autumn). Involving parents in building reading instruction for African-American children. *Theory Into Practice, 31*(4), 350–359.

Edwards, P.A. (1994a). Connecting African-American families and youth to the school's reading program: Its meaning for school and community literacy. In V.L. Gadsden & D. Wagner (Eds.), *Literacy among African-American youth: Issues in learning, teaching and schooling* (pp. 263–281). Cresskill, NJ: Hampton.

Edwards, P.A. (1994b). Responses of teachers and African-American mothers to a book reading intervention program. In D. Dickinson (Ed.), *Bridges of literacy: Approaches to supporting child and family literacy* (pp. 175–208). Cambridge, MA: Blackwell.

Edwards, P.A., & Garcia, G.E. (1981). Parental involvement in mainstream schools. In M. Foster (Ed.), *Readings on equal education: Qualitative investigations into schools and schooling* (pp. 167–187). New York: AMS Press.

Farron, D.C. (1982). Mother-child interaction, language development, and the school performance of poverty children. In L. Feagans & D.C. Farron (Eds.), *The language of children reared in poverty* (pp. 19–52). New York: Academic.

France, M.G., & Meeks, J.W. (1987). Parents who can't read: What the schools can do. *Journal of Reading, 31*, 222–227.

Gee, J.P. (1987, March). *What is literacy?* Paper presented at the Mailman Foundation Conference on Families and Literacy, Harvard Graduate School of Education, Cambridge, MA.

Giroux, H.A. (1991). Series introduction: Literacy, differences, and the politics of border crossing. In C. Mitchell & K. Weiler (Eds.), *Rewriting literacy: Culture and the discourse of the other* (pp. ix–xvi). New York: Bergin & Garvey.

Heath, S.B. (1982a). What no bedtime story means: Narrative skills at home and school. *Language in Society, 11*, 49–76.

Heath, S.B. (1982b). Questioning at home and at school: A comparative study. In G. Spindler (Ed.), *Doing ethnography of schooling: Education anthropology in action* (pp. 102–129). New York: Holt, Rinehart and Winston.

Heath, S.B. (1983). *Ways with words*. New York: Cambridge University Press.

Huey, E.B. (1908). *The psychology and pedagogy of reading*. New York: Macmillan.

Leichter, H.J. (1973). The concept of educative style. *Teachers College Record, 75*, 239–250.

Michaels, S. (1981). "Sharing time": Children's narrative styles and differential access to literacy. *Language in Society, 10*, 423–442.

Pflaum, S.W. (1986). *The development of language and literacy in young children* (3rd ed.). Columbus, OH: Merrill.

Schieffelin, B.B., & Cochran-Smith, M. (1984). Learning to read culturally: Literacy before schooling. In H. Goelman, A. Oberg, & F. Smith (Eds.), *Awakening to literacy* (p. 3–23). Portsmouth, NH: Heinemann.

Snow, C.E., Barnes, W.S., Chandler, J., Goodman, I.F., & Hemphill, L. (1991). *Unfilled expectations: Home and school influences on literacy*. Cambridge, MA: Harvard University Press.

Snow, C.E., & Ninio, A. (1986). The contract of literacy: What children learn from learning to read books. In W.H. Teale & E. Sulzby (Eds.), *Emergent literacy: Writing and reading*. Norwood, NJ: Ablex.

Spewock, T.S. (1988). Training parents to teach their pre-schoolers through literature. *The Reading Teacher, 41*, 648–652.

Swift, M.S. (1970). Training poverty mothers in communication skills. *The Reading Teacher, 23,* 360–367.

Taylor, D. (1983). *Family literacy: Young children learning to read and write.* Portsmouth, NH: Heinemann.

Teale, W.H. (1981). Parents reading to their children: What we know and need to know. *Language Arts, 58,* 902–911.

Vukelich, C. (1984). Parents' role in the reading process. A review of practical suggestions to communicate with parents. *The Reading Teacher, 37,* 472–477.

Vygotsky, L.S. (1978). *Mind in society: The development of higher psychological processes.* Cambridge, MA: Harvard University Press.

Chapter 5_____

# The Family Writing and Reading Appreciation Program

Lesley Mandel Morrow
with Jody L. Scoblionko and Dixie Shafer
*Rutgers University, New Brunswick, New Jersey*

*H*arriet *walked into the school library. Although this was the second meeting in our intergenerational family literacy program, I could tell from the expression on her face that she was hesitant about joining us, so I went to greet her. We found a place for her to sit, next to a parent she knew. I brought her a plate of cookies and a cup of juice and a* new Highlights for Children *magazine, a material we use in the program at home and in school.*

*Keisha, Harriet's grandchild, was with her. We had activities and refreshments for the children in the school cafeteria, supervised by my college students. Keisha went to join the rest of the children during the parent meeting.*

*Harriet, who is about 45 years old, has three grandchildren in her custody, and she is raising the children alone. She is on welfare and has trouble supporting the family. Keisha is not doing well in school, and Harriet is very concerned.*

*We began the meeting with a discussion of what the parents or grandparents had done with their children since last we met. The parents had a list of suggested activities to choose from, such as working in the* Highlights *magazine, noticing printed words at home or in the community, writing in their journals together, and so forth. Each parent mentioned one activity worked on with his or her child. When it was Harriet's turn, she said, "Well, I tried these* Highlights *but them stories are too long to read." I realized that Harriet was probably having trouble reading the stories. We talked about features in the magazine that she could use with her grandchild, such as finding the "Hidden Pictures" or doing the "Matching Pictures." These required limited literacy skills.*

*A week later I happened to meet Harriet in the hallway of the school. I asked how her meetings were going with Linda, a college student working on the family literacy project who meets weekly with Harriet. Harriet was very animated, much different than she had been at the parent meeting. She said, "Oh, our meetings are goin' fine. Linda showed me these little stories I can read to Keisha in the* Highlights, *and we love them. That Linda is such a nice girl."*

*When talking to Linda, I told her how enthused Harriet was about the section of* Highlights *she had introduced her to. Linda said, "I showed her the 'Dear Highlights' letters sent in by children who are responding to articles in the magazine." The magazine pages are divided into three columns and each "Dear Highlights" entry is about one-third of a column long. Harriet referred to them as stories and felt comfortable reading them to her grandchild. She was delighted with her success, and we were pleased that we found something for her to share with Keisha.*

This appears to be a small success story, but to us it represents a very important achievement. Harriet was feeling more confident about

*Linda, a Rutgers University student, meets with Harriet and her granddaughter Keisha to review reading and writing activities to do together at home.*

her ability to help her grandchild and about her own literacy ability. She was not only helping Keisha, but by using *Highlights*, she was practicing her own literacy skills as well.

In a short time, Harriet and Linda formed a close relationship. They respected and cared about each other. When it was parent-teacher conference time in the school, Harriet asked Linda to come to the meeting because she was nervous about what she would hear concerning Keisha's schoolwork and was not sure she would understand everything. Linda sought permission from Keisha's teacher who was happy to have her accompany Harriet. After the conference, Linda helped Harriet understand the ways in which she could work with Keisha. As a result of the family literacy program, Harriet was not as fearful about coming to school as she had been; she was willing to share her concerns, ask questions, and seek help. Harriet commented, "I always wanted to help my grandchildren, but I didn't know how. I thought the teacher knows more than me, and I really don't know what to do. Now I have someone to ask about how to help. I can do the things she shows me, and I feel I'm really helping Keisha now."

In this family literacy program we have observed the effects of home literacy activities on children, especially their increased interest in reading and writing. We have seen how the adults involved develop more confidence in their ability to serve as both teacher and parent to their children, how some parents improve their literacy skills as a result of their involvement, and how teachers participate to help promote literacy activities at home.

## The Importance of Families in Children's Literacy Development

As argued in previous chapters, parents are the first teachers children have, and, beginning at birth, children's experiences affect their success in becoming literate individuals. It is also known that the success of the school literacy program often depends on the environment at home. Because of this, the characteristics of the many children who come to school reading and writing without formal instruction and their homes have been investigated. This line of study has revealed home practices that could be successful in school settings and information concerning the crucial role families play in the development of their children's literacy (Clark, 1984; Cochran-Smith, 1984; Morrow, 1993; Teale, 1984). These studies carried out in homes have been a catalyst for the new innovations in early literacy strategies. This research also points out that literacy experiences practiced in some homes are not congruent with literacy activities encountered in school. Despite the fact that literacy behaviors are present in one form or another in most families, the type of events that some parents share with their children may have little influence on school success. Conversely, the kinds of literacy practiced in classrooms may have little meaning for those children or their parents (Auerbach, 1989; Heath, 1983; Morrow et al., 1993; Taylor & Dorsey-Gaines, 1988).

With this conflict, it is difficult for some parents to integrate school-based literacy events into their homes. Therefore, we must learn about the literacy that occurs in homes of families from diverse cultural backgrounds and how these parents or other caregivers and children share literacy on a daily basis. We need to explore how such events can serve school learning. Rather than approaching parents who speak languages other than English and those who have not acquired mainstream literacy skills from a deficit point of view, we need to identify and build first on the strengths they possess from their cultural backgrounds. According to Delgado-Gaitan (1987), all parents, regardless of education level, recognize the importance of a positive home literacy environment. Parents with less education, however, need to be informed about community resources and shown how they can be role models for their children. Delgado-Gaitan found that parents who participated in school activities and family literacy programs realized that they were an important link in their children's education. She also found that the parents who did not participate did not consider the activities as important and felt the teacher was in charge when their children were at school. As stressed in Chapter 1, if we do not attend to the home when we plan literacy programs, whatever strategies we design for the school will never be completely successful. Therefore, family literacy programs are necessary for helping parents understand how important they are in the literacy development of their children. We need to help parents realize that they do have skills from their own cultures that they can share with their children, and we need to empower them with new skills that will enhance their understanding of literacy development. It is possible to provide programs that are sensitive to diverse cultures by using the resources already within the family and by offering additional strategies for parents to help their children.

## The Family WRAP Program

The purpose of the Family Writing and Reading Appreciation Program (WRAP) is to help parents appreciate and understand the importance of their role in the literacy development of their children. Materials and methods are provided for parents or other caregivers to help enhance their children's motivation for reading and writing. We are also interested in heightening teachers' awareness about how important parents are in the literacy development process, so teachers are involved in this project that includes activities that link home and school. We want the program to motivate parents' interest in helping their children and to increase their confidence in their ability to do so. An indirect goal is for parents with limited literacy skills to enhance their ability to read and write by participating in the activities in the program with their child. The Family WRAP program is now taking place in Redshaw School, an inner-city public elementary school in New Brunswick, New Jersey, where the population is 95 percent African American and Latino. All parents with children in the first, second, and third grades are invited to participate.

The Family WRAP program was conceived to provide a mirror image of an initiative we had already organized in the school called the WRAP (Writing and Reading Appreciation Program) program designed to promote interest in reading and writing.[1] With the WRAP program we wanted to motivate children to read voluntarily for pleasure and for information. We wanted children to be able to approach literacy as a social activity by engaging in activities together and seeking the help of others to achieve goals (National Reading Research Center, 1991). The WRAP school program is a literature-based reading and writing initiative that includes classroom literacy centers with a variety of activities available to children. Materials found in the classroom centers are bookshelves to place featured books that hold five to eight books per child for three to four grade levels and represent varied genres of children's literature. The books can be checked out to take home from the classroom library. Pillows, rugs, stuffed animals, and rocking chairs add comfort to the area. Manipulatives such as feltboards with story characters and taped stories with headsets are available for the children's use. There is also an "Author's Spot" equipped with paper, blank booklets, and writing utensils.

The teacher models activities to create interest in books by reading aloud and telling stories using techniques such as chalktalks, felt stories, puppet stories, and so forth. Children engage in story retelling and rewriting, creating original stories, and sharing books that have been read. Activities emphasized include journal writing, collecting words, and learning elements of story structure, styles of authors and illustrators, and literal and interpretive discussions related to stories. *Highlights for Children* magazines are used regularly in all classrooms.

WRAP Time, part of the WRAP program, gives students choices within a structure. It occurs three to five times a week for 30 to 40 minutes and provides children with the opportunity to choose from a variety of literacy activities. Children can read a book, read to a friend, listen to a taped story, tell a story with the feltboard, or write in their journal. They can work alone or with others. Students are also expected to complete tasks and present them to the class.

### Components of the Family WRAP Program

The Family WRAP program has the same goal as the school WRAP program, with many of the same materials provided for parents. We wanted a home program that was pleasurable and familiar for children. As parents introduce activities, children can relate to them and help their parents with them as well because they have done them in school. The teachers support the home program, and the home program supports what is happening in school.

*Materials for parents or other caregivers.* The shopping bag of materials provided for the parents is similar to that used in school and includes the following:

◆ a *Highlights for Children* magazine;

◆ two spiral notebooks for journals;

◆ a file box with blank 3″ x 5″ cards for recording Very Own Words;

◆ a storyboard for storytelling; and

◆ *The Parent WRAP Program* parent handbook.

Parents receive a *Highlights for Children* magazine to become familiar with its use. Children regularly receive a copy of the magazine in school then another to take home and keep each month and share with their parents. Because this literacy material is used both in the home and school, the same list of lessons that relate to the magazine is provided for parents and teachers so that students will recognize the activities when doing them at home with their family members. Children can also show parents with limited literacy ability what to do with *Highlights*. An excellent feature of the magazine is that there is something for everyone—for all interests and abilities. Because parents enjoy using the magazine, children are able to enlist their help with the activities as well.

We also give parents two spiral notebooks, one for their child and one for them to write in together. They can write whatever they please, such as what each did during the day, or they can make shopping lists, draw pictures, and so forth.

Parents receive a file box containing blank 30 x 50 cards for their children's "Very Own Words." These are words that are new for students that they find in schoolwork or in print within the home or community. Very Own Words are written on the cards and stored in the file box. Children and parents are to read the words, copy them, and use them when they are writing stories or in their journals.

Each parent is provided with a storyboard made of corrugated cardboard. The triangular shaped material has a piece of felt on one side, and the other side is designed for showing "roll stories." The storyboard also serves as a puppet stage. Each parent receives felt story characters, stick puppets with accompanying storybooks to use with their storyboard, and roll paper (white shelving paper from the supermarket) to create stories that are rolled as they are read. Children can write and draw their own stories or re-create stories they have read by making felt figures, stick puppets, or roll stories. The parent packet also includes a book of chalktalks—simple stories that are read and drawn at the same time (Olsen, 1963). (See *Super Tips for Storytelling*, Morrow, 1992.)

Also included is a parent handbook entitled *The Family WRAP Program*—a short guide explaining the importance of the parents' role in the literacy development of their children. The handbook first points out things parents are probably already doing at home that help their children with literacy, such as making shopping lists, sending greeting cards for special occasions, and following directions for preparing recipes. By noting literacy activity already present in the home, we hope to bolster parents' self-confidence in their ability to help their children and to serve as role models. The next section of the booklet lists the things we provide for parents, which were described earlier, and what we ask parents to do in the program. Following is a section called "Things to Look for and Have in Your Home." The list includes scissors, tape, pencils, paper, space for children to work, magazines, newspapers, and children's books. The last two sections are lists of "Things to Do with Your Child at Home," which reflect the activity checklist in Figure 1.

Some sample suggestions include read or look at books together, tell stories using the storyboard with puppets or felt figures, watch TV together and talk about the program or story, let your child see you reading books, magazines, and newspapers, and make your child aware of print in the home. Next is a list of "Things to Do with Your Child Outside Your Home," such as visit the library and check out books, go on outings together to the supermarket, post office, or zoo, and note the

*Morrow, Scoblionko, & Shafer*

## Figure 1
## Parent Weekly Activities

Check the things done with your child:

| Inside Our Home | M | T | W | Date TH | F | S | S |
|---|---|---|---|---|---|---|---|
| played with my child | | | | | | | |
| read to my child | | | | | | | |
| listened to my child read | | | | | | | |
| looked at books together | | | | | | | |
| read silently together | | | | | | | |
| told stories together | | | | | | | |
| did puppet stories | | | | | | | |
| did felt stories | | | | | | | |
| drew pictures about stories | | | | | | | |
| made roll stories | | | | | | | |
| did chalktalks | | | | | | | |
| looked at the newspaper together | | | | | | | |
| did reading and writing for my work | | | | | | | |
| read my own book | | | | | | | |
| went through the mail together | | | | | | | |
| read *Highlights* magazine together | | | | | | | |
| pointed out print at home | | | | | | | |
| helped my child with homework | | | | | | | |
| wrote with my child | | | | | | | |
| wrote a note to my child | | | | | | | |
| helped my child with writing | | | | | | | |
| asked child about school activities | | | | | | | |
| made shopping lists together | | | | | | | |
| made things by following directions | | | | | | | |
| cooked together following recipes | | | | | | | |
| selected TV shows to watch together | | | | | | | |
| discussed what we watched on TV | | | | | | | |
| **Outside Our Home** | | | | | | | |
| attended school activities | | | | | | | |
| visited the library | | | | | | | |
| borrowed books from the library | | | | | | | |
| visited the bookstore | | | | | | | |
| noticed print outside | | | | | | | |
| visited the post office, park, or other place and talked about what we saw | | | | | | | |
| shared talents or cultural customs at school | | | | | | | |

print all around. The last section of the parent book is called "Things to Do and Say to Make Your Children Feel Good About Themselves, About You, and About Reading and Writing." Here we suggest that parents answer children's questions about reading and writing; reward reading and writing activities with words such as, "What nice work you do," "I'm happy to see you are reading or writing," or "Can I help you?"; display your child's work at home; attend parent conferences at school; attend school if your child is in a play; and attend other parent events.

*Parent responsibilities.* We asked the parents in the program to undertake the following responsibilities:

◆ Attend monthly group meetings with other parents and individual sessions every week with a mentor. The mentor is a Rutgers University student pursuing certification in education. The sessions are for sharing ideas that parents do at home, to learn from each other, and to present new ideas.

◆ Find a place for the program materials in your home so children can locate them easily.

◆ Look for materials suggested in the parent booklet that you might have in your home. Place them with the other materials from the program for reading and writing.

◆ Participate in school periods set aside for children to read and write independently called WRAP Time.

◆ Keep records of activities done on sheets provided, and share what you do with the group (see Figure 1).

The activities that we asked the parents to do with their children at home are as follows:

◆ Look at, read, and talk about the pictures, stories, and puzzles in *Highlights for Children*. Follow the plans provided.

◆ Write together with your child in your spiral notebook journals. You can write stories, copy writing from a book, or write about how it feels to work with your child. You can write a lot or a little. The same suggestions for writing apply to children.

◆ Make your child aware of print all around you by pointing it out inside and outside of your home. Read mail, road signs, store signs, and directions on medicine. Record Very Own Words on 30 x 50 cards and place in file box.

◆ Read to your child as often as you can, listen to your child read, read together, and talk about what you read.

Morrow, Scoblionko, & Shafer

*Preparations are made for a parent meeting, with refreshments, childcare, and materials for parents to take home.*

◆ Use the storyboard or other storytelling ideas we have given to you, or make your own materials for storytelling.

At our first monthly meeting with the parents, some of the materials were distributed with demonstrations of how to use them. At subsequent meetings parents have shared activities they have done with their children. At the end of the meetings the children join us, and we do activities together. Children also tell what they have done with their parents. In addition to these group monthly meetings, Rutgers students meet with their assigned parents and act as mentors, as mentioned earlier. The parents and university students have formed strong bonds and look forward to their meetings together.

### Getting the Program Started

To begin the program, all materials had to be prepared for the parents. Teachers were provided with an inservice workshop to describe the elements of the program and how it blended with the school WRAP program. We asked their cooperation in observing the children whose parents were involved. We also asked that after the program began parents be able to come to WRAP program activities in school to participate occasionally. We asked teachers to work with *Highlights* and to continue WRAP program activities including journal writing, storytelling activities, and keeping Very Own Words to provide a model for what was to happen at home.

Letters were sent home to the 120 parents of the children in the first, second, and third grade classes asking for their participation. We received 50 responses from interested parents. Before our first parent meeting we wanted to meet separately with each interested parent to find out their thoughts about helping their children and themselves. When the program is finished, this information will be compared to post interviews to determine if parents' attitudes and ideas about helping their children change.

After trying to contact all 50 parents we were only able to carry out 35 initial interviews. Many of the parents have no phones. They did not respond to letters or notes sent home through the mail or by the teachers. When we did make contact, and dates for meetings were agreed upon, parents often did not keep their appointments. Some interviews were done over the phone.

At our first meeting we expected 35 parents, and 23 attended. To attempt to assure attendance a letter was sent 10 days in advance. We sent another note the day before, and we called each parent to remind him or her of the meeting. We had refreshments, provided childcare and transportation if needed, and scheduled meetings at times that parents indicated were convenient. We still had difficulty maintaining good attendance. We believe that the parents are interested in participating; however, we encountered serious illness in families, grandparents and single parents caring for many children and overwhelmed by the responsibility, family members moving in and out of the homes regularly, and families relocating frequently. From one meeting to the next we did not know who would attend and who was still in the program.

## The Success Stories

This program has been underway for only four months at the time we are writing this chapter. Therefore, we have no definitive findings concerning achievement gains or other test scores. We do, however, have some evidence of success. Parents have expressed that they are learning new ideas. We have rich samples of parent-child journal entries, large collections of Very Own Words, and chalktalks and roll stories displayed at our meetings. Parents feel more comfortable about coming to school and participating, and they have more self-confidence about being able to help their children. They have expressed apprecia-

Morrow, Scoblionko, & Shafer

tion to those carrying out the program for the materials and the attention they are receiving. They demonstrate pride in their accomplishments. We see parents more willing to share their ideas, express their concerns, and ask questions. Parents are enthused about the program and eager to participate and help their children.

There are many success stories about individual parents or caregivers, such as Harriet's story at the beginning of this chapter. These stories illustrate what we have learned about the families we are working with, what their problems and concerns are, and how they are helping their children as a result of the program. Another example concerns Tameka, who is from Trinidad and came to the United States when she was 16 years old. She is married and has three children. Tameka never finished high school but completed a GED. Her husband presses clothing in a cleaning store. Tameka is ambitious; she works the night shift as an aide at a medical center and has a part-time job in a supermarket. She hopes to become a nurse and has been attending a county college. She drops in and out of school depending on finances. She is intelligent and has potential for success, but with responsibilities of childcare and work, it is difficult for her to reach her goal. Tameka confided to a teacher that she is abused by her husband, who has been arrested. Tameka stated that she will not allow her children to have boyfriends until they finish their education. She wants them all to go to college.

Tameka has been very enthusiastic about the program. She never misses a meeting and always completes several activities on the checklist. Tameka lacks self-confidence and is always concerned about doing a good enough job. One week she was only able to do one or two of the activities on the checklist. She mentioned that maybe she should drop out of the program because she was not doing her part. We assured her that she was doing more than enough and that whatever she could accomplish was better than not doing any of the activities at all. Tameka has always helped her children with their homework. She says she has learned new ideas from the program, such as collecting Very Own Words from print in the home environment and community. Journal writing is another activity that she had not participated in with her child prior to the family literacy program. One of the entries in their journals was a biography of each other. There was a biography of Ray Charles in an issue of *Highlights* that was featured by the teachers at school and suggested as an activity for the parents. After reading the story, parents and children were asked to write biographies of each other. Figure 2 presents Kim's biography of her mother Tameka. Tameka was proud of her daughter's writing and shared it at the parent meeting.

Brenda is the university student who works with Tameka. Tameka told her,

> This program helps me remember to work with my kids when things get so busy or not so good at home and I would forget. I'm learning new ideas I wouldn't have thought of before. You make me have more confidence that I am a good mom who does good things with my children. I want them to grow up like you and go to college.

"The meetings with Tameka are gratifying," said Brenda. "She is always cooperative. But the meetings are a challenge." Tameka's two-year-old attended all of them, which caused problems. Tara is a handful: she cannot sit still for a minute and gets into everything. It is difficult to share

### Figure 2

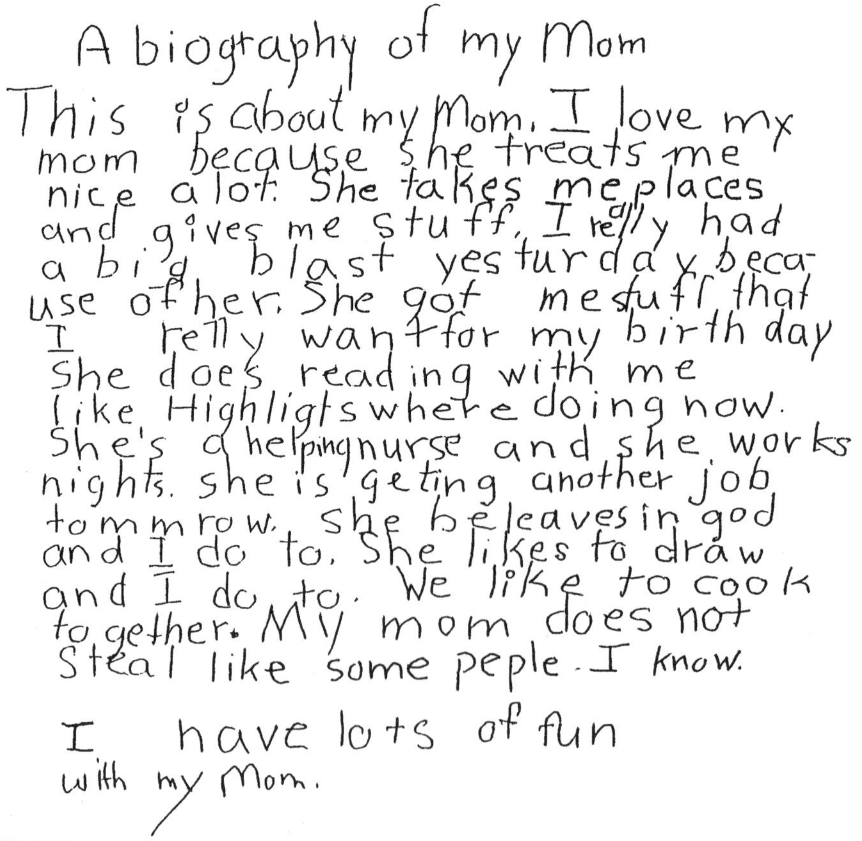

A biography of my Mom

This is about my Mom. I love my mom because she treats me nice a lot. She takes me places and gives me stuff, I relly had a big blast yesturday because of her. She got me stuff that I relly want for my birth day She does reading with me like Highligts where doing now. She's a helping nurse and she works nights. she is geting another job tommrow. she beleaves in god and I do to. She likes to draw and I do to. We like to cook together. MY mom does not steal like some peple. I know.

I have lots of fun with my Mom.

Morrow, Scoblionko, & Shafer

accomplishments and carry on conversations about activities. However, Tameka could not come to the meetings if she did not bring Tara, because she has no one to leave her with.

Our next story is about the only father in the program, Rinaldo Alvarez. Mr. Alvarez is a single parent who has raised Gloria alone since she was a baby. He has never discussed Gloria's mother. We learned from Gloria's teacher that her mother abused her as a baby and left Rinaldo when Gloria was two. He works as a mechanic and has completed two years of high school. He seems to be very concerned about his daughter and suggests that he wants to help her as much as he can. He is a quiet man who does not show much expression. Mr. Alvarez comes to every meeting, but sometimes he forgets to bring his materials and looks a little distraught when we discuss the parent and child activities. Ariadas is the college student who is Rinaldo's mentor. She said, "Although he has good intentions, by the time he gets home from work and prepares dinner for Gloria and himself, he says he is too tired to do much with her."

Gloria is quiet like her dad. She does not do well in school. Her father gets exasperated when she does not cooperate when he tries to help her. She often gets angry with him and then ignores him. Rinaldo said he had not been doing any of the activities with Gloria because "she won't cooperate, and I don't have the patience." We went over the list, and when we got to the activity about looking for different types of print, his eyes lit up and he exclaimed, "Oh yeah, we did that when we went to church Sunday. I showed Gloria all the print. When we got home she asked for the word Bible to put on a Very Own Word card." We also found that Gloria had been doing chalktalk stories in her journal, but Rinaldo thought they were "just drawings," not reading or writing. We explained that when Gloria did the chalktalks, she had to read them to draw the pictures. We found Mr. Alvarez to be very interested in his child but lacking in self-confidence. He did things with Gloria but gave himself little credit for his accomplishments.

### Reflecting on Our Stories

Harriet, the grandparent we described earlier, knew she had limited literacy ability and felt she could not be of help to her grandchild. Tameka also lacked confidence, possibly because of an abusive home situation. She tried to do as much as possible for her children to assure them a better future than her situation. No matter how much she did, however, she never felt it was enough. Rinaldo had a sense of hopelessness. He tried to help Gloria but did not feel successful. He was surprised to find that we felt he was doing good things with her and that she was responding, which gave him the initiative to continue.

These parents or caregivers all lacked self-confidence for one reason or another. They did not realize how important they are to their children; they did not realize that they could help and that what they were doing was extremely productive. In a very short time, we have been able to let them know how successful they have been and have given them incentive to continue.

One of the most successful parts of the program seems to be the *Highlights for Children* magazine used at school and at home. Teachers, parents, and children consistently comment on what a valuable resource it is. Teachers report that parents who never worked with their children before are doing so because they like the *Highlights* themselves. They report that the children's reading ability has improved because they are using the magazine with family members at home. Parents and children note that it is fun to use *Highlights* together. Children speak of their parents' helping them with reading using *Highlights*, and children help Spanish-speaking parents with English when using the magazine. Parents say that working with the magazine provides quality time with their children; they say it is relaxing and that they are learning together with their children. When children are absent from school on days that *Highlights* is distributed, parents often come to pick up the magazine. Several parents have requested extra issues, so they could have one for themselves.

## Looking Toward the Future

Our main problem with the program, as we mentioned earlier, has been attendance. One way to enhance participation is to make family literacy programs an integral part of the curriculum. Schools need coordinators to design programs that include administrators, teachers, parents, and children. All individuals must view family literacy as an essential part of a child's education. Parents must attend this type of program just as their children must attend school.

The Family WRAP program is a collaborative effort, which adds to its strength. The administration of the district has supported it by providing space in the school building for parent meetings and childcare. The teachers are an integral part of the project. They do activities in school similar to those that we teach the parents to do at home. Children repeat the activities at home and get help from parents. In some cases the children help their parents. Regardless whether the child or parent is directing the activity, the interaction is most important. As part of the university community, we have been able to bring something to the school district that did not already exist. My university students have prepared materials, provided childcare during meetings, and worked with parents. The parents they have mentored have found them to be an important part of the program. Many of the students will not be able to continue as mentors in following semesters, but new students will be taking their places. The parents were upset by this because they had become close with their mentors, and at the last meeting, there were hugs and kind words exchanged between parents and university students.

Although it is still in its early stages, we can see the benefits of this program. Children have expressed in interviews that they enjoy working with their parents at school meetings and at home. Parents also talk about enjoying the work they are doing with their children. They mention that they are gaining confidence in their ability to help and becoming aware of their importance in the literacy development of their children. Some also say that their own literacy skills are improving. Teachers admit that they had not realized how important such a program was in bringing parents, students, and teachers closer together in working toward the literacy development of children. They have found that many of their students are beginning to show greater interest in reading and writing and that some are also improving in their literacy skills.

## Notes

Gloria Lettenberger, a first grade English as a second language teacher in Redshaw School, thought of the term WRAP Time for the school program.

This chapter is dedicated to the memory of Linda Glanzberg, a Rutgers University student who participated in the project.

The original research described in the chapter was supported in part by the National Reading Research Center, University of Georgia and University of Maryland, and administered by the Office of Educational Research and Improvement, U.S. Department of Education, and *Highlights for Children* magazine.

We would like to extend our gratitude to all individuals who made this project possible: Rutgers students, New Brunswick School District teachers, administrators, children, and parents. The *Highlights for Children* magazines in this project were donated by Highlights for Children, Inc. We are grateful for their generous contribution to this project.

## References

Auerbach, E.R. (1989). Toward a social-contextual approach to family literacy. *Harvard Educational Review, 59,* 165–181.

Clark, M.M. (1984). Literacy at home and at school: Insights from a study of young fluent readers. In H. Goelman, A. Oberg, & F. Smith (Eds.), *Awakening to literacy* (pp. 122–130). Portsmouth, NH: Heinemann.

Cochran-Smith, M. (1984). *The making of a reader.* Norwood, NJ: Ablex.

Delgado-Gaitan, C. (1987). Mexican adult literacy: New directions for immigrants. In S.R. Goldman & K. Trueba (Eds.), *Becoming literate in English as a second language* (pp. 9–32). Norwood, NJ: Ablex.

Delgado-Gaitan, C. (1990). *Literacy for empowerment: The role of parents in children's education*. New York: Falmer.

Heath, S.B. (1983). *Ways with words*. Cambridge, UK: Cambridge University Press.

Morrow, L.M. (1992). *Super tips for storytelling*. New Brunswick, NJ: Rutgers University Press.

Morrow, L.M. (1993). *Literacy development in the early years: Helping children read and write* (2nd ed.). Boston, MA: Allyn & Bacon.

Morrow, L.M., Paratore, J., with Gaber, D., Harrison, C., & Tracey, D. (1993). Family literacy: Perspectives and practices. *Reading Teacher, 47,* 194–201.

National Reading Research Center. (1991). Conceptual framework: The engagement perspective. In *National Reading Research Center: A proposal from the University of Maryland and the University of Georgia*. Athens, GA, and College Park, MD: Author.

Olsen, M.J. (1963). *Tell and draw stories*. Minneapolis, MN: Creative Storytime.

Taylor, D., & Dorsey-Gaines, C. (1988). *Growing up literate: Learning from inner-city families*. Portsmouth, NH: Heinemann.

Teale, W.H. (1984). Reading to young children: Its significance for literacy development. In H. Goelman, A. Oberg, and F. Smith (Eds.), *Awakening to literacy* (pp. 110–121). Portsmouth, NH: Heinemann.

# Have You Heard Any Good Books Lately?: Encouraging Shared Reading at Home with Books and Audiotapes

**Patricia S. Koskinen**
*National Reading Research Center and University of Maryland,
College Park, Maryland*

**Irene H. Blum**
*National Reading Research Center, College Park, Maryland
Fairfax County Public Schools, Virginia*

**Nancy Tennant**
*National Reading Research Center, College Park, Maryland
Towson State University, Towson, Maryland*

**E. Marie Parker, Mary W. Straub, and Christine Curry**
*National Reading Research Center, College Park, Maryland
Fairfax County Public Schools, Virginia*

*"You always take that book! I want it tonight!" Anna snatched the bookbag and then carefully put the card from* Don't Wake the Baby *on the "Dog Gone Good Reading" chart. After checking to see that she had the audiotape, she put the book into her backpack. Raza knew Anna was right. He loved all the sounds in the baby book, especially the crying at the end. His mom even thought it was funny. Raza had to find*

*something else to take home today and watched as Juan pulled out* The Scrumptious Sundae *from one of the home-school book baskets. When Ms. Barker had read it last week, everyone was talking about their favorite ice cream. Raza loved the candy sprinkles on the top. "That's a good one," he said to Juan. Juan replied, "Yeah, I know, but I'm looking for* The Big Toe. *My sister thought it was scary." After Juan moved to another basket of books, Raza happily dropped the ice cream book into his own backpack. Anna, who had been standing near the door, called to him in her best "teacher" voice, "Raza, you forgot to put the card on the chart."*

The second-language learners and native English–speaking children in this first grade classroom in the United States have been learning to read and write in a literacy program that uses books and audiotapes. In developing this program, these children's teacher expressed her concerns about at-risk second-language learners. Anna, from Vietnam, lives with her brother and parents who come home from their store after nine o'clock every night. Juan's family came from El Salvador a year ago; his mother works in a beauty shop all day and at a fast-food restaurant at night. Raza's mother meets him at the bus every day, and when they get home, she reads to him from the Koran. While all these children have family members who care about their school success, they come from homes where English is not spoken and there are few English storybooks.

Ms. Barker has been sending books and audiotapes home daily to supplement the classroom reading instructional program. All the children in her class have had the opportunity to take the books and tapes home, but the nine children who speak English as a second language were the initial focus of her home-school shared reading program. The Dog Gone Good Reading program provides these students with an opportunity to hear English in their home environment daily using familiar literacy instructional materials from school.

## Home-School Literacy Programs for ESL Students

During the last decade there has been a dramatic increase in the number of ESL students in U.S. schools. Recent estimates suggest that there are more than 2.2 million children currently enrolled in school who have limited proficiency in English and that these numbers will increase by the year 2000 to more than 3.4 million (U.S. Department of Education, 1991). Many of these children are recent immigrants who lack communication skills in their new language. Because second-language learners are in many classrooms across the United States, there is now considerable emphasis on designing learning environments that support these culturally and linguistically diverse students. There is a need to provide many opportunities for these children to develop and practice language and reading skills, particularly within the classroom context that includes native English–speaking peers. As teachers face the challenge of teaching both native English speakers and second-language learners in the same classroom, special emphasis should be given to instructional activities that are appropriate and effective for both these populations.

There is also a need to expand the language and literacy experiences of young readers and to find ways to support classroom instruction in other contexts, such as the home. This is particularly important because children's experiences with language and reading at home are thought to influence substantially their success or failure in learning to read. Second-language learners typically are exposed to 40,000 hours of their home language after six years of schooling and only 3000 hours of English (Elley & Mangubhai, 1983). These children seldom have English books available to them in their homes, either, which may put them at a disadvantage in their early literacy development.

In our efforts to design learning environments that foster literacy, we have concentrated on helping young students understand what they read, learn strategies to improve their reading, and feel successful and motivated to practice (see also Meichenbaum & Biemiller, 1990). We have been especially interested in repeated reading as an instructional strategy to develop fluency (in other words, smooth, accurate, natural, expressive reading) with both less proficient and developmental readers in the early grades. This deceptively simple rehearsal strategy involves multiple readings and provides substantial practice in reading text. It allows novices to feel like experts as they acquire fluency (Blum & Koskinen, 1991). Research with English-speaking students has documented that repeated reading improves reading rate and accuracy (Chomsky, 1976; Dowhower, 1987; Rasinski, 1990; Samuels, 1979), increases vocabulary (Elley, 1989; Koskinen & Blum, 1984), and enhances comprehension (Dowhower, 1987; Yaden, 1988). In addition, repeated reading helps students feel more confident about their reading and is an activity in which they want to participate (Koskinen & Blum, 1986; Topping, 1987).

Recent research indicates that repeated reading in the home environment may also have particular benefits for second-language learners (Blum et al., 1993). In this study, repeated reading of books at home was compared to home reading that included books and accompanying audiotapes. When given the opportunity to practice reading books with audiotapes at home, ESL students showed substantial growth in their ability to read books of increasing difficulty fluently and accurately. In addition, teachers and parents reported that students read more and demonstrated increased confidence and independence in literacy activities.

It appears that support provided by an audio model extends language learning by providing a form of scaffolding, which is critical for beginning readers (Feitelson et al., 1993; Vygotsky, 1978). Hearing the text while reading it encourages beginning readers to make connections between the more familiar oral language and the less familiar written language. Therefore, children begin to recognize vocabulary that was previously unknown. Programs that also include daily access to books are necessary to enhance reading achievement (Elley, 1992). In addition, effective programs provide for several other factors shown by research to increase students' motivation to read (Gambrell et al., 1993), which include choice of materials (Spaulding, 1992) and opportunities for social interactions about books (Guthrie et al., 1993).

## Planning an Effective Program

How do you extend school reading experiences into the homes of children where English is not often spoken and where there are few children's books written in English? How do you help students who speak English but have no one to read to them at home? These are daily challenges for an increasingly large number of teachers as they attempt to design learning environments that will foster literacy skills. They also have been our particular challenges as we have worked with linguistically and culturally diverse students within the regular classroom. As we collaborated with teachers such as Ms. Barker to develop a home-school reading program for the primary grades, we identified a few issues that are especially important. First, there is a need to provide for a range of interests and reading difficulty levels so that students will have successful initial experiences with storybook reading. Short books with repetitive language patterns, which have been used successfully in first grade classrooms, are especially appropriate for home-school reading. Second, it is necessary to provide models of fluent reading in English. Because many parents have limited skill in reading written English, they are not able to assist with or monitor students' reading. Teachers' shared readings of books that are used for home reading are a particularly valuable way to provide a model. This shared reading gives not only an auditory

Koskinen et al.

model but also background vocabulary knowledge. It generally excites interest by the teacher's attention to the book. Audiotapes of the stories for use at home can provide another model and support for oral reading. Third, because some children are not accustomed to daily home reading, consideration needs to be given to encouraging this activity. Developing daily home reading routines, providing access to literacy materials (for example, books, audiotapes, and tape recorders), and packaging these materials are particularly important.

## Ms. Barker's Home-School Program

Ms. Barker is one teacher who has implemented a home-school reading program that reflects her interest in encouraging daily home reading, expanding book access, and providing additional models of fluent reading. Ms. Barker's first grade class of 15 students had 9 second-language learners and several native English–speaking children. She and the ESL resource teacher were particularly eager to make available activities that would support and extend reading opportunities in the children's homes. During the summer they worked with the authors, other teachers, and volunteers to make read-along audiotapes for more than 100 multilevel books that were used in many first grade reading programs. These books ranged in length from 14 words to complex narrative stories. In addition, through a school literacy program, Ms. Barker had procured tape recorders and backpacks for each child to use. As a way of getting started, she brought in the books, tape recorders, tapes, and backpacks that the students would be using for home-school reading. She told the children that they would have an opportunity to take home a book and tape every day and even be able to keep the tape recorder at their home for several months so they could do this special reading homework.

Ms. Barker wanted to acquaint students with the books before sending them home, so she began daily readings of these books. This shared reading took less than five minutes a day and provided her a way to create excitement about the books. Her shared reading included (1) an oral look-through, while the children made predictions and she provided key vocabulary and examples of frequently used language patterns; (2) an oral reading of the book; and (3) a rereading of the book with the children. After reading each book, Ms. Barker put it into a community basket so everyone had access to it for independent reading times throughout the day.

While Ms. Barker was introducing these home-school books on a daily basis, she also sent a letter home to parents or other caregivers telling them about the reading activities that would be starting. Although she had discussed the home-school reading program with the parents who attended back-to-school night, she sent a letter to each family. To ensure that parents could read the letter, she had it translated into the languages the families spoke: Farsi, Spanish, Vietnamese, Laotian, or Korean. Her letter provided information about the importance of practice in becoming a skilled reader and introduced a few details about the home reading activity. Most important, it enlisted their support and interest (see Figure 1).

After about three weeks, when she had read at least 15 books to the children, Ms. Barker introduced a book checkout procedure and began to encourage school use of the tapes and tape recorders. After explaining why it was important to keep track of the books and tapes, she demonstrated how to use the chart and card checkout system she had developed. She also modeled how to use the tape recorder and follow along with the tape. Ms. Barker then provided time each day for one child to model selecting a book and tape set, checking it out, completing the read-along activity, and then checking it in. Although it took several weeks to give each child a chance, at the end of this practice time the students were comfortable with the procedures and able to handle

**Figure 1**
**Letter to Parents**

---

Dear Parents,

We know that the more children read, the better they will do in school! I want to let you know about some special reading homework your child will be doing this year. Every day, your child will choose a book and tape to bring home for extra reading practice.

I will be sending home a tape recorder to use with the tapes. You can keep the tape recorder at your house for the next few months. Please help your child find a place to practice with the books and tapes and a safe place to keep the tape recorder.

This extra practice every day will help your child be a more successful student. We will be contacting you to talk about what we are doing in our class and how you can help with this special project.

Thank you for your help!

Sincerely,
Teacher _____
Principal _____

---

Koskinen et al.

*Students select a book and tape each day to listen to and reread at home.*

them independently. Everyone was ready to teach their parents how to start the tape by pressing the button marked with a green dot, read along with the story, stop the tape by pressing the button with a red dot, and then rewind the tape so that they could begin again. In addition to developing the children's proficiency with the book and tape procedures, Ms. Barker also helped the students plan where and when they would do their daily home reading.

Because Ms. Barker had many beginning readers, she decided to permit only five children to take home books and tapes at one time. After the first group became comfortable with this procedure, five more children began. The more experienced children were able to give advice about where the tape recorder could be stored at home and how to remember to bring the book and tape back each day. One child's advice was, "I put them in my backpack as soon as I finish. Then I don't have to worry about them in the morning."

Ms. Barker continued to introduce a new book each day so there would always be many books from which the children could choose. Because children were excited about the books they had read at home, Ms. Barker established at least one time during the week when students could read their home-school books to a partner. During this time, Ms. Barker listened to several children and made anecdotal notes as she moved among the pairs. Her notes were helpful in guiding students to appropriate books for the home-school reading and have been another valuable source of ongoing assessment information.

Soon after children began bringing books and tapes home on a regular basis, Ms. Barker and the parents noticed an increase in daily reading and conversations about books. Many students wanted to take extra books home for the weekend or their vacation. One parent mentioned that after practicing with the tape, his daughter continued reading to her younger sister when they were in the bathtub. A mother described how her son regularly got up early so he could read to his stepfather at breakfast. Children commented that they liked to read along with the tapes. One child noted, "The books didn't say what the word was the way the tapes did." Another child described how the tapes helped her and told Ms. Barker, "I could hear the story. I put on the tape recorder. I know the words and finish the book." Besides noting increased student interest in books, Ms. Barker and the parents observed a definite increase in children's fluency and reading independence. Further, they noticed children beginning to monitor their reading. As a child exclaimed one morning after taking home only a book, "Ms. Barker, that book was hard. I needed the tape!"

## Practical Suggestions for Getting Started

Ms. Barker is one of many teachers with whom we have worked who has been using books and audiotapes to enhance literacy opportunities at home. The key to a successful program involves careful planning, appropriate materials, and teacher guidance at all phases. The enthusiasm of the children and their parents appears to make teachers' extra time worth the effort. The following are suggestions that teachers of young readers have found helpful when coordinating a home-school literacy program that involves books and tapes.

*Selecting books.* When deciding which books to select for your program, consider using short books with repetitive language patterns that will appeal to a range of interests and ability levels. The shared and repeated reading in our home reading project has been conducted with natural language patterned books that provide an opportunity for emerging readers to have successful experiences with print. These books use familiar concepts and vocabulary with commonly used oral language patterns and have strong links to the experiences of young children. In addition, they contain illustrations that closely portray the meaning and language of the story. The gradually increasing level of language difficulty makes these books particularly appropriate for second-language learners and beginning readers who are native English speakers. When possible, order paperback books, which are more economical and enable you to purchase a greater number.

*Preparing audiotapes.* Because audiotapes provide helpful and gradual steps for learning to read, it is important that they be clear and fluent. The taped reading needs to be smooth and expressive, but slow enough so students can match oral and written words. As we made our tapes, we used the following procedures. The reader first stated the book's title and name of the author and illustrator. Students were then directed to the story and encouraged by the tape-recorded reader to "put your finger under the first word and follow along as I read." The book's text was then read at a pace that would allow beginning readers to follow along. Children were signaled to turn the page with a sound cue, such as a soft whistle, bell, or spoon tapping a glass. Students were also given at least three seconds to turn the page after they heard the cue, which allowed the young readers time to look at the pictures and physically turn the page. On some of the tapes, the story was read twice. The first reading was expressive but slow enough for children to match the speech to print. The second reading was at a faster pace, more typical of fluent oral reading. After making the tape, we first listened to it, and then labeled it with the book's title. As a safety precaution, we removed the tabs on the tape cassettes so children would not accidentally erase the story.

Teachers have successfully involved many people in the making of audiotapes, including parents, older children, school staff, and community volunteers. Teachers have also done some of the taping themselves by reserving specific times before or after school for taping. Some teachers have used shared reading time in class to record tapes. If you do this, be sure to have the tape recorder prepared so that it can be turned on while you read a book to the class. Ms. Barker taped the books she used in her program during the summer, with the help of the ESL resource teacher and several other volunteers.

*Acquiring tape recorders.* To ensure that all your students can listen to tapes at home, you probably will need to provide tape recorders for almost all your class. While some families have a tape recorder, we found that often it is broken or not available for use by a young child. When children in our home-school reading program were given both books and audiotapes for home reading, they were also given a tape recorder for their personal use during the project. We purposely did not use earphones that sometimes come with the machines to encourage the opportunity for others in the family to listen along with the reader. Reasonably priced, battery-operated tape recorders with easy-to-use controls are commercially available for less than US$25. Although small tape recorders are less expensive, we found they are also more appealing to older children and then "lost." Therefore, we used tape recorders that were at least 12 inches long. These were more durable and less appealing to older children who might want to borrow them. You also might want to mark each tape recorder with a number and a school name or project logo. Also, if the controls on your machines are all the same color, consider marking the tape recorder controls with colored dots to help children recognize the words "start" (green), "stop" (red), and "rewind" (blue). Such markings also make the recorder easily recognizable to all family members as the student's special machine for reading homework.

Teachers have appealed to various groups to get support for literacy materials such as books and tape recorders. Parent-teacher groups, professional educational organizations, local merchants, and fast-food chains that offer educational grants have all helped to underwrite these expenses.

*Organizing home-school materials.* To implement a home-school shared reading program, you will need a substantial number of books. Organizing these materials is essential so that you can keep track of them. In our program we began with approximately 150 different books that ranged from emergent to independent first grade level. There were two copies of each title. These were color coded to assist with organization and management of project materials and activities. One copy, marked with a red dot, was used for in-class reading after it had been introduced; another copy, marked with a yellow dot, was packaged with an audiotape of the story for home use. The packages consisted of plastic bags that secured at the top with the book's title written on colored tape on the front. The books with yellow dots were supplied with a library card so that they could be checked out and in as they were transported back and forth from home to school.

Procedures for the daily book exchange need to be designed so that students can work independently. To assist with management of the daily book exchange, teachers who implemented our project used a posterboard chart. This chart, with a project logo (dog mascot) and title "Dog Gone Good Reading," as in Ms. Barker's class, contained library card pockets with each child's name. The children were taught to remove the library cards from the backs of their books and place them in their pockets on the chart when they checked out a book and tape. When they checked materials in, they retrieved the cards from their chart pockets and replaced the cards in the books.

As you design your home-school reading program, consider providing a motivating and convenient way for children to transport materials. We have found that providing some sort of bag not only facilitates the return of materials from home, but also helps children remember to read on a daily basis. Teachers have used plastic suitcases, old briefcases, or lunch boxes for this purpose. Teachers implementing our project used inexpensive backpacks, marked with a project title and designated expressly for the purpose of carrying reading materials to and from school.

*Providing shared reading opportunities.* Shared reading provides an effective and convenient way to build a library of familiar books so that children can make appropriate selections for their home reading. Because this activity is often part of first grade instruction, it easily fits into the daily schedule. Many teachers have a favorite procedure for shared reading, but the activity generally involves the teacher introducing the book and then rereading with the students several times. One teacher's guidelines for shared reading are presented in Figure 2. Some teachers prefer to designate a particular time for sharing the home-school books; others find the activity fits in best during transition times. So that all the children in the class can be successful, especially as the program begins, many teachers have found it helpful to start off with a substantial number of easy books. Afterward, continue introducing at least one book a day so that interesting choices at varying difficulty levels are available to the children. As books are introduced, they can be displayed and made available for use during independent reading times in the classroom. Colorful baskets or other readily available containers can be used for book displays. Several teachers in our project commented that during independent reading time, many children were especially eager to reread the book that had been shared that day. Frequently children asked if they could read the book to peers or to the teacher.

*Introducing the home-school procedures to children.* The success of your home-school reading program is based in part on how comfortable your young readers are with the program's materials and pro-

**Figure 2**
**Guidelines for Introducing the "Dog Gone Good Reading"**
**Project Books**

Time: Approximately 5 minutes

Oral look-through

1. Show children the book, and look at the cover illustration together. Read the title of the book while pointing to the words as you read them. Ask children what they think the book might be about, and accept a few responses. Tell them you will be looking at the pictures to find out what the story is about.

2. Page through the book and look at the pictures together with the children. Point to a concrete object and then to the word naming it. As you go through the book, tell the story, providing key vocabulary and examples of language patterns that children will need to read the book independently. For example, "In this story, different animals tell us where their homes are. The bird said, 'My home is here.' The frog said, 'My home is here.' The pig said, 'My home is here.' Then the dog showed where her home is. Now the dog sees a rabbit. The rabbit wants to get to her home fast. The dog wants the rabbit to come back."

Reading

3. After looking through the book, read it to the children. Continue matching objects and words.

Rereading

4. Read the book a second time, inviting the children to read along. Point to the words as you read.

5. Place copies of the book in the "Dog Gone Good Reading" basket so that it will be available for students to read at school.

cedures. In addition to knowing why reading at home is so important, children will need to understand how to (1) select a book; (2) check a book in and out for home use; (3) operate the tape recorder; and (4) read along with the story three times.

When discussing our home-school reading program with children, we simply told them that they will be reading books in school and then choosing books to take home and read along with a tape so they can become "really good" readers. The children were generally delighted when they realized that the colorful backpacks, books, and tape recorders were for them to take home. Because all books are first shared with the children in class, they become somewhat familiar with them. This procedure helps them select books that are of interest and at an appropriate difficulty level. Teacher modeling, subsequent practice of the checkin and checkout procedures, and knowledge of the use of the tape recorder are essential so that children will be able to engage in the activity independently.

Some teachers spend considerable time discussing, modeling, and practicing home reading activities. Children practice how to follow along with the tape recorder, including following the tape's directions for finding the starting place in the book, turning pages at the signal, and pointing to the words while reading. After reading along with the tape, children then practice rewinding the tape and reading along with the tape a second and a third time. Some teachers hold discussions related to where to do reading at home and where a safe place would be in the children's homes to store the tape recorder. As an extension activity, some children draw a picture of this place in their apartment or house, take it home, and have their parents sign an agreement related to the storage place.

*Introducing the home-school program to parents.* As you are introducing the children to the home-school reading material, you also will want to explain your program to their parents or caregivers. As mentioned earlier, some teachers send a letter home (such as the one in Figure 1) that briefly provides background information about the program. In some schools where parents cannot read English, teachers have held meetings with parents where an interpreter was present, or they have explained the program to an interpreter and asked him or her to call the parents. When possible, teachers have introduced the program during a regular parent-teacher conference.

Teachers have stressed the importance of reading at home and listening to and reading with students. Some teachers have also explained how repeated reading provides much exposure to words and concepts and how children learn from looking at picture books while listening to the tape recorder. Teachers have found that by explaining the classroom routines (book selection and return) and the expectations for home reading (repeated listening and reading on a daily basis), they enable parents to support their children in their daily reading. Many parents who previously had not been encouraging daily reading have become part of the "home reading team" by listening and helping their children assume responsibility for finding a place for home reading and remembering to bring back the book each morning.

*Beginning home reading with audiotapes.* When you feel your students understand the home reading procedures, consider having just a small group begin to take materials home, as discussed earlier. Select a time for regular daily checkout and checkin. Some teachers prefer that children return their books when they arrive in the morning and then choose a new book and tape during the reading and writing period. Because we have been working with young readers, we have had them put the book and tape package and the tape recorder in their backpacks to take home as soon as they have selected their book. Be sure to remind the children that the tape recorder is to stay at home but that the book-tape packages are returned each day so that they can choose a new one. As the initial group becomes comfortable with the home-school reading procedures, they can help introduce these activities to others in the class.

Once children have begun taking books home, you will want to continue introducing one book each day. Keep these books in a special area so children can find and reread them during classroom reading times. Because you will eventually have many books from which the children can choose for home reading, you will also want to keep the books and tapes in some order so students can find books they want. We grouped books in baskets according to difficulty level so that students could easily locate books at their appropriate level.

*Assessing the effectiveness of the program.* The home-school reading program has been suggested as an enjoyable and motivating way to provide materials and opportunities to practice reading at home on a regular basis with hope that this practice will improve students' reading. You will want to think about ways of maintaining the smooth and regular operation of the program. You will want to think about how to assess the program's effect on students' reading. To help monitor whether children are using the procedures and routines to make appropriate book selections, you may want to set aside a few minutes each week to observe different groups selecting books during checkin and checkout. If children are selecting the same book day after day or often choosing books that are too easy or too difficult, you occasionally may want to suggest that they take additional books that are more appropriate choices.

You should anticipate that sometimes children will forget to return their books, and you will probably want to plan a consistent policy. Many teachers permit a child who forgets to return a book and tape packet to take a second one and return both the next day. However, to keep an adequate supply of packages for the class, you will need to limit the number of times this will be allowed. If students frequently forget to return their materials, you will need to contact the parents and remind them of the importance of consistently practicing at home and returning materials on time.

To maintain interest and enthusiasm for the book and tape activity, you may find it helpful to send periodic reminders to parents and students. Some teachers include a reminder about home-school reading in a weekly newsletter that is sent to each family. Others send individual notes or flyers in both English and the child's home language. You may also want to use a few minutes during parent conferences to discuss the reading project. Be sure to ask parents about their child's progress at home and their response to the program.

To evaluate the program's effect on reading performance, teachers have used a variety of observational and interview activities. One of our project teachers developed an activity that provides ongoing assessment information and fits easily into classroom instructional routines, which was mentioned earlier. At least once a week, have students work with a partner to share one of the books they have read at home. Circulate during paired reading and note the children's familiarity and fluency with the book they are sharing. This information will be useful in guiding children's book selections and will also provide useful data on the students' progress.

## Continuing Home-School Reading Programs

The second-language learners and native English–speaking children in our project who had the opportunity to practice reading books with audiotapes at home received substantial benefit from the home-school reading program. It appears that the support provided by the audiotapes enables students to fluently read increasingly more difficult texts. In addition to the critical support of the audio models, the program provides other features important to reading success. Shared reading in school excites interest in the books and provides background information with a model of expressive reading. The books used in our home-school program are especially appropriate for independent reading because they contain short, repetitive language patterns and pictures that facilitate comprehension. Not only does the program provide choice of books and tapes, it encourages reading practice with repeated reading and provides the tape recorder for support.

Parents and teachers have strongly supported our home-school reading programs. They have noted not only increased reading fluency, but also child independence and confidence. The daily expectations and classroom routines for checkin and checkout establish a home reading habit that often is not part of young children's lives. In addition, having auditory models of fluent English in the home environment encourages parent awareness of the student's reading progress and provides a way for parents who do not speak English to participate as a partner and learner in their child's home reading. Repeated reading with an auditory model provides critical support—scaffolding—which enables novice readers to feel like experts. This initial success provides confidence and strong motivation to practice, which is essential to developing skilled, fluent reading.

With the dramatic increase of second-language learners in U.S. classrooms, there is a need to expand these children's language and literacy experiences. All students should have opportunities to feel successful and develop the confidence that will encourage them to become fluent, motivated readers. Because of the extraordinary demands placed on teachers in multicultural classrooms, special emphasis must be given to instructional activities that are effective with both second-language learners and native English–speaking children. Home-school instructional programs that provide books and audiotapes for home environments that currently offer limited exposure to the English language may be one of the solutions to this problem.

## References

Blum, I.H., & Koskinen, P.S. (1991). Repeated Reading: A strategy for enhancing fluency and fostering expertise. *Theory into Practice, 30,* 195–200.

Blum, I.H., Koskinen, P.S., Tennant, N., Parker, E.M., Straub, M., & Curry, C. (1993, December). *Developing children's fluency through shared reading.* Paper presented at the National Reading Conference, Charleston, SC.

Chomsky, C. (1976). After decoding: What? *Language Arts, 53,* 288–296.

Dowhower, S.I. (1987). Effects of repeated reading on second-grade transitional readers' fluency and comprehension. *Reading Research Quarterly, 22,* 389–406.

Elley, W.B. (1989). Vocabulary acquisition from listening to stories. *Reading Research Quarterly, 24,* 174–187.

Elley, W.B. (1992). *How in the world do students read?* Hamburg, Germany: International Association for the Evaluation of Educational Achievement.

Elley, W.B., & Mangubhai, F. (1983). The impact of reading on second language learning. *Reading Research Quarterly, 19,* 53–67.

Feitelson, D., Goldstein, Z., Iraqui, J., & Share, D.L. (1993). Effects of listening to story reading on aspects of literacy acquisition in a diglossic situation. *Reading Research Quarterly, 28,* 78–79.

Gambrell, L.B., Palmer, B.M., Codling, R.M., Berg-Nye, P., Cassell, L., Long, L., & Sherman, J. (1993). *Elementary students' motivation to read* (Technical Rep.). College Park, MD: University of Maryland, National Reading Research Center.

Guthrie, J.T., Schafer, W., Wang, Y., & Afflerbach, P. (1993). *Influences of instruction on reading engagement: An empirical exploration of social-cognitive framework of reading activity* (Research Rep. No. 3). Athens, GA: National Reading Research Center.

Koskinen, P.S., & Blum, I.H. (1984). Repeated oral reading and the acquisition of fluency. In J. Niles & L. Harris (Eds.), *Changing perspectives on research in reading/language processing and instruction* (Thirty-third yearbook of the National Reading Conference, pp. 183–187). Rochester, NY: National Reading Conference.

Koskinen, P.S., & Blum, I.H. (1986). Paired repeated reading: A classroom strategy for developing fluent reading. *The Reading Teacher, 40,* 70–75.

Meichenbaum, D., & Biemiller, A. (1990, May). *In search of student expertise in the classroom: A metacognitive analysis.* Paper presented at the Conference on Cognitive Research for Instructional Innovation, University of Maryland, College Park, MD.

Rasinski, T.V. (1990). Effects of repeated reading and listening-while-reading on reading fluency. *Journal of Educational Research, 83,* 147–150.

Samuels, S.J. (1979). The method of repeated reading. *The Reading Teacher, 32,* 403–408.

Spaulding, C.L. (1992). The motivation to read and write. In J.W. Irwin & M.A. Doyle (Eds.), *Reading/writing connections: Learning from research* (pp. 177–201). Newark, DE: International Reading Association.

Topping, K. (1987). Paired reading: A powerful technique for parent use. *The Reading Teacher, 40,* 608–614.

U.S. Department of Education. (1991). *The condition of bilingual education in the nation: A report to the Congress and the President.* Author. Washington, DC:

Vygotsky, L.S. (1978). *Mind in society: The development of higher psychological processes.* Cambridge, MA: Harvard University Press.

Yaden, D. (1988). Understanding stories through repeated read-alouds. How many does it take? *The Reading Teacher, 41,* 556–560.

## Children's Books

Butler, A. (1989). *The scrumptious sundae.* Crystal Lake, IL: Rigby Education.

Cowley, J., & Melser, J. (1990). *The big toe.* Bothell, WA: The Wright Group.

Melser, J. (1990). *My home.* San Diego, CA: The Wright Group.

Nelville, P. (1989). *Don't wake the baby.* Crystal Lake, IL: Rigby Education.

# Chapter 7

# Enhancing Adolescent Mothers' Guided Participation in Literacy

### Susan B. Neuman
*Temple University, Philadelphia, Pennsylvania*

*D*eria, *an adolescent mother, and three-year-old Kalima are sitting together in the library area in the daycare center reading a book:*

   *Deria: You want to read the popcorn book?*

*Kalima: Yes.*

   *Deria: What's that? (pointing to the cover)*

*Kalima: Popcorn.*

   *Deria: Do you eat popcorn when you go to the movies?*

*Kalima: Yup, I eat lots of popcorn.*

   *Deria: That's a cat, and see those two boys there eating a big bowl of popcorn (takes the book and turns the pages, holding the book so Kalima can see it). Here, do you want to read me a page? Try to tell me what's on this page.*

These simple exchanges lie at the heart of our family literacy program. Here in the setting of storybook reading, caregiver and child are involved in the collaborative process of guided participation. By structuring and adjusting the task and materials to the child's interest and skills, the caregiver is tacitly guiding the child's development and understanding of stories. It is through this activity that parents' educational beliefs and behaviors are transmitted from parent to child and child to parent.

It is the process of and attention to the *transmission* of parents' newly developing skills and strengths to the child that distinguishes family literacy programs from service delivery models. Yet, how to conceptualize this process as it applies to families from diverse economic, educational, and cultural backgrounds presents a challenge to family literacy researchers and practitioners. For our program, we used a conceptual framework based on daily routine involvement of children in the activities of their cultural communities—involvement that is not typically captured in models of interaction based on didactic school lessons. Our goal was to enhance the communication and literacy interactions between adolescent mothers and children.

## Background

It is now estimated that one out of every ten teenage girls in the United States will become pregnant every year (Alan Guttmacher Institute, 1986). Clearly, the consequences of early pregnancy are often tragic and

*Deria, an adolescent mother, and three-year-old Kalima sit closely together and read in the daycare center library area.*

are frequently experienced by those who are least prepared to manage the responsibility accompanying childbirth (Landy & Walsh, 1988). Government statistics, for example, suggest that early pregnancy tends to be tied to the parents' reduced educational achievement, marginal income-earning capacity, and welfare dependency (Alan Guttmacher Institute, 1986; Berlin & Sum, 1988). Further, studies of children born of teenage mothers consistently report evidence of their limited language and problem-solving abilities and significantly lower IQ scores (Anastasiow, 1982; Furstenberg, 1976; Reis & Herz, 1987). These children are less likely to receive educational training during the preschool years, more likely to come from environments where there is little verbal communication, and often in need of foster care (Furstenberg, Brooks-Gunn, & Morgan, 1987; Thormann, 1985; Williams, 1991). Certain factors often occurring in unplanned parenthood—paternal absence, lower education, and economic deprivation—are clearly associated with the children's low cognitive achievement and limited success in school. Consequently, it has been suggested that successful intervention programs should have a multifaceted approach, providing stimulation to the child and education to the parent (Berlin & Sum, 1988; Neuman & Gallagher, 1994).

The focus of our family literacy program, therefore, was not only to strengthen the literacy skills of teenage mothers, but also to enhance their daily language and literacy interactions with children. Of particular interest was Rogoff's (1990) concept of guided participation, which explains how learning occurs between parent and child through everyday events. This concept suggests that during routine activity, parents guide children's participation in relevant events, help them adapt their understanding to new situations, and assist them in assuming responsibility for managing problem solving. From their active involvement, children are thought to "appropriate" an understanding that may carry to future occasions and new situations that resemble those in which they have participated. This communication is considered to occur through two focal processes: creating bridges of understanding from known information to new ideas and structuring children's participation in activities through opportunities that support and challenge their involvement (Rogoff et al., 1993). Thus, by adapting this model of guided participation, we attempted to assist mothers in their efforts to communicate using the tools of language and literacy with their children (Neuman & Daly, 1993).

## The Family Literacy Program

Our project took place in a school district–sponsored adult basic education and General Equivalency Diploma program serving more than

200 women in an urban metropolitan area. The program was designed to allow mothers who had dropped out of school because of the responsibilities of parenthood, poor academic achievement, and economic circumstances to attend a literacy program that provided nearby daycare for their young children. Most of the mothers were African American (95 percent) averaging 19 years of age, and all were on public assistance. Before our intervention, mothers received two and one-half hours of literacy instruction three days a week, followed by a parent education class and an occasional home visit. There was no structured interaction between parents and children during the day.

Our staff transformed these adult literacy classes into a family literacy program, which required several structural changes. First, we refashioned the daycare center to include literacy-related play centers (Neuman & Roskos, 1992, 1993) filled with environmental print, literacy objects, and storybooks in areas that resembled a home kitchen and a grocery store. We also created a small "cozy corner" library area, which included low-lying bookshelves for toddlers' use. Second, we integrated literacy and parent education classes with mothers' regular involvement in the daycare center. Mothers were scheduled on an individual basis to spend one hour a day in the center for 12 sessions. They were mentored by staff to learn how to become involved in the educational activities of the center by reading to children, helping them accomplish goal-directed activities, and playing with them.

Once mothers had become comfortable in the center, we began a four-part intervention designed to enhance their participation with children (Neuman & Daly, 1993). Based on the model of guided participation, we developed metaphorical terms to describe important aspects of the process, which include the following.

1. *Get set.* The process of getting set involves an effort by the caregiver to focus and maintain the child's attention through nonverbal, verbal, and environmental cues. Behaviors to enhance getting set may include orienting a child who is now ready to do an activity and encouraging him or her to focus on a particular topic of interest.

2. *Give meaning.* When they give meaning, mothers share the importance and value of an interaction as well as communicate how this information may promote further understanding. Behaviors that give meaning include labeling objects and elaborating on actions or objects to make them more understandable to the child.

3. *Build bridges.* Once the context and meaningfulness of an activity are conveyed, caregivers may extend children's understanding by linking the activity to something that is either within or slightly beyond the child's own experiences. Behaviors that build bridges may include making connections between what is going on now and other experiences and explaining cause-and-effect relationships.

4. *Step back.* A final crucial feature of participation involves the transfer of responsibility for managing joint problem solving from caregiver to child. Behaviors associated with stepping back include helping the child understand a principle so that he or she can take control of the task, encouraging turn taking, and providing elaborated feedback to cause strategic thinking. The table provides definitions and examples of each part of the guided participation process.

After this part of the program was underway, we involved each mother in a three-part instructional cycle. First, we provided individualized instruction to the mothers on a particular aspect of the process. For example, we might discuss how to get children set for an activity. In the instance of storybook reading, we might describe the importance of getting the child's interest by letting the child touch the book and feel part of the experience by sitting close to the mother. We would try to connect these experiences with those in the home or community by discussing how storybook reading might enter into family daily routines. Following this informal conversation, in the second phase of instruction, mothers were encouraged to engage in the educational activities of the center. They were encouraged to interact not only with their own children, but with two or three toddlers in the center at a time. Working with small groups allowed mothers to experience how these activities might enable children to become increasingly independent as they interacted with their peers—something we had learned was very important to mothers (Neuman et al., 1994). We used ceiling video monitors to videotape these sessions.

In the third phase of the instructional cycle, mothers reflected on their own interactions by viewing parts of the videotape with us together in a small room. Segments were selected to highlight certain features; then we engaged mothers in a spirited discussion of the incident—what they liked, what they might do differently, and what types of activities children seem to respond to best. Of special note were conversations with mothers who seemed to show increasing initiative in working in the center. One mother said, "You know what I'm

## Definitions of the Four Processes in Guided Participation

Get set
- ◆ recruits child's interest in an activity
- ◆ gives child a reason to become involved in an activity
- ◆ focuses child's attention on something observable, "Look at this"
- ◆ attempts to keep child's attention throughout the activity

Give meaning
- ◆ helps child understand what is important to notice and the values associated with it
- ◆ labels objects that are seen in the environment
- ◆ adds descriptive comments or elaborations about an object
- ◆ adds animation to describe objects to make the activity come alive and provoke interest
- ◆ demonstrates or models a behavior

Build bridges
- ◆ makes connection to child's past or future, "Do you ever..."
- ◆ elicits connections from child, "Tell me if..."
- ◆ encourages imagination, "Can you imagine if..."
- ◆ induces hypothetical, cause-and-effect thinking, "What if..."

Step back
- ◆ gives child a strategy for completing a task, "This is a way you can make it work..."
- ◆ encourages turn taking
- ◆ provides elaborative feedback, "No...it works this way..." or "How about trying..."
- ◆ responds to child's initiatives, "So you are building a train"

From Neuman and Daly, 1993.

going to do next time in the center? I'm going to try to work with Fatima on her own. I think she needs some individual time, just with me."

After working in the center, mothers returned to their literacy classes and wrote their reflections in a dialogue journal where they described both positive and negative experiences with the children during the day. Their literacy teacher would often suggest ways they could link center activities with their lives outside school. Mothers revealed through these journals that they rarely had opportunities to talk informally with one another about their children, so we initiated lunchtime discussions where they could share information. In some cases, we showed videotapes of their activities in the daycare centers, pointing out promising practices and important generalizations about children. At other times, mothers began to explore many ideas on their own. One mother explained, "I found after each puzzle I did with Kalief, it was easier to do the next one with him—boy is he smart for his age. After that, I tried to get him to read to me or tell me the story as he sees it. He did a good job, too." We sensed that mothers were using their skills and resources and beginning to feel more confident in their roles as their children's first language and literacy teachers.

## Our Findings

Detailed records of mothers' interactions with children indicated an important phenomenon that we had hoped might occur through their involvement in the daycare center (see Neuman & Daly, 1993, for details). As mothers became increasingly capable of guiding children's participation, they began to adjust their level of support and involvement to meet the level of perceived competence of the child. For example, in the beginning, most mothers' exchanges were quite directive and involved children in getting set or giving meaning, as in the following dialogue between Ruth and Kalief about a storybook.

> Ruth: Who's in the tub? The hipp...
>
> Kalief: Hippo
>
> Ruth: The hippopotamus, that's right (continues and points). That's the dragonfly talking to the mouse. Do you see the mouse?
>
> Kalief: (points to the mouse)
>
> Ruth: Yes, that's right. Oh no, what's the mouse running to? What's that? (points to the picture)
>
> Kalief: (points to the alligator)
>
> Ruth: Yes, that's right. It's an alligator.

Notice in this instance that while Ruth is supporting Kalief's interactions, her role is that of an initiator—guiding and directing him carefully throughout the story. In fact, these sessions tended to reflect a mentor-apprentice relationship, with the caregiver evoking the child's attention and reflecting on specific aspects of the story to convey meaning. Although this relationship was beneficial in eliciting labels of objects, the child's role was primarily that of a responder to the adult's comments and questions. These types of interactions do not provide much opportunity for children's questions and initiatives.

As mothers' exchanges reflected greater bridge building and required more responsibility from the children, storybook reading sessions became far more lively and interactive. In these later situations, we found the children had increasingly become the leader, and the adult assumed the role of interactor and responder to the children's questions, as in the following example.

> Ruth: That's the frog. He lays the eggs and they be the babies like we have in our tank, and then they're going to be the frogs.
>
> Kalief: Where our tadpoles at? (asking about the tadpoles in the tank in the room)
>
> Ruth: Here they go, right here (points to tank).
>
> Kalief: (looks at the back of the book) What's that?
>
> Ruth: See it's a frog.
>
> Kalief: Well, how does it turn?
>
> Ruth: See it got a long tail and then it get smaller. It turns...
>
> Kalief: Why it turn into a frog?
>
> Ruth: It's just like how a puppy turn into a dog. 'Cus a puppy be little then it get big and turns into a dog.
>
> Kalief: Let me see the picture again.

In this active interchange, Ruth helps Kalief extend his understanding of change by talking about an event that is of interest in Kalief's experiences at the center. She also shows similarities between something familiar and something less known. In doing so, Ruth is helping Kalief build cognitive bridges, critical for cognitive development.

## Mothers' Responses

What is not apparent in this example is that, at the time, Ruth's own literacy level was not particularly high; she could read at about an eighth grade level. However, because the processes of guided participation focused more on conveying ideas and meaning to children in storybook reading, it allowed mothers to use stories as playful opportunities to interact with children. It was not necessary for mothers to read every line or even finish every book. But, because of the literacy practice the program did provide, by the end of the year, Ruth was reading well and had passed her GED.

Mothers' journals also documented their involvement in the center and their interest in children's growing development and understanding of literacy. One mother wrote, "Today at the daycare center I worked with Tameika. We made animals out of clay, and we read books together, and it was very inspirational working with her." And another wrote the following,

Since I've been visiting the daycare center, I realize that I do things different-ly; like before now, my little brother would say smart things, and I would hit him or scream, but now I've learned how to just be calm and talk to him. I shock myself but that's what I mean by experience is the best teacher, because this daycare experience has taught me patience and prepared me for work-ing better with my child.

## Children's Responses

Finally, we examined how changes in mothers' actions reflected on how young children interacted with books. Before our program, sto-rybook reading had not been a common event either at home or in the daycare center. Most of the parents, as well as staff, believed children—toddlers and preschoolers—lacked the skills necessary to be able to listen to stories. In fact, the following example of Tanya read-ing to Fatima and Wayne was seen as typical of children this age.

Tanya: (holding a book) See, can you find the mouse in this picture?

Fatima: Where?

Wayne: (looks for the mouse)

Tanya: Where's the mouse at, Fatima? Is that the mouse?

Fatima: Mouse ain't here.

Tanya: (laughs) Where's the mouse at that ain't here?

Wayne: (tries to look at back of cover, but Tanya stops him) Look at the big old...

Tanya: (interrupts, opens book and reads, but children don't listen)

In early sessions, mothers tended to control the situation by defin-ing the pace and establishing the purposes and expectations for story reading. Notice that in this example, it is clear that the agenda was set by the mother and that the child's initiative was extinguished by the mother's goal. As mothers' exchanges became more contingent on the children's increasing competence, however, we began to note important changes in children's interactions around books, as in this example of Tanya reading with Fatima.

Fatima: Turn the page. What are they doing now?

Tanya: They laying down. They tired, see (she reads on very slowly).

Fatima: (interrupts) Turn the page.

Tanya: (finishes studying page in silence, then turns it) Look at what they did (she sounds upset).

Fatima: What happened to the babies?

Tanya: They like—afraid.

Fatima: What happened to them?

Tanya: See the birds are trying to get them. They like (to eat) babies.

Fatima: Where the babies at?

Tanya: Right there in the water. See the bird trying to get them?

Fatima: (turns the page) What they doing here?

Observe Fatima's greater level of attention and interest. Here, she is taking charge by asking the questions, pacing the reading, and physically holding the book, clearly setting the agenda for the parent. Through mothers' careful guiding of children's participation, we found even toddlers began to take control of the storybook reading sessions. In doing so, they increasingly paced their participation to a level that was appropriate to their needs and interest. They also began to set specific purposes for reading, pushing their own development toward new and creative directions. In providing support and meaningful interactions, mothers were establishing a rich foundation for children to take on increasing involvement with and responsibility for their own learning through storybook reading.

## Implications for Teachers and Schools

Our family literacy project was based on several important principles that have relevance to teachers and schools. First, it was rooted in the belief that the central focus of family literacy is on the *transmission* of parents' newly developed skills to the child as it applies to families from diverse economic, educational, and cultural backgrounds. In this respect, our model of guided participation, which displays cultural variations yet shares important universal characteristics across cultures, provides a means for helping parents learn about the processes of conveying meaning to young children. We have focused on storybook reading, but these same processes apply to other routine learning events, such as playing or grocery shopping, which suggests that we can help parents by teaching them these processes and guiding their participation with children.

Second, our program was based on the premise that teen mothers' strong desire to help their children will encourage them to improve their own literacy skills. Our own observations, as well as research studies, have shown that adolescent mothers universally want to be good parents (Furstenberg, Brooks-Gunn, & Morgan, 1987; Neuman & Gallagher, 1994). However, they often face tremendous obstacles of poverty, poor education, and poor self-esteem. Our family literacy program has attempted to break down these barriers by encouraging parents to become valuable teachers by increasing their own literacy skills and knowledge as well as teaching them to respond to their children's learning needs.

Finally, we believe that programs that focus on the tragic consequences of early pregnancy—sometimes subconsciously demeaning these mothers for their life choices—cannot be successful in overcoming the intergenerational cycle of low-achieving families and children. Rather, we believe it is essential to build programs that are guided by mutual respect between parents and professionals. Within this basic framework of respect and collaboration, the overriding intent of family literacy programs should be to empower individuals—both parents and children—to make informed decisions and assume control over their lives.

## References

Alan Guttmacher Institute. (1986). *Teenage pregnancy in industrialized countries.* New Haven, CT: Yale University Press.

Anastasiow, N. (1982). *The adolescent parent.* Baltimore, MD: Brookes.

Berlin, G., & Sum, A. (1988). *Toward a more perfect union: Basic skills, poor families, and our economic future.* New York: Ford Foundation.

Furstenberg, F. (1976). *The social consequences of teenage childbearing.* New York: Macmillan.

Furstenberg, F., Brooks-Gunn, J., & Morgan, S.P. (1987). *Adolescent mothers in later life.* New York: Cambridge University Press.

Landy, S., & Walsh, S. (1988). Early intervention with high-risk teenage mothers and their infants. *Early Child Development and Care, 37,* 27–46.

Neuman, S.B., & Daly, P. (1993, December). *Guiding young children: A family literacy approach.* Paper presented at the National Reading Conference, Charleston, SC.

Neuman, S.B., & Gallagher, P. (1994). Joining together in literacy learning: Teenage mothers and children. *Reading Research Quarterly, 29,* 382–401.

Neuman, S.B., Hagedorn, T., Celano, D., & Daly, P. (1994, April). *Toward a collaborative approach to parent involvement: The implications of parents' beliefs.* Paper presented at the American Educational Research Association Conference, New Orleans, LA.

Neuman, S.B., & Roskos, K. (1992). Literacy objects as cultural tools: Effects on children's literacy behaviors in play. *Reading Research Quarterly, 27,* 202–225.

Neuman, S.B., & Roskos, K. (1993). Access to print for children of poverty: Differential effects of adult mediation and literacy-enriched play settings on environmental and functional print tasks. *American Educational Research Journal, 30,* 95–122.

Reis, J.S., & Herz, E.J. (1987). Correlates of adolescent parenting. *Adolescence, 22,* 599–609.

Rogoff, B. (1990). *Apprenticeship in thinking: Cognitive development in social context.* New York: Oxford University Press.

Rogoff, B., Mosier, C., Mistry, J., & Goncu, A. (1993). Toddlers' guided participation with their caregivers in cultural activity. In E. Forman, N. Minick, & C.A. Stone (Eds.), *Contexts for learning* (pp. 230–253). New York: Oxford University Press.

Thormann, M.S. (1985). Attitudes of adolescents toward infants and young children. In S. Harel & N. Anastasiow (Eds.), *The at-risk infant: Psychological-social medical aspects* (pp. 227–241). Baltimore, MD: Brookes.

Williams, C.W. (1991). *Black teenage mothers.* Lexington, MA: DC Heath.

# Chapter 8

# Let the Circle Be Unbroken:
# Teens as Literacy Learners and Teachers

**Billie J. Enz and Lyndon W. Searfoss**
*Arizona State University, Tempe, Arizona*

*Seventeen-year-old Naomi, a junior in high school, is reading to her daughter, three-year-old Sasha. "Brown bear, brown bear, what do you see? I see a goldfish looking at me.' Sasha, where is brown bear?" asks Naomi. Sasha points. "That's right, Sasha!" says Naomi, as she hugs Sasha. Sasha points to the book and demands, "Read more, Mama!"*

This scene between mother and child, similar to that in the previous chapter, was observed in a daycare center located within Naomi's high school. Sasha attends daycare while her mother has an opportunity to complete her high school education. Naomi's internship in the daycare center is part of her assignment for two courses—child development and life management. Naomi is one of approximately 20 teenage parents (out of a student body of 1250) who currently attend high school classes and work in the daycare center each semester for one hour each day. The center typically serves between 35 and 40 infants, toddlers, and preschoolers and is under the direction of the life management faculty. The center provides services for the children of both teachers and teen parents.

Although she reads fluently to Sasha, Naomi's approximate reading level is grade six. While she recalls her grandmother telling her stories,

Naomi does not remember being read to as a child. The unique curriculum and daycare center in this high school offer a literacy setting in which Naomi can learn to read to her child. This scenario is an example of how dramatic changes in the traditional and conventional U.S. family structure continue to challenge educators in the 1990s. Families come in many varieties, ranging from single-parent households to those families created by combining children and parents from previous marriages and relationships. Schurr (1992) cautions, "As a result, educators can no longer rely on their stereotypic views of what the family represents and how its needs can be addressed" (p. 3). Flaxman and Inger (1991) cite studies reporting that 40 percent of today's school children in the United States will have lived with a single parent by the time they reach the age of 18. They further conclude:

> Conventional parent involvement efforts, aimed at the traditional family, have simply proven ineffective in promoting the involvement of parents of these children. Most schools, as currently structured, with educational practices created for a different population, are less able to deal with the problems of a diverse student population with special needs (p. 2).

The significant numbers of teenagers of all cultures and ethnic backgrounds who become mothers and fathers while still enrolled in public schools present an especially difficult challenge for educators (Scott-Jones, 1993). When teenagers become parents, they face a world in which they must play multiple and confusing roles for which they may be ill prepared: parent, child, learner, and teacher. Within one body, they represent two generations, parents and children, each with its own social and cultural expectations. As learners, many teen parents encounter difficulty and failure as they struggle to read and write, as Neuman discussed in the previous chapter. In fact, their literacy levels may be similar to those of elementary school children. Other teenagers may be fluent readers and writers, but are unprepared for their new role as a child's first teacher. Research clearly demonstrates that growing up in a home where literacy is encouraged by parents gives a child a solid foundation for learning in school (Morrow, 1993; Teale, 1984). Our own work confirms this view: Enz (1990) conducted an informal survey with 400 high school sophomores and found that 70 percent of the remedial readers could not recall being read to by their parents as children, while 96 percent of the advanced students reported their parents had read to them regularly.

It appears that in many cases, children's future literacy and subsequent success in school depend on parents' ability and willingness to provide their children with numerous planned and spontaneous encounters with print. That is why the need for school programs to help *all* teenagers acquire strategies for becoming effective models of literacy for their children is urgent and immediate. Many children learn about literacy early and naturally as they sit on the laps of parents or other family members and share a storybook or other literacy activity. Surrounded by love, these children easily learn about the functions of print and the joys of reading (Clark, 1984; Cochran-Smith, 1986). It is unfortunate that an ever-increasing number of high school students cannot recall such experiences because they have been reared in homes where

*A teen mother provides a literacy model for her child.*

positive experiences with print have been sparse. Because they have not had a parenting model who encouraged literacy activities, they are unlikely to read to or share print with their own children—thus perpetuating the cycle of illiteracy (Nurss, 1991).

If we are to break this cycle, we must acknowledge that all high school students are potential parents. We must dedicate ourselves to teaching these young adults about the critical role they play as their children's first literacy teacher, regardless of when the children are born. Further, we must give them the skills and knowledge they need to accomplish this task.

## Family Literacy in the High Schools

This chapter presents a day-by-day account of a literacy program that focuses on high school students, including teen mothers and fathers. The two-week unit is an example of how educators are trying to meet the challenge of developing a family literacy program within the school context. The objectives of the unit are three fold: (1) to introduce high school students to the genre of children's books and to methods of identifying characteristics of these books that would make them especially helpful in encouraging young children to read; (2) to teach teens fluent and expressive oral reading techniques that enhance the storybook reading experience for both children and teens; and (3) to establish for high school students the connection between early family literacy activities and school success.

*Day one.* To introduce this unit, the instructor brought to class 60 to 70 familiar children's books, such as *I Know an Old Lady, The Three Billy Goats Gruff, The Very Hungry Caterpillar,* and *Green Eggs and Ham.* The students were asked to identify one or two books they remembered and liked in childhood. This simple activity elicited a great deal of interest from the high school students. As observers of this activity, we have often noticed teens who, though resistant initially, became quite animated about a favorite childhood book. It is also not uncommon for several students to like the same book. Next, they were asked if they could recall at what age they first heard this book and identify who might have read it to them. Most of the students could remember this information quite clearly. Finally, they were asked why they thought they remembered this book so fondly. All information is recorded on the questionnaire form in Figure 1.

Through reviewing these questionnaires, we, like other researchers (Auerbach, 1989; Darling, 1992; Taylor & Dorsey-Gaines, 1988), have detected a relationship between socioeconomic levels and access to

**Figure 1**
**Memories**

Name _____ Class hour _____ Date _____
Title of favorite children's book _____
How old were you when you first read this storybook? _____
Who first read this storybook to you? _____
Why do you think you chose this storybook as one of your favorites? _____
_____
_____

books and storybook reading in the home. Most of the students who came from low-SES backgrounds indicated they remembered their books from being read to by a primary school teacher. Middle- and upper-class students were more likely to have remembered a book being read to them by their parents at home.

*Day two.* The students watched a video of a highly animated reading of a book such as *Oh, A-Hunting We Will Go*. The story reader was a well-known, admired high school athlete who completed the course the prior year. He was reading to a group of preschool-age children who attended the daycare center and was modeling many appropriate read-aloud strategies while the preschoolers responded enthusiastically to his reading. The high school students watched the video and were impressed and somewhat surprised at how much the reader appeared to be enjoying himself.

After watching the video, the instructor asked her students if they knew what the most important activity is that a family member can do to help a child be successful in school. Many of the students volunteered suggestions, ranging from "taking children to preschool" and "teaching them to write the alphabet" to "telling them to behave in school." Finally, someone suggested, "Just read to them." The teacher confirmed that all these actions would be helpful, but one of the most important activities that appears to help children achieve success in school is storybook reading. She told the class that the children's literature unit was designed to help them become better teachers to younger siblings, cousins, babysitting charges, and ultimately their own children. She informed them that for the next nine weeks they would be assigned to work with a buddy reader at the adjoining elementary school and that during the hour-long, weekly visit they would be storybook reading with and coaching a beginning reader.

*Day three.* The instructor began by holding up several of the teens' top choices for favorite children's literature books. These included *I Know an Old Lady, The Gingerbread Boy, Drummer Hoff, Caps for Sale, The Runaway Bunny, The House That Jack Built, Green Eggs and Ham,* and *The Cat in the Hat.* She asked the students to listen carefully while she read two stories and to keep in mind these questions: "What is special about these books?" and "Why do you remember them so well?" She read *I Know an Old Lady* and *Green Eggs and Ham* and then asked the students to work in pairs to generate answers. Within a few minutes, the teacher began to solicit the students' responses, which she wrote on the board. The students' answers were similar:

"The stories are funny."

"They have fun pictures and illustrations."

"The pictures help tell the story."

"The words are simple and easy to read."

"The words rhyme."

"The storyline repeats itself (refrain)."

"It was the first book I read by myself."

Congratulating her students for their astute analysis, the teacher revealed that these favorite texts fit a particular category called *predictable books.* She described how predictable books are especially useful in helping young children gain confidence as readers because the illustrations and text match, the repetitive and cumulative refrains encourage initial decoding skills, and the rhythm and rhyme of the words facilitate fluent oral reading (Heald-Taylor, 1987; Rhodes 1981).

*Day four.* The instructor took her students to the high school library, which featured a large children's literature section with multiple copies of favorite books. She asked them to find and check out at least two children's books that fit the predictable book category. The students used the predictable book hunt checklist to help guide their selections (see Figure 2). The teacher found it was important to keep the students on task during this assignment as they often discovered many familiar and new children's books they wanted to review. Before they left the library, the instructor told her class that tomorrow they would begin to learn read-aloud techniques.

*Day five.* Before the students entered the classroom, the teacher had already paired the teens for a read-aloud exercise and made certain each team had at least one competent reader. First, the students watched a video with two segments of a teacher reading aloud a storybook to two six-year-olds. During the first segment, designed to present

**Figure 2**
**The Predictable-Book Hunt**

Name _____ Class hour _____ Date _____

Does this storybook have at least three or more of the following features?

Book 1    Book 2
_____      _____      limited text per page
_____      _____      simple, easy to read words
_____      _____      repeated phrases or refrains
_____      _____      match between illustration and text
_____      _____      rhyming words or refrains
_____      _____      strong rhythm
_____      _____      fun to read

Your selections:
Title _____ Author _____
Title _____ Author _____
Title _____ Author _____

poor read-aloud techniques, the teacher used a monotone voice, sat across from the children, and did not share the illustrations or pictures while reading. The high school students noticed that at first the children were attentive. However, they quickly became restless, and before the end of the story they were beginning to wrestle around with one another. The teacher asked the teens to work with their partners and discuss why they thought the children were misbehaving. In response, the high school students felt that the teacher's dull voice was the biggest problem, and he did not involve the students by asking them questions or showing them the pictures.

The instructor then played a second segment, which demonstrated her reading *The Gingerbread Man* to the same six-year-olds. This time, however, the students observed the teacher reading with great expression, using special character voices. Throughout the story she held the book so that the children could always see the illustrations. In addition, the high school students noticed that the teacher asked the children to join in reading the refrain "I'm a gingerbread boy, I'm as fresh as can be! I can run so fast, you can't catch me!" The teens also noted that at the end of the story the teacher asked several opinion questions, such as, "Why do you think the Gingerbread Man ran away from the little old woman and old man?" Finally, the students remarked that the teacher's enthusiastic reading was the main reason the children were fascinated with the book and listened and participated so well. The students' assignment for the following Monday was to practice reading their predictable books, using all the effective storybook reading techniques they witnessed on the second video segment.

*Day six.* The high school students were first asked to practice their selection with their read-aloud partners and complete the buddy reading observation guide (see Figure 3). This guide was designed to help the partners provide specific feedback to each other regarding the quality of their storybook reading to prepare them for reading to their grade school buddies. After both partners had an opportunity to receive comments and practice their selections, the teacher asked for volunteers to demonstrate their new read-aloud strategies. Both the teacher and observers noticed that even the students with minimal reading levels were fluent, expressive, and very pleased with their performances.

*Day seven.* More students presented their storybook reading skills to the class. Again, the readings were fluent and energetic, and the illustrations were easy to view throughout the entire reading.

## Figure 3
## Buddy Reading Observation Guide

High school buddy _____ Date _____

Grade school buddy _____ Male _____ Female _____ Grade _____

Book title _____ Author _____

Book appropriate for buddy listener? Yes _____ No _____ (reason _____)

| | | |
|---|---|---|
| Illustrations: | visible at all times | hard to see |
| Reading fluency: | articulate/smooth | inarticulate/rough |
| Oral expression: | expressive | monotone |
| Interaction with student: | positive/outgoing | negative/introverted |
| Questions: | open-ended | limited-response |

Comments: _____

_____

Afterward, the students were paired with their first grade buddies. In the separate elementary class, each first grader had written his or her name above a drawn self-portrait for the high school buddy. To help the teens become familiar with each of their reading buddies' educational needs, the first grade teacher had written information concerning his or her reading level and special interests at the bottom of each portrait. The teens and children were paired by the teens' blindly selecting a child's self-portrait from a container. Depending on class size, one high school student might be assigned two first graders.

The instructor asked the high school students to create signs with their first grade reading buddy's name printed on them. The teens would hold these signs when they entered the first grade classroom, and the children would find their reading buddy by recognizing their own names.

*Day eight.* To prepare students for working with their buddies, the teacher discussed appropriate comprehension questions for storybook reading and introduced the idea of story retelling. She encouraged the high school students to use the retelling technique by asking them to work with their teen read-aloud partner and retell each other's story. She told them that the easiest way to retell a story was to guide the children through prompt questions. For example, to begin the teen could say, "Tell me what happened at the beginning of this story." If the child starts to lose his or her place, the teen could give support by saying "After _____, then what happened?" If the child needed help ending the story, the high school student could ask, "What happens at the end of the story?"

The teacher briefly mentioned that first graders are occasionally shy. She suggested that if a buddy was initially timid, the teen buddy should say, "Show me your favorite picture." The teacher also cautioned the teens against interrogating the children about the story. Instead, the teacher encouraged the high school students to use open-ended or opinion questions that would stimulate the children's comprehension and enjoyment of the stories. To help the teens differentiate between open-ended and yes or no questions, they worked through a question typology worksheet (see Figure 4). The night before they planned to present their stories, the teens were asked to write four open-ended questions for both of the predictable storybooks.

*Day nine.* Working with their teen read-aloud partner, the students each planned their 30-minute storybook reading activities (see Figure 5). Their plan was to include the following procedures, which were repeated for the second book:

◆ 3 to 4 minutes to meet their first grade reading buddy;

## Figure 4
## Question Typology

For each question, determine if it is an example of an "O" for open-ended question (questions that encourage inferential thinking and opinions) or "C" for closed-end question (questions that have only one right answer).

_____ 1. What color are bears?

_____ 2. Why do you think the little bunny wanted to run away from his mother?

_____ 3. What do you think happened after the grandmother, boy, dog, cat, mouse, and flea broke the bed?

_____ 4. What did brown bear see?

_____ 5. Why do you think the old lady swallowed the fly?

_____ 6. What did the old lady swallow to catch the spider?

_____ 7. Where would you want to eat green eggs and ham?

_____ 8. What was in the buzzing log?

_____ 9. Who said, "You monkeys you. You give me back my caps"?

_____ 10. Why did the monkeys take the cap sellers' caps?

---

♦ 5 to 6 minutes to read their first story;

♦ 3 to 5 minutes to story retell or discuss favorite pictures; and

♦ 3 to 5 minutes to ask and discuss the open-ended questions.

During the class the teacher circulated through the room to provide guidance, encouragement, and praise. At the end of class the high school students were informed that tomorrow, instead of coming to class, they were to report to the front office, where the bus would pick them up and take them to a nearby elementary school. They were to bring their teaching supplies, which included the name signs they had made, predictable books, and their lesson plans.

*Day ten.* As the high school students assembled at the bus, the teacher made sure the students had all their teaching materials while she took attendance. The teens were excited because most of them had attended the elementary school where they were going, and many had younger siblings there who had heard about the reading buddy project.

As the teens walked into the classroom, the first graders cheered and applauded. The first grade teacher asked the high school students to hold up their buddy name signs and to form a circle around the room. Each first grader then found his or her reading buddy. The bud-

## Figure 5
## Buddy Reading Lesson Plan

Name _____ Class hour _____ Date _____

Minutes

3–4     Describe get acquainted activity.

5–6     Book 1 title _____ Author _____

3–5     *Story retelling*             *Favorite picture*

"Tell me what happened first."    "Show me your favorite picture."

"After _____, then what happened?"

"What happened at the end of the
     story?"

3–5     Comprehension: opinion or open-ended questions

Write four questions.
1.
2.
3.
4.

5–6     Book 2 title _____ Author _____

3–5     *Story retelling*             *Favorite picture*

"Tell me what happened first."    "Show me your favorite picture."

"After _____, then what happened?"

"What happened at the end of the
     story?"

3–5     Comprehension: opinion or open-ended questions

Write four questions.
1.
2.
3.
4.

dy reading teams immediately found a private spot to sit, and the introductions began. The teachers monitored the classroom, and when the storybook reading started, they used the buddy reading observation guide (see Figure 3) to assess the high school students' preparation and performance. Thirty-five minutes passed quickly and, as the high school students were leaving, the first graders gave them special, handmade thank-you cards and hugs.

Once on the bus, the teacher praised the high school students as they completed a self-assessment form similar to Figure 3, which also asked what the students would do again and what they would change in their first buddy session. The teacher reviewed the assignment sheet that informed the students that each Wednesday for the next seven weeks they would learn a new read-aloud strategy and select appropriate books. Wednesday night homework would consist of practicing their read-aloud skills and designing the lesson plan for Friday. Each Friday they would work with their first grade reading buddies.

During the next seven weeks, the high school students learned about echo reading, choral reading, paired reading, storytelling, and chanting. At the end of the nine-week grading period, the teacher videotaped each buddy reading team, and the high school students wrote a paper describing what they had learned through this experience.

## Reading Buddy Program Evaluation: To Teach Is to Learn Twice

We have documented some effects of this family literacy program, including the following:

- Both the high school and elementary classes involved in the program had nearly perfect attendance on Fridays.

- Homework for the unit activities was almost always turned in on time because the high school students discovered they could not read to the buddies on Friday unless their lesson plans were complete.

- High school students began bringing children's books to school that were not in the school library and often shared them with other classmates.

- The high school students asked their teacher to order books for them from book clubs as the first graders often did.

Perhaps the most important and lasting impact was observable in the faces and attitudes of the high school students. Their verbal comments and written reflections provide insights about what they learned from the experience.

"I feel like a hero, you know? Mickey tells me I'm so smart 'cause I read so well to her. She says she wants to be like me. Really, she's the smart one. She already can read most of the stories. I really look forward to being with her on Friday."

"Mostly I don't like reading, but when I read with Shaun it's like different. I want Shaun to grow up likin' this stuff, so I feel good about helpin' him."

"I have a four-year-old sister at home. I was never read to when I was little—my mom had to work nights. But I am reading to my sister. I don't want her to hate school like I did. Cindy (her buddy) is already reading; I want that for Macy."

"I never knew parents were supposed to do this reading stuff. But now I know. I want my son to be smart. His mother is going to take this class next year. I will help her read to him 'cause I read children's books real good. Jose (his buddy) has trouble 'cause, like me, he speaks a lot of Spanish. But Jose, he's gonna be okay, 'cause he said his sister is reading to him all the time."

For very little money and with the cooperation between an elementary school and a high school, family literacy programs can break the cycle of illiteracy too common among teenage parents and their children. The need for these types of programs is urgent and immediate. The teachers and administrators involved in the program described here responded to that challenge professionally and creatively.

## Note

We would like to thank Donald Enz, principal at Coronado High School in Scottsdale, Arizona; Patricia Heck, reading specialist at Red Mountain High School in Mesa, Arizona; and Millie Musson, reading specialist at Challenger Elementary School in Nogales, Arizona. They are the dedicated educators who allowed us the opportunity to work with them and observe the wonderful programs they are creating to meet the needs of their students and the children of tomorrow.

## References

Auerbach, E.R. (1989). Towards a socio-contextual approach to family literacy. *Harvard Educational Review, 59,* 165–181.

Clark, M.M. (1984). Literacy at home and at school: Insights from a study of young fluent readers. In H. Goelman, A. Oberg, & F. Smith (Eds.), *Awakening to literacy* (pp. 122–130). Portsmouth, NH: Heinemann.

Cochran-Smith, M. (1986). Reading to children: A model for understanding text. In B.B. Schieffelin & P. Gilmore (Eds.), *The acquisition of literacy: Ethnographic perspectives* (pp. 35–54). Norwood, NJ: Ablex.

Darling, S. (1992). Family literacy: Parents and children learning together. *Principal, 72*(2), 10–12.

Enz, B.J. (1990). *Sophomore high school students' literacy memories.* Informal survey. Arizona State University, Tempe, AZ.

Flaxman, E., & Inger, M. (1991). Parents and schooling in the 1990s. ERIC *Review, 1*(3), 2–5.

Heald-Taylor, G. (1987). Predictable literature selections and activities for language arts instruction. *The Reading Teacher, 41,* 6–12.

Morrow, L.M. (1993). *Literacy development in the early years: Helping children read and write.* Boston, MA: Allyn & Bacon.

Nurss, J.R. (1991). *Reading together: Times worth remembering.* Dimensions, 19(4), 21–23.

Rhodes, L.K. (1981). I can read: Predictable books as resources for reading and writing instruction. *The Reading Teacher, 34,* 511–518.

Schurr, S.L. (1992). Fine tuning your parent power increases student achievement. *Schools in the Middle, 2*(2), 3–9.

Scott-Jones, D. (1993). Adolescent childbearing: Whose problem? What can we do? Kappan Special Report. *Kappan, 75*(3), K1–K12.

Taylor, D., & Dorsey-Gaines, C. (1988). *Growing up literate: Learning from inner-city families.* Portsmouth, NH: Heinemann.

Teale, W.H. (1984). Reading to young children: Its significance for literacy development. In H. Goelman, A. Oberg, & F. Smith (Eds.), *Awakening to literacy* (pp. 110–121). Portsmouth, NH: Heinemann.

## Children's Literature

Bonne, R. (1961). *I know an old lady.* New York: Scholastic.

Brown, M. (1954). *The three billy goats gruff.* San Diego, CA: Harcourt, Brace.

Brown, M.W. (1942). *The runaway bunny.* New York: HarperCollins.

Carle, E. (1981). *The very hungry caterpillar.* New York: Putnam.

Cutts, D. (1979). *The gingerbread boy.* Mahwah, NJ: Troll.

Emberly, B. (1967). *Drummer Hoff.* Englewood Cliffs, NJ: Prentice-Hall.

Guilfoile, E. (1962). *The house that Jack built.* Orlando, FL: Holt, Rinehart and Winston.

Langstaff, J. (1974). *Oh, a-hunting we will go.* New York: HarperCollins.

Martin, B. Jr. (1967). *Brown bear, brown bear, what do you see?* Orlando, FL: Holt, Rinehart and Winston.

Seuss, Dr. (1957). *The cat in the hat.* Boston, MA: Houghton Mifflin.

Seuss, Dr. (1960). *Green eggs and ham.* New York: Random House.

Slobodkina, E. (1940). *Caps for sale.* Reading, MA: Addison-Wesley.

# Chapter 9

# The Reading Is Fundamental Motivational Approach to Family Literacy

**Ruth Graves and James H. Wendorf**
*Reading Is Fundamental, Washington, DC*

In 1966 a former school teacher and a group of parents created a program to make books and reading more appealing to children. The program provided children with books that they could choose and keep and included events and activities to make reading fun. The program's approach was motivational in nature and was based firmly on the "pleasure principle": kids who learn that reading is fun are more likely to continue reading and learning. That program became Reading Is Fundamental—today the oldest and largest reading motivation program for young people in the United States. The program that Margaret McNamara and her fellow volunteers initiated now serves more than three million children each year throughout all 50 states, the District of Columbia, and the U.S. offshore possessions. More than 166,000 parents, teachers, and other committed citizens volunteer their time to RIF programs at 16,000 schools, libraries, early childhood centers, and other locations serving children and families.

As the RIF program grew, its motivational approach proved to work steadily over time. Today's children, like those in 1966, need to experience the pleasure of reading. They need access to books that relate to their lives and interests and that motivate them to read more. And they need the adults in their lives to encourage their growth as readers and learners. RIF recognizes that parents and other family members play a special role in motivating children to read, and our approach to family literacy emphasizes this role, which is one of the two distinguishing characteristics of our family literacy programs. The other characteristic is RIF's trademark emphasis on book ownership. As stressed by the authors in this work, the positive effect of having books in the home is well documented, most recently in the 1992 National Assessment of Educational Progress (U.S. Department of Education, 1993). A study that analyzed trends in reading over four U.S. assessments (U.S. Department of Education, 1985) concluded, "Children from homes with an abundance of reading material have substantially higher average reading proficiency levels than do children who have few such materials available" (p. 50). Our experience over the past 27 years supports a related conclusion—namely, that choosing books to own is a powerfully motivating activity for children. If children are motivated to read, they will read more and read better. As one major study noted, "Children improve their reading ability by reading a lot. Reading achievement is directly related to the amount of reading children do in school and outside (U.S. Department of Education, 1987, p. 8).

RIF's family literacy initiatives aim to put such research into practice and into the lives of children and families. They share other characteristics that reflect the organization's approach to families. Our programs and materials

- ◆ treat parents as parents, not as instructors; parents are enlisted to encourage reading and guide children in activities, not to teach them to read.

- ◆ build on parents' strengths, regardless of their level of formal education; our programs include roles, activities, and tasks for parents with varying reading skills.

- ◆ provide hands-on opportunities and resources so that parents can translate good intentions into positive actions.

- ◆ acknowledge the powerful aspirations that parents have for their children and that can guide parents in encouraging their children's love of reading.

- ◆ are based on a pleasure principle for parents that resembles the one for children: parents who learn that participating in their children's reading is fun are more likely to affect positively their children's reading behavior and attitudes toward books.

From RIF's beginning, parents have served as volunteers by administering all aspects of the program from choosing and ordering books to raising funds to planning and conducting reading activities. With this foundation, RIF began in 1982 to develop a range of direct services to aid parents in encouraging their children's reading, including the following.

- ◆ "Growing Up Reading" workshops for parents were designed to aid schools and libraries in their outreach efforts to parents. More than 40 workshops were conducted jointly by RIF and community partners and have been incorporated into local programs around the United States.

- ◆ Brochures for parents on topics originally addressed in the "Growing Up Reading" workshops (for example, reading aloud, choosing good books for children, TV and reading, family storytelling, encouraging prereaders and young writers, and building a family library) have been distributed throughout the United States.

- ◆ *Helping Your Children Become Readers* and *Como ayudar a que sus niños sean buenos lectores,* two reproducible brochures offering basic suggestions for parents to nurture their children's interest in books and reading, have been distributed.

- ◆ *The RIF Guide to Encouraging Young Readers* (Graves, 1987), a resource book for parents with activities, annotated book lists, and a guide to children's magazines, book clubs, and helpful organizations, was published.

- ◆ *Reading Is Fun!,* a pamphlet of tips for parents of children up to age eight, was made available. It features ways that parents can help prepare young children for reading and encourage them as they begin to read on their own.

- ◆ Eight pilot programs were developed in cooperation with organizations in six communities. Funded by the John D. and Catherine T. MacArthur Foundation, these experimental programs allowed RIF to explore various of methods and media including storytelling for Spanish-speaking families, informal lending libraries run by parents, radio programs featuring literacy information and activities, and book sharing programs for pregnant and parenting teenagers.

By the end of 1989, RIF began to develop model programs that could incorporate the most effective strategies from our earlier programs and publications for parents and be replicated by schools and community organizations throughout the United States. Two family literacy initiatives evolved: Shared Beginnings and the companion programs Family of Readers and RIF for Families.

## Shared Beginnings

In 1990 RIF developed the Shared Beginnings program to help educators in schools, community centers, and agencies interrupt the cycle of intergenerational low literacy among teenaged parents and their young children. Similar to the programs described in the two previous chapters, this program teaches pregnant and parenting teens how to create literacy-rich homes for their babies and toddlers and why it is important. Our development work was made possible by two foundations concerned with intergenerational literacy: the New York Life Foundation underwrote program development and field testing, and the Hearst Foundations supported program expansion.

Teenage pregnancy is interwoven with various serious health, educational, and social concerns, as explained in Chapters 7 and 8. Though teenage pregnancy and parenthood are not new phenomena in the United States, the social and economic circumstances of early childbearing have changed dramatically, especially over the past 40 years. In the 1950s many pregnant adolescents tended to get married, live in stable families, and get adequate jobs in a world where little formal education was required (Scott-Jones, 1993). Today's young mothers are generally unmarried and were not performing well in school prior to their pregnancy. The sudden, often unanticipated responsibilities of parenthood make it that much harder for young mothers to finish school and find work. They tend to earn lower incomes in an economy that requires more formal education and higher literacy rates than ever before.

Many teens whom RIF has surveyed have had attitudes toward books and reading that can be characterized, at best, as indifferent. Through Shared Beginnings, RIF seeks to change attitudes and behaviors, enabling teen parents to create reading and learning opportunities for their young families. The goals of the program are to

- ◆ help teen parents understand the importance of nurturing the emergent literacy of their infants and toddlers;
- ◆ help teens acquire the skills and the desire to nurture their children's literacy; and
- ◆ strengthen teens' confidence in their parenting ability by giving them practice in a broad range of emergent literacy activities.

Graves & Wendorf

Related program objectives include helping teen parents with the following:

- discover the pleasure of reading aloud to their infants;
- select books that are appropriate to their children's ages and interests;
- understand how other activities—talking, singing, playing, going places together, and telling stories—nurture oral language development and prereading skills and help prepare young children for school; and
- create an environment for learning at home by showing them how to make books and other educational toys using inexpensive, everyday items.

*Program structure, content, and materials.* Shared Beginnings features discussion, modeling, and group activities to encourage teen parents to participate in their children's earliest learning experiences. The activities focus particularly on those experiences that lead to language development, learning, and literacy. The program is structured around eight major themes, each of which can be explored in a week. The program is flexible enough, however, to run for less than eight weeks or for as long as three to four months, depending on the depth or breadth of coverage desired. RIF intends that Shared Beginnings complement a school or agency's regular curriculum, which includes, for example, parenting, early childhood education, or children's literature.

Two publications are provided that present activities: the *Shared Beginnings Leader's Guide* for program coordinators and the *Shared Beginnings Idea Book* for each parent in the program. Both publications cover the eight themes, which focus on varieties of communication between parents and young children: talking, singing with rhyming and rocking; playing; going places; storytelling; choosing books; reading aloud; and writing and drawing. The program's flexibility allows the themes to be presented in any order; although the order suggested here emphasizes increasing attention to books and the written word.

At the start of each Shared Beginnings session, parents are invited to talk about their children and share their parenting concerns and successes. The *Leader's Guide* offers informal narrative and questions on each of the eight themes to help program coordinators guide these peer group discussions, called "baby talks." As the group explores each new topic, program coordinators also model a "book bonding" activity, which demonstrates appropriate ways to share books with infants and toddlers. Because parents' young children are often present at these sessions, coordinators encourage parents to practice stimulating their infants' language and learning. At other sessions, hands-on projects show parents how to make books and other educational toys. Every group activity includes the reminder to "take a baby break"—a few minutes of quiet time when parents' attention is focused entirely on their children. If parents have made books or toys for their children, the "baby break" is time for parents to sit with them and enjoy a story or some play time together.

The themes and activities covered in the *Leader's Guide* are reinforced in the *Idea Book*—a resource and memory book for parents to take home. Group discussions, activities, and discoveries are underscored and enhanced in the *Idea Book* in ways that encourage the parents to try at home what they have learned at school.

The final component of Shared Beginnings is the BABE—Books and Babies Event—where each family is able to choose a book to take home and keep at least three times during the program. While most programs provide infant and toddler books for teen parents to choose and read with their young children, some programs have books specifically for teens as well. As mentioned earlier, book choice and ownership have long been recognized by RIF as natural incentives for reading. Shared Beginnings is no exception, and the BABEs have been a significant factor in the success of the program.

*Program results.* From September 1990 through August 1991, RIF field-tested Shared Beginnings at ten pilot sites. During that time, the program brought resources for parents, 4497 books, and more than 100 reading motivation activities to program participants. Field-test participants included 621 teen parents and 617 infants and toddlers. The young parents represented various socioeconomic and ethnic groups, including monolingual Hispanic families that required Spanish-led sessions and Native Americans. Sites served from 5 teen mothers to 400 mothers and fathers. The pilot sites included schools, clinics, community centers, and a residential home in inner-city as well as rural areas. All the sites provided daycare, which allowed infants and toddlers to participate in activities. At most of the pilot sites, teen parents were already meeting together regularly for educational programs, peer support, or health services.

Surveys and reports submitted to RIF by field-test projects and programs currently in operation point to the following results:

♦ Teen parents learn that language development, literacy, and pre-reading skills begin even before children can talk. A Kentucky parent observed, "Although my son is not old enough for reading or even understanding what is read to him, he loves listening to my voice and looking at the pictures."

◆ Young parents learn and practice specific ways to nurture their children's emergent literacy skills. The result is that parents may actually witness their own power for the first time, as noted by a Massachusetts coordinator: "After the singing, rhyming, and rocking session, one mom came in and told a staff member, 'I sang to my baby for the first time last night. I sang into his face and—oh, my God—how he looked at me!'" Another parent said, "Shared Beginnings has provided me with ideas about how to make different things for my child such as baggie books and magnets. I learned songs to sing to my child, also. Now I know a lot of things that I didn't know before." A Montana teen added, "I like making really neat books out of things you have right in your home. The peek-a-boo book is what I really liked."

◆ In addition to giving teens practice in identifying and sharing books, the program strengthens their parenting skills. A New York coordinator reported, "The teen mothers embraced the 'baby break' concept as a break with baby, not a break from baby. Baby breaks are a very strong part of the program, and the participants liked explaining it to new students." A South Carolina coordinator concluded that the program "helped teens see that bonding was more than just meeting basic needs."

◆ Teen parents develop a more positive attitude toward their own reading, which coordinators said is often the result of happy experiences sharing books with their children.

Our experience with Shared Beginnings reveals that family literacy activities are closely related to such issues as self-esteem, a sense of efficacy and purpose, risk taking, peer support, and motivation. Coordinators of the program consistently report that book sharing and other literacy activities help young parents learn to communicate with their children and to connect with them in powerful and positive ways. Family literacy programming becomes a means of enabling teens to become more responsive and effective parents.

There are currently 51 Shared Beginnings programs operating at 177 sites in 25 U.S. states. More than 3300 teen parents and their 3500 children are participating. In addition, Shared Beginnings program materials are being used by educators of pregnant and parenting teenagers at hundreds of locations across the United States.

# Family of Readers and RIF for Families

In 1992 RIF designed and developed two new initiatives to help educators in both adult- and child-focused programs add a family literacy program to their existing services. Family of Readers is designed for groups offering instructional services to adults, such as in adult basic education and general equivalency diploma courses. The program has been field-tested in community colleges, schools, Even Start programs, and other settings focused on the educational needs of adults. RIF for Families, on the other hand, has been conducted almost exclusively in Head Start and other preschool settings, where the main focus is on the educational needs of young children. Both of these RIF initiatives call upon parents to assume leadership of a book sharing program for their children.

Our program development efforts have been supported by several foundations: Kraft General Foods and the John S. and James L. Knight Foundation have underwritten Family of Readers, and GE Capital, The Prudential Foundation, and Fidelity Investments have made possible RIF for Families.

## Family of Readers

Like all RIF programs, Family of Readers puts books directly into children's hands and engages children in motivational reading activities. It gives parents, most of whom are continuing their own education, the guidance and the means to plan and run such a program for their children. Children in a Family of Readers program learn to love books and think of themselves as readers. Parents develop their skills and self-confidence so that they can take a lead role in supporting their children's reading and learning, regardless of their own reading skills. To accomplish these goals, the program does the following:

- ◆ provides children with three opportunities to choose books to take home, keep, and read—at no cost to their families;
- ◆ gives parents key roles in conducting the RIF program for their children;
- ◆ offers parents ideas, hands-on activities, and practice in creating literacy-rich homes for their children;
- ◆ builds peer support and encouragement among parents—a valuable benefit for adult learners, who confront many challenges while participating in their children's education.

*Program structure, content, and materials.* Family of Readers provides parents and educators with the opportunity to work together to create their own special RIF program—a program with motivational reading activities and books that will appeal to children. Selecting and ordering children's books helps familiarize parents with their children's reading preferences. Planning and organizing reading activities offers parents the chance to show creativity, while reinforcing the message that reading and learning can be fun. And the program offers parents activity ideas to make reading and learning an important and enjoyable part of family life.

Program guidelines and activity ideas are presented in the *Family of Readers Advisor's Guide, Parent's Handbook*, and *Activity Book*. The *Advisor's Guide* gives program advisors a concise and easy-to-follow overview of the RIF program, including book selection, book ordering, motivational reading activities, and themes and ideas for book events. It suggests activities to help parents get acquainted so they can work to-

*RIF's Family of Readers program provides parents with activities that they can try at home to become involved in their children's reading and learning.*

gether to create the program. Exercises familiarize parents with children's books so they can order books that will appeal to their children's interests. There are suggestions for older children to participate in the program as well. The guide also features activity ideas and suggested resources to help build a community of readers in the classroom and the home. The guide underscores the advisor's role in the Family of Readers program. Through quotations and suggestions from field-test participants, the guide explores how educators can work with parents to run the program. Advisors are encouraged to allow parents to assume full responsibility for the program and to provide advice as needed. As a program coordinator in Kansas City noted, "My role in the beginning of the program was definitely that of leader or teacher. Over the next few months it became more of a facilitator. I led discussions and kept parents on track."

The *Parent's Handbook* parallels the *Advisor's Guide* by providing parents with a complete description of the RIF program, including how to select and order books, create motivational activities, and plan and organize book events. The handbook also gives parents examples of book event themes and activity ideas and identifies various volunteer opportunities for family members who wish to help. In addition, the handbook suggests activities for parents to learn more about their children's interests and preferences so they can make informed book selections. There are ideas that families can try at book events or in their own homes and ideas to link home and school. Through these activities, the handbook explores the importance of parental involvement in children's reading and learning and encourages parents to continue their involvement—even after their children are in school. It reinforces the many ways parents already teach their children and encourages them to do more of what they already do so well.

Each family also receives a *Family of Readers Activity Book*. It features activities for families to enjoy together at home including reading, writing, cooking, coloring, and other projects. These activities reinforce the fun of learning for children and parents, while demonstrating that there are many opportunities to learn and enjoy through everyday tasks in family life. The book helps build parents' confidence in their ability to guide their children and support their learning.

The culmination of parents' efforts in any Family of Readers program is RIF Day, when every child chooses at least one book to take home. At intervals throughout the program, children and their families attend the book events, which are held in conjunction with motivational reading activities—all planned and prepared by parents. Each

Family of Readers group provides at least three free books for each child to choose and keep during the program. If groups can offer books that parents may choose for themselves, in addition to books for their children, all the better. By providing books for free, each Family of Readers group ensures that every participating family has books in the home to use during and after the program.

*Program results.* RIF conducted a two-year field test of Family of Readers in several sites around the United States, including an elementary school, a Head Start program, and several community colleges offering ABE, ESL, and GED classes. Although targeted for adult learners, Family of Readers has also been used successfully by child-serving organizations attempting to increase parent involvement. The response from field-test sites has been overwhelmingly positive. Parents are enthusiastic about their own participation in the program and are pleased with its effect on their children's reading. A parent in Miami reported, "Before we got involved my son would not pick up a book. Now, he has gotten very interested in reading." A Kansas City parent noted that his daughter "enjoyed the partys [sic] but she loved the books even more." And another parent wrote, "I wish I could have done this when I was a kid."

Parents also noted that they enjoyed the opportunity to spend time with their families, and they liked having the chance to get to know other families. From a parenting class we heard, "We feel that it is great encouragement for the children and for us all as a family. It also serves as another opportunity to be together as a family unit." A parent in Baltimore echoed the sentiment: "It gives parents and children a chance to meet other parents and children."

Advisors reported that Family of Readers made a significant contribution to the programs they were already running. One advisor noted that it reinforces what parents are already hearing about family literacy in their own literacy classes, and it gives them an opportunity to put that learning into practice. In several cases, coordinators were surprised by some of the dynamics in instructional settings that resulted from the program. A Kansas City advisor reported, "I was surprised! The parents said...they'd like to get to know one another better. Because we're in a classroom situation, we have a very structured atmosphere, and conversation with one another is held to a minimum." Finally, a coordinator at one of the community college sites explained that while the program was unquestionably rewarding to parents and their children, it also had a profound impact on her and the other professional staff. She explained that she and her staff were somewhat conditioned to think of delivering services to the adults in their adult education classes. She said that it required real restraint on their part to allow parents to take the lead in conducting the Family of Readers program. The advisor noted that parents were more than able to run the program, were extremely pleased with the results of their efforts, and were very proud of their accomplishment. She recognized that parents' success in running the program had a positive effect on their self-esteem in addition to achieving the specific literacy goals the program was designed to address.

There are currently 17 Family of Readers programs operating at 22 sites in 9 U.S. states. Approximately 2000 children and 1341 parents are participating.

## RIF for Families

RIF's work on Family of Readers led us to begin development of a companion program to increase Head Start and preschool parents' involvement in their children's education. RIF for Families enlists parents and staff to work together to run the RIF program for their children. Through their involvement, parents take a more active role in encouraging their children's prereading behaviors. Like Family of Readers, this program involves parents in key family literacy activities: selecting and ordering books from publishers and suppliers, planning activities to motivate their children to read and share books, and conducting book events for their children. Parents learn about children's books and take responsibility for selecting authors and illustrators who will appeal to their children. RIF Day offers traditional opportunities for parents to participate by reading aloud, by leading storybook activities, or, more simply, by helping the preschoolers print their names in their new books.

RIF for Families is being field-tested with 1437 children and 65 parents in Head Start and preschool programs in Connecticut, New Jersey, and Kentucky. Field-test advisors and parents receive training and technical assistance from RIF staff. Each family also receives a copy of the *Family of Readers Activity Book* and *The Family Facts Book*—a RIF pamphlet that gives parents a single place to record essential details of family life, such as immunization records and emergency phone numbers. Interspersed with these records are practical tips to help parents encourage their children's reading and learning. These publications underscore the importance of reading and place it among the most important aspects of family life.

# A Look Toward the Future

This is a time of great promise for parent involvement and family literacy. Although the literacy needs of children and their families far outstrip currently available resources, voices at the national and community levels are having considerable success in alerting the public and potential funding sources to the value of family programming. Practitioners are also demonstrating the kind of resourcefulness that characterizes effective programs; they are developing projects by choosing from the growing array of approaches, methods, and materials becoming available.

It is no coincidence that this is also a time when the value placed on the parent's role in encouraging a child to grow up reading has never been greater. That is as it should be. We believe that parents have the clear upper hand over all others when it comes to motivating their children to embrace books and reading. If we have a concern, however, it is this: as important as parents are to the process, we must ensure that children receive the support and encouragement they need, whether or not their parents can participate in a family literacy or parent involvement program. We should never diminish our outreach to parents; yet it is a stark reality that, for a variety of reasons, there are simply too many parents we cannot reach. We do, however, have access to children, especially in their school years, which can help educators break the cycle of low literacy. Today's children are, after all, tomorrow's parents. We should have no less a goal than to give them all the gift of literacy—a legacy they can bequeath to future generations.

## Note

Shared Beginnings and Family of Readers are registered servicemarks of Reading Is Fundamental.

## References

Graves, R. (Ed.). (1987). *The RIF guide to encouraging young readers*. New York: Doubleday.

Reading Is Fundamental. (1992). *The family facts book*. Washington, DC: Author.

Reading Is Fundamental. (1993). *Shared beginnings idea book*. Washington, DC: Author.

Reading Is Fundamental. (1993). *Shared beginnings leader's guide*. Washington, DC: Author.

Reading Is Fundamental. (1994). *Family of readers activities book*. Washington, DC: Author.

Reading Is Fundamental. (1994). *Family of readers advisor's guide*. Washington, DC: Author.

Reading Is Fundamental. (1994). *Family of readers parent's handbook*. Washington, DC: Author.

Scott-Jones, D. (1993, November). Adolescent childbearing: Whose problem? What can we do? *Phi Delta Kappan*, K1–12.

U.S. Department of Education. (1987). *What works: Research about teaching and learning* (2nd ed.). Washington, DC: Author.

U.S. Department of Education, Office of Educational Research and Improvement. (1985). *Reading report card: Trends in reading over four national assessments, 1971–1984, national assessment of educational progress.* Washington, DC: Author.

U.S. Department of Education, Office of Educational Research and Improvement. (1993). *Reading report card for the nation and the states: National assessment of educational progress 1992.* Washington, DC: Author.

# Chapter 10

# Helping First Graders Get a Running Start in Reading

**Linda B. Gambrell**
*National Reading Research Center and*
*University of Maryland, College Park, Maryland*

**Janice F. Almasi**
*State University of New York, Buffalo*

**Qing Xie**
*National Reading Research Center and*
*University of Maryland, College Park, Maryland*

**Victoria J. Heland**
*Reading Is Fundamental, Washington, DC*

It is clear that home, school, and community literacy environments are important elements in fostering the literacy development of young children. There is currently a renewed interest in how connections among the home, school, and community can be made to support young children in their literacy learning and increase their motivation to read (Elley, 1992; Teale & Sulzby, 1987). The RUNNING START program was designed to support the literacy development of first graders by providing them with high-quality children's literature books and increasing their opportunities for reading at school and at home. The motivational program brings the school, home, and community together in a 10-week celebration of reading that is designed to help children develop a love of reading and books that can serve as the foundation of lifelong literacy.

The RUNNING START program supports literacy development in several important ways. The program is designed to (1) increase the number of books in the classroom; (2) increase the number of books in the home; (3) increase opportunities to read at school and at home; (4) foster reading success for all children; and (5) provide home, school, and community support for literacy development. The following comments from parents who have participated in RUNNING START reveal some of the reasons this program positively affects the literacy lives of young children and their families:

> "RUNNING START prompted us to form a habit of reading together on a regular basis."

> "During the RUNNING START program we could hear our daughter reading early in the morning before she even got out of bed."

> "Since the RUNNING START program started my child reads to her infant sister, and it is such a joy to watch this."

> "One night Angelica was reading a story to us. She was so excited, she read it all by herself! Last year she wanted so much to learn to read. And now a whole new world has opened up for her."

And here is what teachers say about RUNNING START:

> "RUNNING START has given my students and their parents an opportunity to get hooked on reading. The RUNNING START Reading Rally is so fantastic...you can't help but be motivated to read!"

> "My students were highly motivated to read by the RUNNING START program. It was the spark that helped to light the fire I had already started."

> "The best thing about the RUNNING START program is that it gets parents involved with their children!"

> "This year I had many different people come into the classroom to read stories to the class (the principal, lunch aides, and parents). Our class read a total of 1565 books! I can't think of a better way to start students reading when they are young."

> "I think the most important aspect of the program is that children get to choose what *they* want to read!"

> "Parent involvement in RUNNING START is so important. It validates what we are doing in the classroom."

## Rationale and Program Description

RUNNING START is a motivational program created by Reading Is Fundamental under a grant from the Chrysler Corporation Fund. As with the RIF programs described in the previous chapter, RUNNING START supports and nurtures literacy development by encouraging children to read. The program is designed to give first graders a "running start" toward becoming readers for the 21st century. The three primary goals of RUNNING START are to increase children's motivation to read so that they eagerly turn to books for both pleasure and information, to involve parents in their children's literacy development, and to support schools and teachers in their efforts to help every child become a reader.

Parents and teachers agree that first grade is an important time for shaping subsequent reading achievement. During this critical period, it is essential that children be supported in their literacy development (Alexander & Entwisle, 1988; Lau & Cheung, 1988; Snow et al., 1991). Rich literacy environments in the school, home, and community must be a priority if the United States is to increase the literacy levels of to-day's youth (Allington, 1991; Morrow, 1992). Innovative literacy programs that create connections across schools, homes, and communities reflect the value of literacy in society and can provide motivation and support for young children in their literacy learning.

Programs that encourage children to spend their time reading, both at school and at home, are important for several reasons. First, we know that children who are motivated and who spend more time reading are better readers (Anderson, Wilson, & Fielding, 1988; Morrow, 1992; Taylor, Frye, & Maruyama, 1990). Second, some children arrive at school with far more experience with print, books, book language, and home support for reading than others (Allington, 1991). Third, supporting and nurturing early literacy development in both home and school environments is crucial to improving the educational prospects for children who find learning to read difficult (Allington, 1986, 1991; Smith-Burke, 1989).

## The Running Start Challenge

The RUNNING START program recognizes that the availability of books is a key factor in reading development, so funds are provided for teachers to select and purchase high-quality fiction and informational children's books for the classroom. Teacher book selection is an important aspect of the program because teachers know about the kinds of books that will be appropriate and appealing to their particular students. The theme of the RUNNING START program is "Creating Readers for the 21st Century," and children are challenged to read, or have someone read to them, 21 books during the 10-week program. This challenge is two-fold in that individual children strive to meet the

21-book goal, and each classroom tries to have all its students reach the goal. Books read either at home or at school count toward achieving the goal. It is important to note that the RUNNING START program is not a competition; there is no special recognition for those who read more books or who finish reading more quickly than others. Teachers, parents, and other family members are encouraged to read to the first graders to assure every child's success. When children meet the challenge of reading 21 books (or having someone read 21 books to them), they are rewarded with a book of their own choosing for their home library.

Teachers receive a handbook of creative classroom ideas and activities that engage children in reading and stimulate book sharing. A packet of colorful materials designed to create interest and excitement among children about the RUNNING START program is also provided. The packet includes a theme poster, stickers, bookmarks, bookplates, certificates, and other incentives for the program that are linked to reading. For each child in the classroom, the teacher receives a personal challenge chart and stickers so that the child can keep track of his or her individual progress. In addition, bookmarks are provided to be used as "reminders to read" and as rewards as children finish reading books. Finally, when the children reach the goal of reading 21 books, they receive a RUNNING START certificate to take home.

To promote family involvement teachers receive a packet of practical suggestions for reading activities for parents and family members to do with their children. The materials are nonthreatening, require only a few minutes of time, can be accomplished at home, and do not require the purchase of any additional items.

*Encouraging a reading-rich classroom environment.* Teachers support children in their efforts to meet the challenge of reading 21 books by creating classroom opportunities for reading and book sharing. For example, in some classrooms first graders are paired with older students who either read to them or listen to them read. In other classrooms teachers have guest readers come into the classroom to read to individual students and small groups. One school enlisted the support of an organization of young business men and women, who came into the classrooms one day each week during the 10-week program to read to children. Other teachers support children by having cafeteria workers, senior citizens, and high school students read with the first graders.

*Encouraging a reading-rich home environment.* The RUNNING START program promotes and supports family literacy by encouraging parents and all other family members—grandparents, sisters, brothers, aunts, uncles, and cousins—to become reading partners with the first graders. Families are encouraged to engage in shared reading activities with their children by listening to them read or by reading to them. Teachers also suggest that children take home books from the classroom library to share with their families.

*Encouraging a reading-rich community environment.* One of the most exciting aspects of RUNNING START is the Reading Rally, a festive celebration of reading. Similar to the rallies in the RIF initiatives described in Chapter 9, the Reading Rally involves the school, parents, and community in celebrating reading, and it provides children's books for the home. It is a visible demonstration that the community values and supports literacy development. The Reading Rally features speakers who focus on motivational aspects of reading and the value of reading. In addition, there are skits, readings, music, and other motivational presentations that emphasize the pleasure and importance of reading. At the rally, parents and families of first graders are provided with practical ideas for supporting children's reading. Most important, children are encouraged to bring all their family members and friends to the rally because every person who attends receives a children's literature book to share with the first grader.

# Can a Motivational Reading Program Make a Difference in the Literacy Lives of Young Children?

Several incentive programs designed to motivate children to read have been developed and implemented across the United States. However, there is little documentation of the effectiveness of these programs. In RUNNING START there have been enthusiastic testimonials from teachers, parents, children, and communities about the motivation the program has provided. We were interested in gathering information about the program and how it has influenced children, parents, and teachers, so we conducted two studies. The studies evaluated the effects of the RUNNING START program on the reading motivation and behaviors of participating children and on family literacy practices.

## Pre- and Posttest Assessment

This first study involved approximately 7000 first grade children, their 4000 parents, and 320 classroom teachers who participated in the RUNNING START program (Gambrell, 1993). The study was conducted in 49 schools located in 9 states across the United States. These schools reflected a wide range of economic levels, urban and suburban areas,

*Parents and children come together at school to learn about their part in the RUNNING START program.*

and ethnic diversity. Before the RUNNING START program was implemented, children responded to the "Me and My Reading Scale," parents answered a family literacy survey, and teachers filled out a brief survey of classroom literacy practices. The Me and My Reading Scale was designed to assess children's motivation to read and engagement in literacy behaviors. This survey was read aloud by the classroom teacher, and students responded by circling their answers. For example, one item asked children, "Do you like to read during your free time?" The response alternatives were (1) yes! (2) It's okay, or (3) I would rather do something else.

The family literacy survey consisted of 10 items designed to elicit parents' views of their child's motivation to read and of family involvement in literacy activities. One item on the survey was, "How often do you read to your child?" The response alternatives were (1) less than

Gambrell et al.

once a week, (2) once a week, (3) several times a week, or (4) almost every day.

The classroom literacy practices survey consisted of various questions about classroom literacy practices and reading instruction. Teachers gave descriptive information about their background in children's literature, classroom reading instructional materials and instructional procedures, and teacher read-aloud practices. In addition, teachers were asked to estimate the percentage of students who, in their opinion, were highly motivated to read and the percentage of parents who read to their children on a consistent basis.

At the conclusion of the 10-week RUNNING START program, the same assessment instruments were again administered to children, parents, and teachers. Pretest to posttest differences were calculated to provide information about the effects of RUNNING START throughout the program. The results of the pre- and posttest analysis revealed statistically significant increases in children's reading motivation and involvement in literacy activities. Children's responses to the reading scale revealed that RUNNING START motivated them to read, spend more time engaged in independent reading, take more books home to read, and participate in family reading activities. Parent responses to the family literacy survey showed evidence that their engagement in family literacy practices increased during the program. There were statistically significant increases in the amount of time parents and family members reported spending with their children reading books and discussing books and stories. In addition, parents reported that the program increased their child's motivation to read and reading proficiency level.

Teacher responses to the classroom literacy practices survey revealed several interesting insights about the program. Teachers indicated that they encouraged children to take books home to read more frequently during the program. Teachers were enthusiastic about sending the RUNNING START books home because, as one teacher explained, "These books belong to the children and their families—that's what RUNNING START is all about." Another teacher noted that he felt comfortable sending the books home with children because he did not have to be accountable for them at the end of the year. Finally, teachers reported that they learned a great deal about children's literature from being involved in RUNNING START. There was a statistically significant increase in self-rated knowledge of children's literature for teachers who were participating in the program for the first time.

The results of the pre- and posttest assessment of the RUNNING START program documented the positive effects it had on a wide range of schools, children, parents, and teachers across the United States. Because pre- and posttest assessments are primarily descriptive and have a number of limitations, a more rigorous experimental-control study was conducted.

## The Experimental–Control Study

This study was designed to investigate the effect of the RUNNING START program on the reading motivation and behavior of first grade inner-city children from minority backgrounds (Gambrell, 1993). Four schools in an urban area in a northern U.S. state that were participating in the RUNNING START program for the second year were identified to serve as the experimental group. Four nonparticipating schools served as the control group. The schools were matched on various factors including percentage of students enrolled in the free and reduced lunch program, percentage of students eligible for compensatory reading services, and ethnic distribution. All the schools served primarily minority students. Approximately 500 children, 350 parents, and 23 teachers participated in the study. The four control schools were told that they had been selected to participate in a study of early literacy and were informed that each classroom would receive a bookshelf library of 8 to 10 books for their participation. At the end of the 10-week RUNNING START program children, parents, and teachers in both the experimental and control schools responded to the reading scale (for children), family literacy survey (for parents), and classroom literacy practices survey (for teachers). In addition, 109 children from the four experimental schools and 109 children from the control schools were randomly selected to participate in in-depth interviews about their reading motivation and behaviors.

The results of this experimental study provided compelling evidence of the positive effects of the intervention program for inner-city minority children and their families. The results of the reading scale and the individual interviews revealed that, when compared to the children in the control schools, the children in the RUNNING START program were more motivated to read, spent more time reading independently and with family members, engaged more frequently in discussions of books with others, and took more books home to read. During the individual interviews, children in the RUNNING START program mentioned more often than the control-group children that their parents read aloud to them, discussed stories and books with them, and purchased books for their home libraries. Most important was the fact that children in RUNNING START more frequently said that their parents were instrumental in getting them interested or excited about books and reading. In addition, when asked to retell a favorite book or story they had read during the previous week, the children in the program were able to do this more often than children in the control group. Experimental-group children were also more aware of other stories and books they wanted to read than children in the control group. Overall, the interviews with the children demonstrated supporting evidence of increased motivation to read as well as an increase in the number and quality of family literacy practices due to involvement in RUNNING START.

The results of the family literacy survey indicated that, when compared with parents in the control schools, parents involved in RUNNING START spent more time reading to their children, discussed books and stories more often with them, and purchased more books for them. In addition, parents in the program reported that their children enjoyed reading to a greater extent than parents in the control group reported of their children.

The classroom literacy practices survey revealed that teachers in the RUNNING START classrooms encouraged children to take books home to read more often than did control-group teachers. The experimental-group teachers also reported that, in their judgment, more parents read to their children (57 percent) as compared to the control group (30 percent). Perhaps the most important finding was that teachers in the RUNNING START program reported that more of their students were highly motivated to read. In the experimental schools, teachers noted that more than 80 percent of their students were highly motivated to read, as compared to the control teachers who claimed that only 63 percent of their students were highly motivated. This suggests that the RUNNING START program positively influences teachers' perceptions and expectations of their first grade students as readers.

Together, these two studies conducted on the RUNNING START intervention program reveal compelling and converging evidence from children, parents, and teachers that the program positively affected the reading motivation and behaviors of first grade children and promoted home and school reading engagement. These studies also suggest that book access and socially interactive book reading experiences are significant factors in learning to read. As mentioned, one of the most interesting findings was that teachers in RUNNING START encouraged children to take books home to read to a much greater extent than did teachers in the control group. This influx of books in the home environment may explain the persuasive evidence that parents in the program read more frequently to their children and were a more powerful motivational influence on their children than parents in the control group.

## Implications for Practices and Programs

The RUNNING START program provides the conditions, encouragement, and support for first graders to read widely and frequently both at school and at home. The success of the program in motivating children and their families to engage in reading activities has clear implications for the development of literacy programs linking the home, school, and community:

1. *Access to books is a key factor in motivating children to read.* The positive effects of RUNNING START document the importance of book-rich classroom libraries. The results of the two investigations of the program suggest that even a modest increase in the number of books in the classroom (approximately two per child) can result in increased reading motivation and engagement.

2. *Encouraging children to take books home from school to share with others promotes family literacy.* The RUNNING START program illustrates the value of teachers' extending the use of the classroom library to the home. The results of the studies on RUNNING START suggest that a motivational, book-rich program can dramatically affect engagement in family literacy practices, which include having more books in the home, sharing books, and discussing books more often. It is indeed noteworthy that parents in the program spent more time reading with their children and discussing books and stories with them. This suggests that the support provided by the program encouraged parents to cultivate a more nurturing literacy environment for their children. An interesting finding from the experimental RUNNING START study was that parents who participated in the program purchased more books for their children than control parents, even though the children in RUNNING START were bringing home a considerable number of books from school each day (Gambrell, 1993). This finding is even more surprising because the schools in which the studies were conducted are located in a low socioeconomic–status area.

3. *Books are the best reward.* Businesses, organizations, and corporations have supported numerous reading incentive programs at local and higher levels. Such programs have typically offered ex-

trinsic rewards such as pizza, games, or prizes. In keeping with theory and research that suggests that intrinsic motivation is fostered when rewards are closely linked to the desired behavior (Anderson & Stokes, 1984; Deci et al., 1991; Myers, 1986), the primary incentive in RUNNING START is books. First grade children, parents, and other family members are rewarded with a book for attending the Reading Rally, and children are given a book for meeting the challenge of reading 21 books during the 10-week RUNNING START program. As mentioned earlier, other motivational incentives are used in the program that are consistently linked to the desired behavior of reading. The success of RUNNING START suggests that if we want to develop intrinsic motivation to read we would be well advised to develop programs that offer books as an incentive.

Creating motivated and engaged readers for the 21st century is a worthy and challenging goal for society. It is clear that the responsibility for meeting this goal must be shared among teachers, parents, children, and the community. If we are to make a real difference in the literacy lives of young children we need programs that will support the enrichment of classroom and home libraries and encourage and support family reading practices. The RUNNING START program provides a promising model of a home-school-community effort to support and nurture first graders in their literacy development.

## References

Alexander, K.L., & Entwisle, D.R. (1988). Achievement in the first 2 years of school: Patterns and processes. *Monographs of the Society for Research in Child Development, 53*, 1–157.

Allington, R.L. (1986). Policy constraints and effective compensatory reading instruction: A review. In J. Hoffman (Ed.), *Effective teaching of reading: Research and practice* (pp. 261–289). Newark, DE: International Reading Association.

Allington, R.L. (1991). The legacy of 'slow it down and make it more concrete.' In J. Zutell & S. McCormick (Eds.), *Learner factors/teacher factors: Issues in literacy research and instruction.* Chicago, IL: National Reading Conference.

Anderson, A.B., & Stokes, S.J. (1984). Social and institutional influences on the development and practice of literacy. In H. Goelman, A. Oberg, & F. Smith (Eds.), *Awakening to literacy* (pp. 24–37). Portsmouth, NH: Heinemann.

Anderson, R.C., Wilson, P., & Fielding L. (1988). Growth in reading and how children spend their time outside of school. *Reading Research Quarterly, 23*, 285–303.

Deci, E.L., Vallerand, R.J., Pelletier, L.G., & Ryan, R.M. (1991). Motivation and education: The self-determination perspective. *Educational Psychologist, 26*, 325–346.

Elley, W.B. (1992). *How in the world do students read?* Hamburg, Germany: The International Association for the Evaluation of Educational Achievement.

Gambrell, L.B. (1993). *The impact of RUNNING START on the reading motivation and behavior of first-grade children* (Research rep.) College Park, MD: University of Maryland, National Reading Research Center.

Lau, K.S., & Cheung, S.M. (1988). Reading interests of Chinese adolescents: Effects of personal and social factors. *International Journal of Psychology, 23*, 695–705.

Morrow, L.M. (1992). The impact of a literature-based program on literacy achievement, use of literature, and attitudes of children from minority backgrounds. *Reading Research Quarterly, 27*, 250–275.

Myers, D.B. (1986). *Psychology* (1st ed.). New York: Worth.

Smith-Burke, T.M. (1989). Political and economic dimensions of literacy: Challenges for the 1990s. In S. McCormick & J. Zutell (Eds.), *Cognitive and social perspectives for literacy research and instruction* (pp. 1–18). Chicago, IL: National Reading Conference.

Snow, C.E., Barnes, W.S., Chandler, J., Goodman, I.F., & Hemphill, L. (1991). *Unfulfilled expectations: Home and school influences on literacy.* Cambridge, MA: Harvard University Press.

Taylor, B.M., Frye, B.J., & Maruyama, G.M. (1990). Time spent reading and reading growth. *American Educational Research Journal, 27*, 351–362.

Teale, W.H. (1986). Home background and young children's literacy development. In W.H. Teale & E. Sulzby (Eds.), *Emergent literacy: Writing and reading* (pp. 173–206). Norwood, NJ: Ablex.

Teale, W.H., & Sulzby, E. (1987). Literacy acquisition in early childhood: The roles of access and mediation in storybook reading. In D.A. Wagner (Ed.), *The future of literacy in a changing world* (pp. 111–140). New York: Pergamon.

Chapter 11 _____

# The Even Start Family Literacy Program

### Patricia A. McKee and Nancy Rhett
*U.S. Department of Education, Washington, DC*

> You just can't believe the pride these parents feel. You know they're going to
> believe in the importance of education even more. I can't think of a more
> powerful way to help children than to get their parents back into education.
> Think of the effect on a kid, seeing his mom and dad doing their homework
> (Jim Varney, Even Start coordinator, West Aurora, Illinois).

Family literacy, as a broad concept, is not new. For decades, we have
acknowledged the intergenerational nature of literacy and education
and recognized the family, not the public schools, as the first and most
important educational institution. It is only in recent years, however,
that educators have begun to see the potential of family literacy as a program tapping family strengths to improve the literacy and life circumstances of adults and children. Family literacy as a program combines
or integrates education for adults with the education of their children.
Successful programs start with family goals, accentuating the positive to
meet the individual needs of the family as opposed to individual family
members. The Even Start Family Literacy program is currently a large
federal investment in full-scale family literacy integrating adult education or literacy training, parenting education, and early childhood education into a unified program designed to serve the most disadvantaged

families in the United States. Even Start programs offer at-risk children and their families a chance to "start even" with other families.

## The Program's Background

Even Start is a program that supports education reform by addressing three of the eight U.S. national education goals to be achieved by the year 2000.

- ◆ Goal 1: All children in America will start school ready to learn.
- ◆ Goal 6: Every adult American will be literate and will possess the knowledge and skills necessary to compete in a global economy and exercise the rights and responsibilities of citizenship.
- ◆ Goal 8: Every school will promote partnerships that will increase parental involvement and participation in promoting the social, emotional, and academic growth of children.

All three goals are equally important in Even Start. This program represents an innovative combination of adult, parenting, and early childhood education. Even Start's design is based on the notion that these components build on one another and that families need to receive all three services to effect lasting change. It is the intergenerational approach and the integrated family education focus that makes Even Start unique in addressing the needs of disadvantaged families.

The U.S. Department of Education began Even Start in 1989 as a demonstration program that provided school districts with four-year discretionary grants from the federal government for family literacy projects. In 1992 the program, while remaining a competitive, discretionary-grant program, became state administered. There were also specified funds that would be handled directly at the federal level for migrant and Native American tribe Even Start projects. Even Start began with a US$14.8 million budget in 1989 funding 76 projects in 44 states. When the program switched to state administration the budget was US$70 million with approximately 340 projects operating in all 50 states, the District of Columbia, and Puerto Rico. By the summer of 1994, Even Start was serving more than 26,000 families in approximately 474 projects, with an appropriation of US$91.3 million. Nine of these projects were funded with special grants to federally recognized Native American Indian tribes and tribal organizations, and 14 were for programs serving migratory families. In July 1995, US$102,024 million will be available for local Even Start projects.

## A Mother's Experience in Even Start

When my oldest child entered first grade, she started to bring papers home which I couldn't read. I always had to go to my neighbor's house to ask her to translate them for me. I decided then I had to go back to school if I was going to be able to help my children with their school work.

I learned about Even Start from a friend of mine who told me I could learn English and study for my GED at the same time.... That was two years ago. My goal was to learn how to speak, read, and write English. When I started, I really thought that it was a good program because it offered me and my family the opportunity to learn together. At that time, I had two of my three children, Jaime and Juan Karlos, in Even Start.

As we went through the program, I found that it had a lot more to offer than I had originally thought it would. For instance, the parenting classes have changed our lives in a positive way. I have learned more effective ways to teach and discipline my children. As I was going through these classes I sometimes felt guilty because I was being taught better ways to educate my children, ways that I had already known but hadn't put into practice.

My English skills have also increased greatly. I can help my children with their homework and feel secure about it. I also recently completed a course in personal computers at the local high school.

My son Juan Karlos began Even Start with me.... He spent all of last year in the Even Start child class in the morning and pre-K in the afternoon. When he began school, he wasn't speaking in either language, only mamma, papa, agua. He is now speaking in both languages. When he is home, he is singing the songs and saying the nursery rhymes he learned in Even Start. Since I learned the songs and rhymes in my parenting class, I can help him and sing with him. He also asked me to read to him, sometimes the same book three or four times a day. I was not able to read to my other children because I couldn't pronounce the words, but now I can read to him.

My goal for the future is to have a career in the computer field as a computer engineer and to provide for my family with the best education possible. Even Start has made it possible for me to pursue my goal.

Testimony of Maria Del Pagan at the Congressional Oversight Hearing on the Even Start program before the Subcommittee on Elementary, Secondary, and Vocational Education, July 28, 1992

# Even Start Model

It is the purpose of Even Start to improve the educational opportunities of low-income families by integrating early childhood education, adult basic education, and parenting education into a unified family literacy program. Even Start has three interrelated goals:

- to help parents become full partners in the education of their children;
- to assist children in reaching their full potential as learners; and
- to provide literacy training for their parents.

The Even Start program simultaneously recognizes and addresses the educational and support needs of parents and their children. It is the first large-scale federal effort to combine all three educational components into one program and develop and demonstrate its effectiveness among disadvantaged families.

*Family eligibility.* To be eligible for Even Start, a family must have an adult who is eligible to participate in an adult education program under the Adult Education Act (which requires a person to be at least 16 years old, to not be enrolled or currently required to be enrolled in a secondary school, and to lack mastery of basic educational skills) and who is a parent of a child younger than eight years old. Once one family member becomes ineligible (a child reaches the age of eight, or a parent completes an educational program and is no longer eligible for adult basic education), the family may continue to participate in appropriate Even Start activities until all family members become ineligible. Participating families must be determined locally as among those with eligible individuals most in need of Even Start services. The new Even Start legislation of 1994 extends eligibility to include teen parents, who are among those most in need of the types of services provided by Even Start, as long as the school district provides the basic educational component.

*Services.* Even Start projects must provide all participating families with an integrated program of early childhood education, adult basic skills training or English as a second language instruction, and parenting education, and family members must participate in all core services to stay in the program. Even Start is family focused, not parent or child focused. Services are not limited to one or two years, and continuity of services is encouraged by serving families through the summer months and for the full period of their eligibility. The Even Start statute calls for program applicants to state how they will use the services to encourage participants to remain in the program "for a time sufficient to meet program goals." Even Start may reach children at birth and continue to serve them and their families through second grade. Although the school is most likely providing the core educational program once the child reaches kindergarten, Even Start may continue to provide the other family education services including home-based instruction, parenting education, and adult literacy. Support services such as childcare, transportation, crisis intervention, counseling, nutritional services, social services, and health referrals are also provided as needed.

*Integration of services.* A key feature of Even Start is that it builds on existing programs, such as Head Start, Chapter 1 preschool (a compensatory reading program), adult basic education, and the Missouri Parents as Teachers Program, among others and melds them into family literacy programs without duplicating services that already exist. Even Start projects are required to collaborate with other agencies because many existing programs already address specific needs of parents and children eligible for Even Start. Rather than duplicate, replace, or compete with those programs or resources, Even Start funds are intended to build on them to create a new range of family literacy services. Moreover, the key components of Even Start must not operate separately; to the greatest degree possible they are to be integrated into a new program or, as the statute states, "a new range of services" that is greater than the sum of the parts.

*Collaboration.* Even Start, even in the early years of its implementation, has been successful in initiating collaborative arrangements. The national evaluation of the program (St. Pierre et al., in press) reports an average of 20 collaborative arrangements for core services and 7 collaborative arrangements for support services in each local project. With the limited size of the Even Start appropriation and the large number of other local, state, and federal programs focused on adult literacy and early childhood education, it is critical that project-director applicants use Even Start funds as the link to provide a comprehensive family literacy program combining all sources of support. Even the application requirements to set up an Even Start program require a collaboration. This requirement helps to ensure practical and effective ways to identify and recruit eligible families, identify relevant programs with which the project should coordinate, and identify research and other information needed to design high-quality proposals.

*Local contribution or matching requirement.* Even Start projects are required to provide a local or matching contribution that increases with each year of a four-year grant. The federal share of an Even Start project may not exceed 90 percent of the project cost in the first year the recipient receives Even Start assistance, 80 percent in the second year, 70 percent in the third year, and 60 percent in the fourth and any subsequent year of operation. The local contribution may come from any local, state, or federal source, public or private, except funds made available under the program Title 1. Some organizations make their local Even Start contribution in cash, but most include at least some in-kind services. Projects use Head Start, adult basic education, Parents as Teachers Programs, literacy volunteers, parent volunteer services, state and local preschool programs, daycare, babysitting, building use, food services, corporate contributions, and a host of other goods and services as the local contribution. This requirement has served to make projects more self-sufficient and improve the likelihood they will continue without federal support; it has also encouraged projects to build on existing resources and to collaborate with a wide range of education, health, nutrition, and social service providers to make Even Start assistance more comprehensive.

*Home instruction.* The statute requires "the provision of integrated instructional services to participating parents and children through home-based programs." The Even Start program allows flexibility to match appropriate intervention to clients' needs for home-based and center-based programs, but some instructional services must be provided in the home. Home-based instruction means that teachers, social workers, or home aides come to the family's home and teach and mod-

*Even Start projects emphasize joint participation by parents and children.*

McKee & Rhett

el ways to develop parents' self-sufficiency and children's developmental and learning skills. Home-based services can provide greater opportunity to tailor services to individual family needs in a more informal setting and can offer a chance to evaluate the utility of materials and training in parenting and other skills. Home visitors can help families find assistance in addressing difficult life circumstances such as inadequate housing or substance abuse, but the primary purpose of home instruction is to attend to the educational needs of children and parents and to improve the literacy environment in the home (Powell, 1991). Home visits should be an integral part of the whole Even Start instructional program and not an add-on activity conducted for the purpose of meeting the statutory requirement.

*Parents and children together.* Finally, Even Start projects are required to include "scheduling and location of services to allow joint participation by parents and children." While not all services must, or should, be carried out in this manner, this requirement is an important asset of Even Start projects. Joint participation by parents and children impresses on parents that they are the key to their children's education. Examples of services delivered to adults and children together include reading and storytelling; developing readiness, social, and gross motor skills; working with numbers; asking children questions that stimulate thinking and promote verbal problem solving; using television appropriately; doing arts and crafts; and learning about health and nutrition. Parents also learn that valuable literacy experiences occur within routine family interactions in the home and community and that ordinary events can be "teachable moments" (Powell, 1993). Parent and child activities may take place in the home and in the center or school.

## Profile of Even Start Families

The national evaluation of Even Start (St. Pierre et al., in press) has provided detailed information on the families served by local Even Start projects. Fifty percent of the Even Start participant families are headed by couples, and 37 percent are single-parent households. The remaining families are extended families of three or more adults or children living with grandparents, stepparents, or guardians. Forty percent of the Even Start adults are white, 26 percent African American, 22 percent Hispanic, 8 percent Asian or Pacific Islander, and 4 percent Native American.

As intended, Even Start is serving a needy population. Although there is no absolute income requirement for Even Start families, the average income is very low. Nearly half of the families report government assistance as their primary source of financial support. Forty-four percent have a family income of less than US$15,000 per year, and 76 percent of the adults who participated in Even Start core services in 1993 were unemployed at the start of the program year.

Even Start also serves an undereducated population. Nearly 80 percent of the adults who participate in Even Start core services have not completed high school. Moreover, data show that adults who enter Even Start with a diploma or GED are not functioning at a higher level than their less credentialed counterparts. In recent years Even Start children have scored very low—at the ninth percentile nationally—on a vocabulary test that is given when they enter the program. Seven percent of children served by Even Start are identified as having a disability.

Even Start also serves a large population of families with limited English proficiency. Thirty-four percent of Even Start adults are considered in this category. Spanish is the primary language for 26 percent, and the remaining 8 percent speak Hmong, Vietnamese, Chinese, Creole, and other languages. There has been an increase in the percentage of limited English–proficient families in each year of Even Start operation. These families, many of whom are recent immigrants, have other needs in addition to the need to become more proficient in English. Sixty percent of Even Start adults who have limited English proficiency did not reach the ninth grade; 78 percent are unemployed; and 83 percent, a much higher percentage than their English-speaking Even Start counterparts, have an annual family income of less than US$15,000.

## The National Evaluation of Even Start

The Even Start legislation requires that the U.S. Department of Education implement a national evaluation of the program's effectiveness to provide information needed by local program directors, federal administrators, and congressional staff who are developing family literacy policy. The national evaluation started in January 1990, soon after the first grant awards were made, with the charge to evaluate the first four years of the program's implementation. A contract was awarded to Abt Associates and its subcontractor, RMC Research Corporation, to conduct the study, which had three components:

1. A universal survey of all local projects in which local staff collected and submitted data on participants and services.
2. In-depth studies of 10 typical sites that had fully implemented designs with some variation in location and service population. This

component of the study included a small experiment, in which 5 of the 10 sites randomly assigned participants to treatment and control groups for evaluation of Even Start's effects.

3. Encouragement and training for projects to implement a local outcome evaluation that would provide evidence of the projects' effectiveness and enable them to qualify for the National Diffusion Network, the U.S. Department of Education's data system that provides information on individual sites for all those interested.

Basic research questions for the national study included the following:

1. What are the characteristics of Even Start participants?
2. How are Even Start projects implemented?
3. What Even Start services are received by participating families?
4. What are the effects of Even Start projects?

The national evaluation provided three types of useful information: early data on implementation that were used by local projects and the federal government to make mid-course corrections, common data on child and adult outcomes and services that provided benchmarks for local projects to judge their own effectiveness, and final study results for use in improving Even Start and judging its impact. Early findings about problems that several projects had with getting parents to participate in adult basic skills instruction enabled the Department of Education to provide direct guidance and arrange for technical assistance to projects to improve participation. Early evaluation data and information gained by department staff during monitoring identified the perverse effect of an eligibility requirement that limited families' ability to participate after they achieved success in the program, which was revised. Two local projects—Oklahoma City Public Schools in Oklahoma and Webster Groves School District in Rock Hill, Missouri—were able to use the common data available from the national study, along with locally collected data, to show how their programs were especially effective. As a result, they gained entry into the Department's National Diffusion Network, an honor granted to projects that have documented evidence of their program's exemplary effectiveness.

## Implications of the Evaluation for Teachers and Schools

As might be expected, national evaluation findings on the effects of Even Start were mixed. The evaluation did not find significant effects on children by the average Even Start project. The evaluation did confirm the importance of intensive early childhood education and parenting education in improving children's readiness for school and literacy. In one of the most important findings of the study, the vocabularies of Even Start children (ages three to five) whose parents had a substantial amount of parenting education increased significantly more than Even Start children whose parents did not have much parenting education. Evidence that direct instruction of parents in how to support their children's education development can have a clear effect on child literacy gains is very encouraging.

> Parenting education in Even Start includes activities to help parents be their child's first teacher and to enable parents to enhance their child's development. This analysis suggests that the Even Start model has added benefits for children beyond the benefits that would be derived from a traditional early childhood program, and, more specifically, that parenting education is associated with positive educational gains for children (St. Pierre et al., in press)

The Even Start program did have positive effects on the likelihood of parents obtaining a GED, and when parents stayed in adult education long enough, they made literacy gains. However, the evaluation did not find a direct relationship between parents' literacy gains or amount of participation in adult basic skills instruction and their children's scores for school readiness or literacy skills. Nor did adult education have an effect on parents' employment or family income. It may be that effects from adult literacy gains or credentialing by getting a GED may not show up within the year or two that the families were studied. However, the lack of effects is consistent with other studies, which show minimal or, at best, moderate effects for adult basic skills instruction. The study was not able to identify effects of Even Start's parenting education component on parents' own attitudes and behaviors, either. The measures available to assess these changes, however, are not very sensitive. Many parents know "the right way" to respond to interviews. Future studies will need to find or develop better measures.

The home-based instructional visits were clearly a successful strategy for service delivery as they motivated parents to stay involved with the Even Start program. Projects that used a lot of home visiting had lower participation turnover than those that were primarily center based. However, home-based instruction is not as intensive as instruction offered to parents in centers and does not achieve the same learning gains, so it is necessary to find a balance between home visits and group instruction.

In general, the evaluation confirmed what would seem to be a common-sense idea—the more hours spent in instruction, the more is learned. Even Start families benefit from intensive and continuous service. Projects need to keep track of the time their families spend in educational activities, and they need to plan their programs to provide a substantial amount of instruction in the core services. Parenting education once a month does not result in literacy gains for children.

Implementation of family literacy programs that are as comprehensive as Even Start take extra time and cost more during the first years. Nevertheless, few Even Start projects failed in their task: almost all successfully developed a program that provided the three core services and multiple support services and that established collaborative arrangements with local community agencies and organizations. As projects matured, they improved their recruitment of families, serving larger numbers with the same staff—so costs per family decreased after the first year of a typical project.

## Even Start Reauthorized

On October 20, 1994, the U.S. President signed into law Pub. L. 103-382, the "Improving America's Schools Act of 1994," amending the Elementary and Secondary Education Act of 1965 (ESEA). This law reauthorizes, for five years, programs currently under Chapter 1 of Title I of the ESEA, including Even Start. The new legislation puts an even greater emphasis on the family focus of program goals and activities, both through its purpose and through the inclusion of family members other than eligible participants in appropriate family literacy activities. It also strengthens targeting of services to families most in need by (1) specifying that projects must include active recruitment and preparation of these families; (2) giving priority to projects serving families in areas with a high concentration of poverty; (3) requiring that a high percentage of families served include children who reside in Title I attendance areas; and (4) requiring that projects consider, at a minimum, individual levels of adult literacy (or English language proficiency) and poverty in recruiting families most in need. The new law also extends eligibility to include young teen parents who are among those most in need of the types of services provided by Even Start. In response to the lessons learned from the national evaluation about the importance of intensity and continuity of services, the new law also requires program designs to provide services for at least a three-year age range and to operate on a year-round basis. Finally, it improves connections between schools and communities by requiring stronger collaboration, through partnerships, in the application process and implementation of programs.

## Reflections

Family literacy is an important part of the U.S. education agenda for the 1990s. At its best, Even Start, with its family and community orientation, is comprehensive, intensive, integrated, and collaborative. Its goal is to empower parents and other caregivers by increasing their educational skills and parental abilities while improving the educational opportunities of the young children. Even Start connects families to much-needed resources, supports parents' efforts to help their children to succeed in school, and offers parents their own opportunities to be successful. It brings together parents with children as learning teams and improves the bonds among families, communities, and schools so they support one another. Family literacy is not a quick or an easy fix. Those who have worked with it over the past five years know Even Start is a complicated model and difficult to implement. But family literacy is working in many places, and it is showing promise for breaking the intergenerational cycle of undereducation—a key to reaching U.S. education goals.

### Note

This chapter was written by the authors in their private capacity. No official support or endorsement by the U.S. Department of Education is intended or should be inferred.

### References

Congressional Oversight Hearing on the Even Start Program. (1992, July 28). Hearing before the Subcommittee on Elementary, Secondary, and Vocational Education of the Committee on Education and Labor, House of Representatives (102nd Congress, 2nd session) Serial no. 102–136.

Powell, D.R. (1991). *Strengthening parental contributions to school readiness and early school learning.* Paper prepared for the Office of Educational Research and Improvement, U.S. Department of Education, Washington, DC.

Powell, D.R. (1993). Beliefs and behaviors: Parent contributions to children's school success come from complex patterns. *Look at Even Start*, issue three. Portsmouth, NH: RMC Research Corporation.

St. Pierre, R., Swartz, J., Gamse, B., Murray, S., Deck, D., & Nickel, P. (in press). *National evaluation of the Even Start Family Literacy Program: Final report.* Washington, DC: U.S. Department of Education.

# A Comprehensive Approach to Family-Focused Services

Meta W. Potts and Susan Paull

*National Center for Family Literacy, Louisville, Kentucky*

*D*onna, a talented artist, dropped out of school when she was 14 years old because her mother ridiculed her drawings and paintings, teased her about wasting her time, and admonished her for spending family money on art supplies. "The last time she tore up one of my pictures, I just screamed and ran away," said Donna. Married and a mother at 16, Donna spent her days in front of the TV with her son on the floor beside her. "I hated everybody," she said, "and I thought they hated me." When her husband left and took 3-year-old Jerrod with him, Donna had no income, no place to live, no future, and no hope.

"If you want your son back," the judge told her, "you will have to prove that you can take care of him, not just his daily needs, but take care of his future, too. I mean I want to know that you're doing something with him besides setting him in front of the television set."

When Donna found out about the family education program, she reluctantly tried it, and she stayed. Jerrod came with her every day, and they became family literacy students together. Two years later, Donna, with her general equivalency diploma in hand, enrolled in her local community college, and Jerrod enthusiastically went off to kindergarten.

From reading this and the many stories presented in earlier chapters about how family literacy education helps parents or other caregivers and their children, it is not difficult to understand why family literacy appeals to teachers. They know it makes sense. It made sense to the founders of the Parent and Child Education program in Kentucky because they represented both generations in literacy development: adult and early childhood educators began to look for ways to bring parents and children to school to learn together, and the PACE program was born under the leadership of Sharon Darling, then Kentucky's Director of Adult Education. PACE was begun in six rural counties in 1986 and now operates statewide. In January 1988 the William R. Kenan, Jr., Charitable Trust of Chapel Hill, North Carolina, gave a major grant to expand the program even further to seven sites in Kentucky and North Carolina. In September of that year, the Ford Foundation and Harvard's Kennedy School of Government named PACE/Kenan one of ten outstanding innovations in state and local government in the United States. Since then, the PACE/Kenan model for family literacy has been adopted and adapted by hundreds of organizations across the United States and has come to define the family literacy movement for many in the field.

## Program Background

These successful family literacy programs employ a comprehensive strategy to get at the root of school failure and undereducation. The programs are based on the assumption that parents are powerful: their attitudes convey a critical message about schooling, the work and joy of learning, and the connection between education and quality of life. Most children who succeed in school learned early that reading and learning are important and that educational goals are attainable. But in some families, children absorb very different attitudes concerning what is expected, what is desirable, and what is possible, as described in earlier chapters. Parental messages often reflect their own low self-esteem and limited expectations. The PACE/Kenan programs aim to change those messages; they provide opportunities for parents and other caregivers to develop the skills and confidence that enable them to see possibilities in place of dead ends. They also offer programs for young children to build social skills and improve their readiness to learn. But they understand that educating parents does not necessarily improve parental interactions with children. PACE/Kenan directors know that educating children might not have long-term effects if the messages in the home do not support their learning, so they offer parent education and support groups where adults can learn parenting and life-coping skills and develop a network of friends. They also provide time each day for parents and children to play together, so parents can practice the skills they are learning to support their children's emerging literacy.

The PACE/Kenan programs are based on common sense as well as education research in related fields. A detailed discussion of the adult and early childhood education research is included in *Generation to Generation: Realizing the Promise of Family Literacy* (Brizius & Foster, 1993) and is summarized here. Although the research base for adult education is thin, most educators agree on these issues:

1. Adults learn best when instruction relates to real-life needs and important life roles such as job skills and parenting.

2. Strong motivation and frequent positive reinforcement are essential for adults who often have low self-esteem and pressing responsibilities. (Most practitioners find that motivation for adults is improved when they are working toward their individual goals, which often include helping their children.)

3. Other support services, such as childcare, transportation, and informal counseling, must be provided to enable adults to take advantage of learning opportunities.

Research in early childhood education emphasizes the importance of developmentally appropriate learning experiences for children and the benefits of early intervention, especially with low-income children. The Perry Preschool study (Berreuta-Clement et al., 1984) looked at a group of children who attended a program with a curriculum similar to the High/Scope Preschool Curriculum, which is based on active learning, "plan-do-review," and key experiences. The study followed the group into young adulthood and found the subjects had a higher degree of education and better work experiences and social behaviors compared to a control group, which did not attend the program. This and other studies described by Berreuta-Clement and colleagues indicate that "early childhood education can have an immediate and positive effect on children's intellectual performance" (p. 102). As these researchers point out, however, the quality of preschool education matters; early childhood instruction must be developmentally appropriate and must include parental participation and competent leadership. Effective family literacy programs provide learning experiences for young children and their parents that reflect the research findings.

# The National Center for Family Literacy

Because of the early success of the PACE and Kenan projects, Darling and her associates were nearly overwhelmed by requests for information. In response to this demand, the Kenan Trust provided the resources to establish the National Center for Family Literacy in the United States. Since then, with continued funding from the Kenan Trust and other sources, the Center has become the primary source of advocacy, training, information, and research for the growing family literacy movement.

The mission of the NCFL is to promote and support the family literacy movement through activities in four areas: (1) leadership, advocacy, and policy; (2) training and technical assistance; (3) research; and (4) dissemination. Through program funding, teacher and coordinator training, awareness activities for policy makers, and public education efforts, NCFL staff work toward the ultimate goal of establishing a family literacy program in every U.S. school system. The NCFL has been instrumental in the national expansion of family literacy through its support of Even Start programs (described in the previous chapter) at state and local levels, its work with administrators and policy makers across the United States, and its training and technical assistance for program providers. NCFL staff have trained family literacy teachers in programs in all 50 states.

# The Comprehensive, Center-Based Program Model and Variations

The programs funded by the Kenan Trust have lent their name to a program design called the Kenan model or the comprehensive, center-based program model. As the name implies, these family literacy programs offer comprehensive services aimed at ambitious goals. The programs work with at-risk families and offer multifaceted services that meet educational and other needs of both parents and children. The intent is to provide intensive, long-term intervention with four basic program components: (1) adult literacy, basic, and life skills education or English-language instruction for parents; (2) early childhood education for their young children; (3) a parent education and support group; and (4) regularly scheduled parent and child interaction. These components reflect the objectives and goals of the programs, which are to provide holistic, family-focused program services that improve (1) the skills and educational level of undereducated parents or other caregivers, (2) the developmental skills of their young children, (3) the parenting and coping skills of adults, and (4) the quality of parent-child interactions in support of children's learning.

The critical factors in quality family literacy programming are the four components or service areas, the integration of the components to form a unique, comprehensive service, and sufficient intensity and duration of services to effect lasting changes. Programs adapt this basic model to suit the characteristics of their communities and the priorities of their sponsors, so they vary in agency sponsorship, location, intensity and duration of instruction, scheduling of components, curriculum, participant demographics, funding source(s), or community collaborations. The center-based model has also been adapted by many programs that have added a home visit component. The home visit allows for individualized services and offers an opportunity to reinforce classroom learning in the home setting. Programs in rural areas or those serving a hard-to-reach population have made the home visit the core of their services, with periodic group-based activities as a supplement. Still others offer "levels of service," with home visits as a transitional option for those not ready or able to attend group sessions, and center-based services for other families. The four components outlined earlier may be addressed through home visit programs if they are carefully structured with attention to the goal of empowering families and providing for high-quality educational opportunities, including regular group activities. (See Figures 1 and 2 for a summary of the four components in home- and center-based formats.)

## Implications for Teachers and Practitioners

Successful family literacy programs are dynamic: they change and grow as practitioners and administrators reflect on lessons learned, as Paratore stressed in Chapter 3. To begin with, family literacy, like most literacy programs and classes in the 1980s, focused attention on the adults who needed literacy education; we even divided our thinking and our language into recognizable but inappropriate terms—the literate and the illiterate. But it did not take the NCFL long to redefine literacy as a continuum of skills and in terms relating to the specific issue of family literacy. Our focus changed from being another adult basic education or general equivalency diploma program to becoming a program that recognizes the multiple roles of parents and the literacy needs within each role. We expanded our goals and set new ones. We rejected the deficit model, explained by Auerbach in Chapter 2, and developed a strengths model, which views the learner as capable and in possession of healthy traits and prior knowledge, which establish a base for learning (Potts, 1992). We believe firmly in emergent literacy, for both children and adults.

# Figure 1
## Quality Home-Based Family Literacy Programs

*Adult Education Component*
- attention to noneducational and educational needs
- joint parent- and teacher-initiated approach
- meaningful, functional, and individualized instruction
- whole language strategies
- interdisciplinary curriculum
- critical and creative thinking mode
- prevocational training

*Parent Component*
- content driven by self-identified needs of parents
- information for family growth
- opportunities for some group activities for the purpose of mutual peer support
- advocacy and referral services
- coping and problem-solving strategies
- community collaboration efforts act as single point of referral

Quality Home-Based
Family Literacy Programs

- build on strengths
- empower families
- integrate all components
- include opportunities for some group activities
- are parent focused
- have a consistent structure
- have an individualized focus
- apply assessment to instruction
- incorporate goal setting
- use daily routines of families
- provide activities to work on between home visits
- celebrate diversity
- collaborate with community service providers
- have consistent documentation procedures
- secure qualified staff
- provide systematic and ongoing staff development

*Early Childhood Component*
- attention to noneducational and educational needs
- parental involvement in planning and implementing activities
- specific and developmentally appropriate activities
- ongoing developmentally appropriate assessment
- use of daily routines and household items to reinforce skill development
- whole language strategies

*Intergenerational Component*
- child-initiated activity
- opportunity for positive parent-child interaction
- opportunity to practice newly acquired skills
- staff in supportive role
- some opportunity for group-based parent-child interaction

**Figure 2**
**Quality Center-Based Family Literacy Programs**

*Early Childhood Component*
- attention to noneducational and educational needs
- specific and developmentally appropriate curriculum
- developmentally appropriate assessment
- appropriate teacher to child ratio
- small group size
- parental involvement

*Intergenerational Component*
- child-initiated activity
- opportunity for positive parent-child interaction
- opportunity to practice newly acquired skills
- staff in supportive role
- activities to support transfer to home

Quality Center-Based Family Literacy Programs
- build on strengths
- empower families
- apply assessment to instruction
- incorporate goal setting
- facilitate active learning
- integrate components
- use whole language strategies
- include some home-based services
- celebrate diversity
- collaborate with community service providers
- use a team approach
- secure qualified staff
- provide systematic and ongoing staff development

*Adult Education Component*
- attention to noneducational and educational needs
- joint parent- and teacher-initiated approach
- balance of group and individual instruction
- interdisciplinary curriculum
- cooperative learning strategies
- critical and creative thinking mode
- prevocational training

*Parent Component*
- content driven by self-identified needs of parents
- information for family growth
- mutual peer support
- advocacy and referral services and single point referral
- coping and problem-solving strategies
- community collaboration efforts

We then learned to target particular groups to achieve our goals and make the most of limited resources. No one program can meet the needs of all families who might seek our services. Therefore, our target group became parents who did not work outside the home, who had a preschool child from three to five years old, and who could devote several hours each week to an intensive program. Some programs target families with children from birth to age eight; a few target those parents with upper elementary and middle school children. In any case, the choice of target group affects recruitment and retention efforts. We learned that when funds are limited, it is advisable to be selective and collaborate with others who have chosen to work with different groups. These collaborations and others serve as tools that help family programs reach multiple populations. One way of accomplishing this task is to link a center-based program with one that is home based to consult and plan together while each has its own focus and resources.

Reaching out to and retaining a collective audience that has been discouraged by the educational system may demand alternative rules and regulations. For example, in many school districts adults are not allowed to ride school buses. An addendum to the rules may be required to include adults who are parents and students as legitimate school-bus riders. Some adults in the program may smoke, which also may be cause for school boards to bend their rules to designate a smokers' room or outside area for these parents. Other districts may alter school rules to include free or reduced-cost lunches for enrolled parents and subsidized infant and toddler care for those who have children eligible for the program and younger babies as well.

These issues may seem commonplace, even superficial to some, but we found that noneducational or affective issues are important in successful programs. We handled those issues early and were able to concentrate on what we care most about—quality education for families. We learned to develop and refine standards for quality programs. Persistent efforts to observe various programs with many participants enabled us to extract quality indicators, worthy objectives, and valuable outcomes. An important lesson is this: a family literacy program cannot be just another literacy service, duplicating those already in existence.

*Early childhood education.* Deciding what should be taught was our next major issue. With the whole family in mind, the first objective was to select a quality approach to early childhood education, one that is child centered and developmentally appropriate. In response to identified strengths, needs, and interests of children, we structured an environment that stimulates active learning with materials, manipulation,

Potts & Paull

*Down the steps of the school bus and off to family education classes, a mother and son stride toward achievement.*

choice, and adult support for exploration and discovery. Assessment is based primarily on observations of children, and teacher-led instruction is driven by that assessment.

*Adult instruction.* Confident in our selection of approaches to early childhood learning, we were left with questions about parents' needs. Should we recruit only adults interested in earning a GED and focus instruction on the five areas of the GED examination? Should we seek participants whose major objective is to become better parents and focus instruction on parenting issues? Should we reject applicants who possess a high school diploma because we believe that our services and instruction would not fit their needs? Answers to these questions surfaced in what we know about how people learn—both adults and children. We learn best when we have reasons to learn (motivation); when we are recognized for what we already know (the use of prior knowledge in a strengths model); when accumulated knowledge is linked with new information (the introduction of strategies and techniques); when we are given opportunities to practice without being made to feel inadequate; and when the learning is interesting and exciting.

For these reasons, the adult education curriculum in effective programs is individualized based on the academic, vocational, or personal goals of the learners. Goals may include improving reading or math skills to enter college or a vocational program, earning a GED or an alternative high school diploma, developing employment interview skills, exploring career options, or improving skills to help children with homework. To address these varied goals and to offer adults a second chance at learning, most family literacy programs have adopted a schedule that allows time for both group-based activities and individual study. In the NCFL program describing what should be taught and deciding on an approach to instruction became connected in an adult-oriented approach to learning, which we call "whole language for adults." This approach is based on the premise that knowing how to learn is the key to the future, whether the future lies in further academic pursuits or in the workplace; it applies to all categories of learners; and it is learner centered and productive. It incorporates all the language modes—reading, writing, speaking, and listening—and is process rather than product oriented. Successful strategies include the following:

♦ mind-mapping, clustering, and other techniques that link prior knowledge to new information;

♦ prediction exercises, including the use of children's literature as predictable books;

♦ strategic questioning, using prereading, embedded, and postreading inquiry;

♦ analyzing, clarifying, and summarizing to improve comprehension;

♦ process writing (prewriting, drafting, revising, rewriting, and publishing);

♦ critical thinking, including collecting information, analyzing, and synthesizing;

♦ problem solving; and

♦ evaluating.

*Parent support groups.* Because these strategies and others that motivate adult students combine both cognitive and affective elements, relate to real-life situations, and are useful and meaningful, we found that we could not confine our teaching to academic needs. So, we added parent groups as a third component. A parent group is a planned, focused time for parents for discussion, problem solving, learning, and peer support (see also Paull, 1993a, for detailed information on implementing parent groups). As the concept developed, the varied needs and interests of the parents served by these programs came to define the purposes of parent groups:

- ◆ to provide information, new ideas, or skills in subject areas that include health care, nutrition, child development, budgeting, career exploration, interview skills, legal rights, the preschool curriculum, and public school expectations;
- ◆ to offer encouragement and support; and
- ◆ to identify needs and make referrals to other services including legal assistance, counseling or therapy, housing assistance, respite care, emergency shelter, or substance abuse treatment.

*Parent-child interaction.* During group sessions parents learn new skills and techniques for managing children's behavior and supporting their learning. The program also provides parents with opportunities to practice their newly acquired skills with their children during the parent-child interaction component. This session is a regularly scheduled time for parents and children to play together, for parents to listen to and learn about their children, to observe them as they learn through play, and to encourage language use and literacy skills. It may also be a chance to practice new parenting or behavior management techniques. Parent-child interaction sessions are regularly scheduled, child-led, play-focused opportunities for quality time between parents and children (see also Paull, 1993b). A typical session looks like this:

1. Children plan. They decide what they want to do with their parents.
2. Children communicate their plans. Teachers often find ways to make this fun by using colorful symbols and other ideas.
3. Parents prepare. During parent group meetings, adult education classes, or a presession meeting, parents and staff members may talk about ways to support children's plans—ideas for play, questions to ask, and so on.
4. Parents and children play. If children change their plans, parents follow their lead. The emphasis is on ensuring a positive experience and learning through fun.

5. The whole group participates in circle time. This might be a game, a song, a finger play, or a story that concludes with an idea for a follow-up home activity to reinforce new learning.

6. Parents and children review. They talk about their play as they clean up, which encourages a habit of review and reflection.

7. Parents debrief. During parent group sessions, parents may discuss or write in a journal their reflections on their children's learning and their time together, as they internalize new understandings and skills.

*Integrating components.* Participation in the four components results in a complex array of new learning in all three domains for adults and children. We found that the most effective programs learned how to integrate the components, weaving themes, issues, and ideas into each period of the day. To accomplish this, the staff must become a team by meeting together to discuss their assessments, observations, and ideas and incorporating them into integrated lesson plans (see Figures 3, 4, and 5, which illustrate ways to integrate these components).

*Assessment.* Even the best instructional strategies must be adjusted to fit the learning needs and styles of multilevel students. To measure these changes and adjust instruction, appropriate and ongoing assessment is vital. We learned that no one assessment tool adequately measures what students know, need, and want; therefore, we elected to use informal and formal tools. Informal assessments can be as basic as a teacher-student conference or as multidimensional as a graphic representation of wishes, dreams, and goals. When selecting a formal assessment, we found that a "life skills" approach works well when it matches learners' goals. Other standardized assessments also fit into the family literacy schema when dealing with multiple populations, such as speakers of English as a second language, home based and homeless, inner-city and rural communities, young mothers, and older, extended family members.

Other standards are also needed to judge the effectiveness of a family literacy program. Many sites decide to gather anecdotal information; others develop a quantitative database for reporting results. Both are important because we believe that to describe the total effect of this program on families, the rich detail must unfold in stories, and many aspects of growth and development must appear as numbers. Many programs are also documenting growth in family portfolios as described in Popp (1992). Research must also be ongoing and follow families and their changing expectations into the workplace, school,

# Figure 3
## Integration of the Components: Adult Education Perspective

Planning together, the Family Literacy team coordinates cognitive and affective elements of the daily plan. One way to address curriculum integration is to take an *adult education perspective* and focus on the need for specific skills. For example, when parents begin their search for a job, they will need specific and appropriate skills for keeping a job and getting a promotion.

| Adult Education | Early Childhood | Parent-Child Interaction | Parent Group |
|---|---|---|---|
| Strategies:<br>◆ active reading<br>◆ analyzing<br>◆ discussing<br>◆ cooperative learning<br>◆ writing<br>◆ computer graphing<br><br>Adult students will read *Your Attitude Is Showing* and discuss in groups, using a guide sheet.<br><br>After visiting at least three places of employment, adult students will write a comparison essay, which addresses behavior and dress. At the computer, students will create a histogram to demonstrate distribution of survey data on skills needed for various jobs.<br><br>After viewing the film *Take Interpersonal Skills to the Bank*, students will use the film viewer's guide to discuss ideas. After reading the manual *Safe Work Attire*, students will work in groups to prepare an employees' guideline sheet. | Items will be added to the book area to create an office:<br>◆ computer<br>◆ typewriter<br>◆ desk<br>◆ rulers, stencils<br>◆ clock, timer<br>◆ index cards<br>◆ labels, folders<br>◆ briefcase<br>◆ books on occupations<br><br>Items will be added to the block area:<br>◆ junk for various jobs<br>◆ occupational hats<br>◆ toolbox<br>◆ workbench<br><br>Items will be added to the music area:<br>◆ tapes of the songs "That's My Job," "I've Been Working on the Railroad," "Hi Ho, Hi Ho, It's off to Work I Go."<br><br>Opening circle: Children will tell stories using the magnetic board and characters to talk about "workjobs." | Children may choose to introduce parents to the new materials in the work areas, or parents may choose to read one of the books on occupations to the children.<br><br>Parents may show children how to use tools.<br><br>In the closing circle parents and children will listen to the tape *That's My Job* and then practice a sing-along.<br><br>Take-home activity: Families will be given information about adding tools of literacy to a work area in the home to support emergent literacy. | Parents will create a prop box for the children's classroom in which they will place various work-related clothing:<br>◆ lady's dress<br>◆ man's suit<br>◆ shoes, boots<br>◆ uniforms<br><br>Parents will practice the reading strategy of "prediction" by reading the book *The Little Red Hen*. |

**Figure 4**
**Integration of the Components Using Children's Literature**

Another way to address curriculum integration is the *adoption of themes, issues, and ideas using children's literature.* This plan was developed in a Native American family and child education program. The complete lesson plan is based on "The Story of Jumping Mouse" by John Steptoe. The frog's quote sets the tone: "Your unselfish spirit has brought you great hardship, but it is the same spirit of hope and compassion that has brought you to the far-off land."

| Adult Education | Early Childhood | Parent-Child Interaction | Parent Group |
|---|---|---|---|
| Strategies:<br>◆ reading for fun<br>◆ learning to sequence<br>◆ reflecting<br>◆ geography mapping<br>◆ vocabulary building<br>◆ writing<br><br>Adult students will analyze the story to discover the sequence involved with having a goal or dream and reaching that goal.<br><br>Topic for writing: Tell your own story. Looking back, what gifts did you give to others that may have slowed your journey toward your own goal? | Focus on the key experiences:<br>◆ time<br>◆ social or emotional development<br>◆ language development<br>◆ seriation<br>◆ music and movement<br><br>Opening circle: Teacher will read the story.<br><br>Small group time:<br>1. Children will be given "sense sacks" that contain moist dirt, fur, pine boughs and cones, rocks, and sand for touching, smelling, guessing.<br>2. Children will cut out pictures of animals and compare sizes. They will have measuring tools such as rulers and measuring tapes.<br><br>Throughout the day, we will encourage the exploration and use of words such as far, farther, easy, hard, harder, little, big, bigger, biggest. Children will have a jumping time, trying to jump high, higher, highest. | Parents will support the key experiences selected as the focus in the early childhood classroom.<br>During recall or review, they will talk about first, next, last.<br><br>In the closing circle parents and children will sing "Frog Songs" and imitate a mouse, a frog, and a fox.<br><br>One parent will reread the story before the lunch break.<br><br>Take-home activity: Families will be given models of each of the characters in the story, which they can make into finger puppets. | Parents will learn various strategies for reading aloud to their children. We will discuss questioning techniques.<br><br>Strictly for parents: We will discuss gift giving and receiving. We will role-play the positives and negatives of giving and receiving gifts.<br><br>We will focus on the unselfish giving of parents and discuss the need for balance in our lives.<br><br>We will make felt board characters depicting the story of "Jumping Mouse" that will be used in the early childhood classroom. |

## Figure 5
## Integration of the Components: Focus on Parental Concerns

Another way to address curriculum integration is to focus on *parental concerns*. Often parents are embarrassed because their children do not share toys willingly. The parents do not understand the developmental process of sharing as a social skill.

| Adult Education | Early Childhood | Parent-Child Interaction | Parent Group |
|---|---|---|---|
| Strategies:<br>◆ active reading<br>◆ building a child's vocabualary of sharing<br>◆ cooperative learning groups<br><br>The early childhood teacher will visit the adult education classroom to introduce the concept of social and emotional development and cooperative play.<br><br>Adult students will read two newspaper articles:<br>◆ "Mine's Mine; Yours Is Mine Too"<br>◆ "Children Can Learn How to Share"<br><br>Students will compare the child's vocabulary of sharing (show, share, lend, give) with the adult vocabulary of sharing (negotiation, compromise, cooperation, ownership.)<br><br>The ideas and concepts of cooperative learning groups will be further developed. | Opening circle: Teacher will read the story "What Mary Jo Shared."<br><br>Other books on sharing will be added to the book area.<br><br>Small group time: Teacher will introduce a new prop box to each group, and the children will share the clothes and other contents among the small group.<br><br>Children will have the opportunity to participate in joint planning, another way of sharing.<br><br>Teacher will introduce new symbols for sharing and limiting time in the computer areas where there are only one or two computers. | Parents and children will be given cookies to share in the house area. Children will pass out the cookies on a one-to-one correspondence.<br><br>Parents and children will be introduced to new puzzles and games, which they may choose to share.<br><br>Closing circle: Focus on the concept of taking turns by standing up to share worktime experiences.<br><br>Take-home activity: Families will be given a box of cookies to take home as a family sharing experience. | Parents will brainstorm their own experiences, during which they were forced to share something—material possessions, time, or personal information. Once they share, they will be asked to assume their child's perspective and write a journal entry.<br><br>At a follow-up meeting, a developmental psychologist will discuss sharing—its rewards and frustrations. |

and community. Longitudinal studies will construct for us an understanding of the long-term effects of family education.

*Program funding.* The key to the permanent success of family literacy programs is institutionalization of the program because initial funding usually lasts, at best, three to four years. We encourage program providers to begin the search for a permanent base as soon as they learn about their first grant award. Finding an administrator, school board member, or community member who will speak up for the program and champion the cause for institutionalization often begins the process for establishing a permanent home.

Even when the family literacy program becomes grounded, however, no one funding source can carry the entire financial burden. We learned to identify a range of funding alternatives and to seek multiple sources. Many programs depend on two or more of the following sources to assist with funding: government agencies, literacy volunteer organizations, corporations, local and national foundations, and private individuals (see also National Center for Family Literacy, 1993). The fear always exists that funds will disappear, that the hunt for sources will intensify, and that outside interest in the program will wane. But, as studies are reported and outcomes revealed, new funding sources do develop.

## Follow-Up Studies

A research summary reveals that in general parents in our PACE/Kenan family literacy program have developed a positive self-concept, view education differently than they did before their participation in the program, help their children with homework, spend more time reading to their children, attend more school functions including teacher-parent conferences, and better understand teachers' and administrators' problems. Many volunteer in schools and communities, making an increased commitment to the greater society. The parents have a more positive view of their future after obtaining a GED or alternative high school diploma, and many seek more learning opportunities in colleges and technical schools. Others, who have never worked before, join the labor force. A very significant finding is that these parents dedicate themselves to the task of keeping their children in school.

The children, whom many would have previously considered at-risk, are enthusiastic about school and are generally in the upper half of their primary classes as indicated by test scores and teacher rankings. Academic performance is only part of the story; the rest involves their positive attitudes, good attendance, motivation to learn, and social maturity. In general, as a recent follow-up study concluded, the comprehensive model for family literacy provides hope of breaking the cycle of undereducation and poverty.

## Broad Initiatives

Because of the positive effects of family literacy programs on individuals, families, and communities, broad initiatives have been established on both national and state levels in the United States. Even Start and The Barbara Bush Foundation are both federal projects to support family literacy, which are described in this volume. In 1990 the Bureau of Indian Affairs joined the National Center for Family Literacy with the Parents as Teachers National Center in St. Louis, Missouri, to serve Native American families with children from birth to age five. In 1991 the Head Start program began a family literacy initiative to enable Head Start families to enhance and develop their literacy skills. And Hawaii, New York, North and South Carolina, Illinois, Louisiana, and Kentucky have established statewide family literacy initiatives.

In response to the proliferation of varied programs resulting from these initiatives, the National Center for Family Literacy and the National Diffusion Network of the U.S. Department of Education have joined forces to provide a means for identifying and validating model programs in family literacy. The National Family Literacy Project will make available information on high-quality program models to practitioners and others. This project is an example of the movement to develop a national infrastructure for the field—a development that will support the growth of family literacy and the attainment of its potential to effect change among families who need help the most.

### References

Berreuta-Clement, J., Schweinhart, L., Barnett, S., Epstein, A., & Weikart, D. (1984). *Changed lives: The effects of the Perry Preschool program on youth through age 19.* Ypsilanti, MI: High Scope.

Brizius, J.A., & Foster, S.A. (1993). *Generation to generation: Realizing the promise of family literacy.* Ypsilanti, MI: High Scope.

National Center for Family Literacy. (1993). *A guide to funding sources for family literacy.* Louisville, KY: Author.

Paull, S. (1993a). *Empowering people: Parent groups.* Louisville, KY: National Center for Family Literacy.

Paull, S. (1993b). *The power of parenting: Parent and child interaction.* Louisville, KY: National Center for Family Literacy.

Popp, R.J. (1992). *Family portfolios: Documenting change in parent-child relationships.* Louisville, KY: National Center for Family Literacy.

Potts, M.W. (1992). *A strengths model for learning in a family literacy program.* Louisville, KY: National Center for Family Literacy.

Chapter 13_____

# Parents and Children Reading Together: The Barbara Bush Foundation for Family Literacy

Benita Somerfield
*The Barbara Bush Foundation for Family Literacy, Washington, DC*

*Standing behind a podium in the East Room of the White House in Washington, DC, Anna radiated self-confidence and spoke with passion as she told her story to an audience of policy makers, business executives, educators, and First Lady Barbara Bush. A 30-year-old woman with 5 young children, Anna had been a drug abuser and dealer only two years prior to her enrollment in the family literacy program sponsored by her community health center. Her children had been taken away from her and placed in the city's child welfare system, which "got her attention" finally and made her determined to get her children back and take control of her life.*

*After one successful year in a drug rehabilitation program, Anna did get her children back. She also enrolled in a family literacy program because she wanted to get an education and build a better life for herself and her family. According to the director of the family literacy program, Anna had become a leader and an example for many of her classmates as a result of her hard work and dedication. This had become particularly clear during the program's popular parent time at which the participants shared their problems, debated solutions, and offered support to one another.*

*Anna continued in the drug rehabilitation and family literacy programs and was hired by a community women's organization to be a part-time workshop coordinator. After obtaining her general equivalency diploma about one year after her enrollment in the family literacy program, Anna registered at her local community college to begin courses in early childhood education. Her children are thrilled by the changes in their mother, and her very obvious commitment to her education sets an example that they try to emulate in their own schoolwork. She is also more capable of helping them with their homework and demonstrates a commitment to their education as well as her own.*

*The director of the family literacy program, who grew up in the same predominantly Hispanic, urban community as did Anna, told the audience at the White House that news about the positive changes in the lives of the majority of the women enrolled in the program had spread throughout the neighborhood by the end of the first academic year. As a result, a long waiting list of interested families developed, and two local foundations offered to fund the program when the initial Barbara Bush grant finished.*

## Foundation Background

The Barbara Bush Foundation for Family Literacy was founded in 1989. During its first five years the Foundation funded the implementation or extension of 52 family literacy or family reading programs in 32 different U.S. states in urban (34 programs) and rural (18 programs) settings. Sites include homeless shelters, housing projects, libraries, Native American reservations, schools, community centers, and universities. Instructional designs include curricula targeted to the specific strengths and goals of the learners as well as structured curricula such as High/Scope for children and GED for caregivers. Services are usually delivered by teams that include professional educators, community activists, volunteers, and representatives of government agencies—a wide variety of stakeholders in the outcomes of this innovative educational intervention.

Projected outcomes of these family literacy programs are often similar, regardless of program type. A guiding principle is that in the process of helping their children, adults can improve their own literacy behaviors and skills. Most program directors believe that explicit literacy instruction directed at the parents' personal, nonparenting goals can increase that effect. Further, some programs include behavioral goals that have no direct link to the improvement of reading, but rather relate to the improvement of the self-esteem of parent and child, their relationship to each other, and their quality of life. Observations in this area have proven most interesting. For example, many parents reported an improved ability to handle discipline issues because of better communication with their children.

In support of the Foundation's commitment to family reading, which is an integral component of family literacy, five holiday season editions of *Mrs. Bush's Story Time* have been broadcast. This ABC radio program designed by the Children's Literacy Initiative has been aired on hundreds of stations in the United States, Canada, Mexico, and China. During the program, Mrs. Bush, along with well-known personalities such as Ben Kingsley, Lily Tomlin, and General Norman Schwarzkopf, reads children's literature and offers family reading tips. The positive effect of these programs has been supplemented by ABC's outreach activities directed to libraries and community centers as well as by publications generated by the Foundation, particularly *Barbara Bush's Family Reading Tips* (The Barbara Bush Foundation for Family Litera-

---

### Barbara Bush's Family Reading Tips

1. Establish a routine for reading aloud.
2. Make reading together a special time.
3. Try these simple ways to enrich your reading aloud:
   - ◆ Move your finger under the words as you read.
   - ◆ Let your child help turn the pages.
   - ◆ Take turns reading words or sentences or pages.
   - ◆ Pause and ask open-ended questions such as, "How would you feel if you were that person?" or "What do you think might happen next?"
   - ◆ Look at the illustrations and talk about them.
   - ◆ Change your voice as you read different characters' words. Let your child make up voices.
   - ◆ Keep stories alive by acting them out.
4. Ask others who take care of your children to read aloud.
5. Visit the library regularly.
6. Let your children see you reading.
7. Read all kinds of things together.
8. Fill your home with opportunities for reading.
9. Keep reading aloud even after your children learn to read.

---

cy, 1989) (see the figure). Response to this pamphlet (available in both English and Spanish) from schools, libraries, literacy and Head Start programs, women's clubs, parent-teacher associations, newspapers that reprint the *Tips*, and individuals has been very strong.

The Foundation's goal in its first years has been to encourage innovation and experimentation in program design and implementation often in venues not eligible for government funding. This chapter is based on the data collected from program grantees as a result of these first five years of activity. Specifically, in addition to developing the original grant proposal and responding to regular monitoring calls, each grantee is required to submit quarterly progress reports as well as final reports, which include questionnaires completed by program participants (learners and project directors). In some cases, an outside evaluator was used to document results.

## Establishing the Foundation

Newspapers all over the United States shocked us with this headline news on International Literacy Day: according to a recent survey of adult literacy in America, 47 percent of us—90 million adults—function at only the lowest literacy levels.

Once I realized that the report did not mean that these adults couldn't read, write, or use numbers *at all*, I felt a little better. However, the results clearly indicated their skills are so poor that their productivity at work, participation as citizens, and ability to be their children's "first teachers"—a critical factor in preparing children to start school ready to learn—are suffering.

The National Adult Literacy Survey left me momentarily daunted. Illiteracy in this country obviously is still an enormous problem. But now it's time to get over our shock, roll up our sleeves, and get to work. We have to—the stakes are too high (Bush, 1993, p. 13A).

Not that long ago, the fact that tens of millions of U.S. adults have serious literacy problems was not well known to the general public and the consequences of this rather startling reality not generally accepted by many of the policy makers responsible for enacting education legislation and authorizing funding. In the 1980s, however, that changed: the problem of low literacy skills among adults was brought to the forefront of U.S. consciousness by excellent and sustained public affairs campaigns such as Project Literacy U.S., the first partnership of its kind between a major commercial television network (CAP CITIES/ABC) and the Public Broadcasting System (WQED in Pittsburgh, Pennsylvania); new federal legislation spearheaded by Senators and Congressmen, particularly Paul Simon of Illinois and William Goodling of

Pennsylvania; new state literacy initiatives led by governors and their wives such as the Virginia Literacy Foundation created by Jeannie Baliles of Virginia when her husband was in the statehouse; and efforts by then First Lady Barbara Bush.

By November 1988 Mrs. Bush's very visible advocacy for a wide variety of literacy programs, particularly those targeted at adult learners, had prompted the suggestion that a foundation focusing exclusively on these areas be formed in her name. Familiar with the research that says that one of the most important things a parent can do to help a child succeed in school is to read to that child early and often, Mrs. Bush determined that a foundation that funded family literacy activities could make a difference in many families' lives.

On March 6, 1989, The Barbara Bush Foundation for Family Literacy was launched at a luncheon given at the White House. It would be operated by a volunteer board of literacy and education experts, of which Mrs. Bush was to be Honorary Chairperson. Money would be raised in the private sector by a committee of corporate leaders, and the Foundation was to be established as a fund of the Foundation for the National Capital Region in Washington, DC.

Coverage of the event in the national media was extensive and provided many "quotable items" that literacy providers and advocates could use later when approaching state legislatures and other potential funding sources. The media coverage also proved helpful in introducing family literacy to the general public. Before this event, the concept that it was important for adults to develop their literacy skills, not only for themselves or to improve the workforce, but also as a critical element in the educational development of their children had not been given much publicity.

## Setting the Mission

In formulating strategies for improving literacy skills among adults and children, the Foundation focused on stimulating intergenerational program activity and improving the climate for recognition of the value of literacy, both to the individual and to society, without demeaning those who lack it. It became clear that two separate, although parallel and interdependent, tracks would be required. The following mission statement, which seeks to reflect these goals, was developed.

The mission of The Barbara Bush Foundation for Family Literacy is

◆ to establish literacy as a value in every family in America...by helping every family in the nation understand that the home is the child's first school, that the parent is the child's first teacher, and that reading is the child's first subject; and

◆ to break the intergenerational cycle of illiteracy…by supporting the development of family literacy programs where parents and children can learn to read together.

To accomplish our mission, the Foundation will

◆ identify programs that are successful;
◆ award grants to help establish family literacy initiatives;
◆ encourage parents and children to learn and read together;
◆ recognize volunteers, teachers, students, and effective programs; and
◆ publish and distribute materials.

## What We Have Learned from Our Programs

Following is a book review from *Fathers for Better Family Values*, a publication of the program When Bonds Are Broken: Family Literacy for Incarcerated Fathers and Their Children, located in a Pennsylvania county prison and funded by the Foundation.

> I read *Leo, the Late Bloomer*. This was the first book I ever read. I feel very happy because I read my first book. Leo was on a different time schedule for learning and so am I. I think my little girl is too, but it's OK. We will both learn to read (William P., incarcerated father).

In completing final program questionnaires, participants enthusiastically stated that they had increased the range and frequency of literacy activities with their children as well as improved their own reading skills. Although many of the parents entering the various programs had basic skills sufficient to read children's books, they did not read. According to a program director, "While they [the parents] could read, none of them used this skill to share books with their children. They simply didn't know they should, or how to do it effectively." The literacy activities most frequently cited by the parents included telling stories to their children, reading books to them, drawing or painting with them, talking about the shape or color of things, talking with their children's teachers, helping their children with their homework, and taking their children to the library. When asked how the project helped them be better parents, over and over again parents responded, "I know I must be more involved in their learning."

In program directors' final reports, they supplied results of standardized pre- and posttests using measures such as the Test of Adult Basic Education, the California Adult Skills Assessment System, or the general equivalency diploma test to document gains in adult reading

*Parents and children play together at The Sunset Park Family Literacy Program of the Lutheran Medical Center in Brooklyn, New York.*

ability. Documentation of children's increased skill levels was provided using observation and measures such as the Batelle battery.

Most programs reported some gains in literacy skills. However, the narratives describing other behavioral changes have proven to be quite thought provoking. For example, in visiting program sites and having the opportunity to talk with participants about the parts of the program that were most important to them, I learned that many parents had just learned how to play with their children. They had not played as children themselves and did not know how. As a result, in some cases, program directors felt it was important to set aside time during the week for the adults to also play without their children.

Directors' narratives describe specific nonreading-related outcomes of the programs that emerged with remarkable consistency and similarity across programs, particularly in those programs with well-established parent-child time and parent group discussion components. These outcomes included:

♦ significant positive changes in the parents' relationship to their children;

- changes in children's ability to act independently of their mothers and relate to other children;
- improvements in parents' self-esteem;
- parents' interest in continuing education; and
- parents' ability and willingness to become involved in their children's education either by participating in prekindergarten or becoming more involved in local school activity.

Further, observations suggest that the holistic approach taken in a family literacy program can positively affect the quality of life and literacy skills of the family. For example, parents' improved ability to handle discipline problems with their children was frequently cited as a program outcome by both parents and program directors. Following are two representative statements from a parent and program director at the Sunset Park Family Literacy Program, located in a community health center in Brooklyn, New York, geared to the literacy and parenting skills needs of single mothers and young children in the community.

> Before I couldn't stand their fighting. Now, instead of scolding or hitting, I talk to them more. I couldn't sit and do things with them before. Now I have more patience, and I enjoy working with them. The project has affected my husband, too. He sees how I am with the children. I can talk to him more about discipline (parent).

> Once visibly frustrated and seemingly helpless over behavior problems repeatedly occurring in their children, mothers are seen "talking things out" with their youngsters instead of striking them out of desperation. Once confused about what constitutes appropriate parenting interactions based on children's age and development, mothers are now seen actually fostering independence in their own children (program director).

If these positive behavioral changes continue beyond the program cycle, then the potential impact of family literacy could be truly significant. This is an area of inquiry that we believe merits further study.

## What the Results Have Demonstrated: Elements of Successful Programs

Following are the key elements of family literacy programs that were most successful in accomplishing their goals.

*1. A strong charismatic leader with a vision.* Family literacy programs are typically developed outside of the institutionalized education systems. Their initial and continued existence is therefore often the result of the vision, advocacy, and hard work of one or more individuals. The following anecdote tells the story of how one such program was born:

> A few years ago, I spent several mornings in the waiting room of one of our county health clinics on well-baby day, observing the ways in which young mothers interact with their babies. While sweeping generalities are abhorrent, it was difficult to avoid one general observation: there was very little interaction between parent and child, and most of that was negative. Mothers—most of them teenagers—sat with infants thrown over their shoulders, toddlers sitting on the floor at their feet, preschoolers screaming distractedly and running in circles...the only words the mothers uttered were "No! Don't! Stop that!" There was no one reading a book to a child or telling a story, no conversation, no singing of lullabies to fretful infants.
>
> I went away with the strong conviction that the library had to find a way to help these young moms learn the value of communication—the value of talking with their children. After all, children can only develop language skills by listening to language. They must be talked to, listened to, and surrounded by words and books. Language skills are the basic building blocks of literacy, and literacy is the library's lifeblood. So, the concept of the Building Blocks program was born. The DeKalb County Public Library in Decatur, Georgia, wanted to help parents learn to play with their babies in ways that encouraged the development of language and cognitive skills. We wanted to model successful behaviors, and we wanted it all to be fun (Sherry Des Enfants, Youth Services Coordinator, personal communication, June 27, 1993).

Building Blocks has become a recognized success in its own community, a model library literacy program, and the winner of a 1993 National Association of Counties Award for addressing a significant concern in DeKalb County.

*2. Effective recruitment and retention strategies.* Positive "word of mouth" resulting from a program that met and expanded participant goals proved to be by far the most effective recruitment strategy. Even with programs that drew exclusively from mandatory, welfare-related projects, talking about them positively was always cited as the best way to recruit new participants.

Critical factors in retention centered around overcoming the many barriers to attendance. Programs that did best in this area, like others described in this volume, provided round-trip transportation, on-site meals, quality childcare, and counseling and home visits by teachers and social workers.

An interesting factor that contributed significantly to high retention rates, according to parents, was their children. Participants often reported that their children insisted on going to school. A number of program directors also noted the critical influence children had on their parents' desire to continue coming to class. Following is an excerpt from a quarterly report from Project FREE, in New Iberia, Louisiana, located in a subsidized housing facility in the Louisiana bayou:

> The staff has had several meetings to discuss and analyze why we have not had more success in attendance and retention, problems we know exist nationwide. Pooling the insights of our three aides, who are close to the experience of the participants and articulating our own gut feelings, we have come up with this analysis: our target group consists of individuals who have been trapped in poverty all of their lives. They have known deprivation and oppression and all the frustration and despair that result. Their hope, if they ever had any, is just about used up. They have given up trying to envision the invisible, touch the intangible, and achieve the impossible. They do, however, continue to want the best for their children, and this is the spark we try to ignite.

*3. Qualified and supportive staff who meet regularly to develop integrated curricula and discuss progress and problems.* The most successful programs included staff with expertise in early childhood and adult education as well as support staff, such as counselors, social workers, community liaisons, and other volunteers. In strong family literacy programs, adult and early childhood staff work together, integrating curriculum objectives to serve the individual and mutual literacy and parenting needs of adults and children. Adult and early childhood educators do not have a history of working together. Because their bureaucratic entities are different and their training and background frequently dissimilar, an effort often must be made for this critical relationship to work optimally.

Further, an effective staff is characterized by sensitivity to the culture of the participants, flexibility, creativity, initiative, commitment, and willingness to try new things. As one project director put it, "We looked for a staff that possessed the ability to accept others as they are and to treat them as they are capable of becoming."

Volunteers are also used in most programs and often provide support services such as clerical or library assistance; serve as storytellers and workshop presenters; feed, rock, read, and play with the children; or provide individual tutoring.

*4. Program design that includes four integrated components: literacy instruction for primary caregivers; prereading instruction for children; parent and child together time; and parent group time.* (In the Foundation's experience, family reading programs that seek to instill a love of reading, improve the quality and frequency of shared reading activity, and create a print-rich environment do not require these four components to be effective. We do, however, make a distinction, for the purposes of determining strategy and setting funding priorities, between these family reading programs and the more intensive instructional family literacy programs.)

As a result of the work of the National Center for Family Literacy and the Even Start legislation, there are many examples of this four-component model currently in existence, as described in some of the chapters in this book. As one such program, the Elgin YWCA Family Literacy Project in Illinois provides six levels of English as a second language instruction for adults and three classes of age-appropriate ESL activities for their preschool children, both taught by professional educators. Family literacy classes for parents and children are delivered by both adult and early childhood teachers. The project represents a successful collaboration among a number of service providers: the YWCA, the local library, the Illinois State Board of Education, and other community agencies. In its first cycle of operation, it served 75 families (81 adults and 93 children). Parents received 10 hours of ESL instruction per week; their children received 10 hours of instruction; and there was one hour per week of parent-child time, one hour of parent time, and one hour of special events such as field trips.

Most materials are teacher developed, and the teachers work very closely with one another, meeting on a weekly basis for family literacy class planning sessions. For example, staff developed a family literacy curriculum for ESL families, which was later published, and a blueprint for a personal storybook entitled *Kindergarten Here I Come*, which parents and children completed together in the spring and read over the summer before school started. Some commercial texts such as dictionaries were also used, and computer literacy was part of the instruction offered. Describing her program, the project director stated:

> All components foster self-esteem and encourage personal growth through participation and conversation built around daily living themes. The family literacy modules helped parents acquire skills to take a more active part in their child's growth and development. Participation in their child's learning provided a comfortable and natural setting for acquiring and reinforcing their own English.

*5. Evaluation of program effectiveness and assessment of participants are part of the program design.* This is an area in which many programs were lacking. The major problems were lack of assessment for one of the two generations involved; standardized test measures that did not capture relevant behavioral changes; and measures that did not always match stated program goals. It is also too soon to be able to gauge the long-term impact of these programs on participants, although a number of programs such as When Bonds Are Broken: Family Literacy for Incarcerated Fathers and Their Children in Pennsylvania have plans in place to do so. In describing the major outcome looked for as a result of the program, the director states:

> The fathers' change in behavior that allows for positive and lasting reintegration into the family and community is the primary measure. Currently recidivism is approximately 70 percent within a six-month period of time. Records will be maintained on these individuals for reincarceration into our institution. During the coming year, contact with all of the families will be continued where possible in order to support and follow the children of these fathers.

It is vitally important for these programs to document results, both to show outcomes and to provide ammunition for future funding and program development.

## A Look Forward

Although we are still in the early stages of development and dissemination of these family literacy programs, results are interesting and encouraging both in terms of improvements in literacy and preliteracy skills as well as in the effect these family literacy efforts may have on the solutions to other social problems. It seems important then, when evaluating these programs, to look at them not simply as literacy skills programs, but as strategies that may be part of broader efforts designed to attack problems such as violence, homelessness, welfare dependency, and health care reform.

### References

Barbara Bush Foundation for Family Literacy. (1989). *Barbara Bush's family reading tips.* Washington, DC: Author.

Bush, B. (1993, November 9). Illiteracy in America. *USA Today*, p. 13A.

Chapter 14_____

# Linking Families, Childcare, and Literacy: *Sesame Street* Preschool Educational Program

Iris Sroka, Jeanette Betancourt, and Myra Ozaeta
*Children's Television Workshop, New York, New York*

*M*s. C., a parent of two children, volunteers in the afterschool program. She begins today's session by passing out the Sesame Street *Muppets and asking the children, "Are these Muppets anything like us?" Receiving a "no" from the group, she asks, "What is different?"*

*The children reply, "They are blue," "Ernie has a red nose like a reindeer," and "Elmo has fur." Ms. C. encourages the children to talk about the differences.*

*When the children talk about the Muppets having fur, she asks, "What do you have?"*

*"Skin!"*

*Ms. C. announces that they are going to watch a short segment from* Sesame Street *and then talk about it. The clip features Ernie and a human friend discussing their similarities and differences. Ms. C. asks the children how some of the* Sesame Street *characters are the same as they are.*

*Afterward, Ms. C. holds up the book* We're Different, We're the Same, *making sure everyone can see it. The group talks about the differences between the children on the cover. Ms. C. asks questions, pauses when she turns to a new page, and invites the children to talk about the illustrations as she reads. When Oscar the Grouch is brought into the discussion, Ms. C. explains, "We don't always feel the same. Sometimes we are grouchy, and sometimes we are sad, and sometimes we are very..." The class answers, "Happy!"*

*When they finish reading the book, Ms. C. passes out sheets of paper and invites the children to draw a picture of themselves. She spends time with each child talking about the drawing.*

Children's Television Workshop, the producer of *Sesame Street* and other educational television shows for children, has as its mission "to help educate children and young people through high-quality and entertaining media...and outreach efforts, with a special commitment to reach minority and poor children" (Britt, 1993, p. 1). It was with this mission's outreach component in mind that the Community Education Services Division of CTW developed a project called the *Sesame Street* Preschool Educational Program. The program reaches childcare professionals and the children in their care across the United States with the primary goals of encouraging children's natural curiosity and love of learning and fostering an enthusiasm for reading. This is achieved by using three components: the *Sesame Street* show (which has a curriculum of more than 200 cognitive and socioemotional developmental goals), children's books related to the goals of the show, and related activities extending those goals. *Sesame Street* PEP is an educational framework specifically designed to support coordinated implementation of these key components that extend the goals of the *Sesame Street* show, which range from developing emergent literacy to appreciating human diversity, and contribute to quality childcare experiences.

*Sesame Street* PEP includes training and a handbook with sections on developmentally appropriate practice, tips on reading children's books, suggested book lists, and follow-up activities that guide childcare professionals in the implementation of the program. The activities are organized around four main areas: children and their world, human diversity, symbols, and thinking skills. The handbook is designed to be used by childcare professionals in daycare centers and family day homes to enhance their preschool education programs and support quality opportunities for and interactions between them and the children in their care.

With the same principle, *Sesame Street* PEP is extending its outreach efforts toward the families of preschool children with the following goal:

> To get (adult family members) involved as early as possible in their children's education, become aware of the potential that *Sesame Street* and reading have for developing their children's motivation to learn, and view *Sesame Street* and read books in an active way with their children on a regular basis to help strengthen bonding and communication (Community Education Services Research Department & RMC Research, 1993, p. 1).

Another primary goal of *Sesame Street* PEP is to introduce television to families as an educational tool, instrumental in the preschool development of their children, as *Sesame Street* PEP has in the childcare setting. To promote the involvement of adult family members in *Sesame Street* PEP, CTW is developing materials especially for families in accordance with the CTW model of collaboration between experts in curriculum and program development, materials development, and research. The *Sesame Street* PEP–related materials currently available to families, in both English and Spanish, include a family activity book and a brochure informing families about the themes featured in the *Sesame Street* show, the goals of *Sesame Street* PEP, and what they can do at home to encourage quality interaction. These materials are designed to provide adult family members with suggestions for getting involved in the education of their young children. The family activity book includes activities related to the four major goal areas of *Sesame Street* PEP and suggestions of books for children up to age 10. It also provides families with tips for taking advantage of everyday situations, fostering their children's love of reading, and selectively and actively viewing television as a family activity. The reading tips offer strategies for making books come alive for both adults and their children so that they may read books together in easy and enjoyable ways.

## Background

Research conducted by CTW and others has addressed the issue of family involvement in preschool education. As mentioned in earlier chapters, this research shows that families' involvement in their children's education has overwhelmingly positive effects on both the children and their adult family members. Other research has explored issues related to the potential of television to educate. Anderson and Collins (1988) found that children are engaged in various thinking processes while viewing TV. Educational programming has been found to support and enhance children's acquisition of vocabulary and literacy skills (Rice et al., 1990) and math skills (Fisch & McCann, 1993). Television can contribute to children's developing social skills and attitudes as well. For example, Brown and Bryant (1990) found that programming content can play a role in children's understanding of family roles, interactions, and values. Dorr, Kovaric, and Doubleday (1990) discovered that children's judgments of social realism on TV are sensitive to program content.

The overwhelming evidence of the potential of television viewing to contribute in positive ways to the cognitive and social development of children qualifies the medium's use as an educational tool. As with the *Sesame Street* PEP and materials for the childcare setting, *Sesame Street* PEP for families uses educational TV as an innovative approach to promoting family literacy and involvement in the educational experiences of their children. In the words of one teacher, it is necessary to build a "bridge between television viewing and learning...to help children understand that learning and fun go hand in hand" (Community Education Services Research Department, 1993c, p. 14).

A study by KRC Research & Consulting (1993) for the Public Broadcasting System explores the perceptions, reactions, and evaluations of kindergarten through third grade teachers, childcare professionals, and adult family members of preschoolers to PBS's Ready to Learn Service. The service establishes a block of broadcast time and an outreach strategy designed to meet the educational needs of preschoolers. Though the research indicates there is a positive effect as a result of family involvement in their preschoolers' education, the KRC study and our own findings suggest there is a tendency for limited interaction between families and childcare professionals. Constrained family involvement in preschool education was reported due to time demands on families. However, it also suggested there is a range of involvement among adult family members in their children's education and a range of monitoring of preschoolers' TV viewing.

Another study, conducted by the Center for Research on the Influences of Television on Children at the University of Kansas, investigated the characteristics of individual children, families, and environmental conditions that affect TV viewing patterns of preschoolers (Wright & Huston, 1993). This study, called the Early Window Project, examined the effect of educational TV on young children and their families over four years (from 1989 to 1993) and indicated that families and the home environment play an important role in determining what kinds of TV programs children watch and what children learn from those programs.

These findings, among others, are helping to guide the development and refinement of *Sesame Street* PEP materials for families.

## CTW's Program of Formative Research

A great deal of CTW's research has been conducted in relation to families and their perceptions of their preschoolers' education, and in particular, of *Sesame Street* PEP. The four key studies that contributed to the preliminary development of *Sesame Street* PEP for families are briefly outlined here.

### National Study on Early Implementation

The *Sesame Street* PEP National Study on Early Implementation, an extensive program of research, in part surveyed and interviewed adult family members throughout the United States to determine their involvement in *Sesame Street* PEP and their children's care program (Community Education Services Research Department & RMC Research, 1993). Among other things, the results of this study indicated a common lack of communication between childcare professionals, especially those center based, and families. Interviews with childcare professionals, daycare center administrators, and families indicated these professionals perceived a general lack of involvement on the part of adult family members in their preschoolers' education. Many family members reported interest in becoming more active, but attributed their lack of involvement to time constraints. We were encouraged to find that *Sesame Street* PEP, as a part of their children's childcare program, was received positively by a majority of the families included in the study. Many said they wanted to become more involved in *Sesame Street* PEP and to do the program at home with their children.

### Sesame Street PEP New York City Demonstration Site Project

In the *Sesame Street* PEP New York City Demonstration Site Project: Daycare Centers and Family Day Homes study, childcare professionals trained in *Sesame Street* PEP were interviewed about a range of issues, including their relationships with the families of the children in their programs (Community Education Services Research Department, 1993a; 1993b; 1993d). In addition, a survey of adult family members of children attending the demonstration site programs was conducted. The findings from this effort confirmed what was learned from the national study: there is a general lack of communication between childcare professionals and families and limited involvement on the part of adult family members in their children's preschool education. The lack of involvement, once again, was attributed to time constraints and also to the difference in primary language between childcare professionals and adult family members.

Another issue that surfaced in the results from this research was the apparent lack of agreement between families and childcare professionals regarding the prioritization of preschool educational goals. Childcare professionals placed a great deal of emphasis on the children's acquisition of social skills, while families emphasized the need for children to learn reading and writing. Both groups, however, agreed that more communication and involvement is necessary to maximize children's preschool educational experiences.

### The P.S. 43 Demonstration Site

Public School 43, also a *Sesame Street* PEP New York demonstration site, was unique in that it was the only site located in a public school and implemented by volunteer mothers who were trained in the program (Community Education Services Research Department, 1993c). During the course of the study, the volunteer mothers' implementation of *Sesame Street* PEP was observed. In addition, interviews were conducted with school personnel, the volunteer mothers, and other mothers who were trained in *Sesame Street* PEP but did not volunteer in the program.

P.S. 43's model of implementation of the program is very encouraging. The volunteer mothers' participation in *Sesame Street* PEP has supported family participation in P.S. 43's afterschool program and has promoted selective and educationally appropriate TV viewing in the home. *Sesame Street* PEP has influenced family interaction, fostered involvement in family literacy activities, and heightened awareness of the importance of celebrating ethnic diversity and developing self-esteem.

## Implications for Childcare Professionals and Early Childhood Programs

There were many insights gained from the implementation of *Sesame Street* PEP by childcare professionals in daycare centers and family day homes and by mothers at P.S. 43. The lessons learned can assist other childcare professionals to use TV as an educational tool to enhance literacy and link the experiences of the childcare program and the home.

◆ *Engage in selective viewing in your childcare program.* Select television and video programming content that reinforces and ex-

*Shared reading experiences contribute to quality family involvement.*

tends your program's educational goals. While viewing with your children, sing, dance, describe what you see, and predict what may happen next.

♦ *Prerecord appropriate TV segments.* Prerecord segments of programming that supplement the goals of your curriculum. This will allow you to review the content, design ways to engage children in viewing the segment, select a children's book that will highlight the goal of the segment, and choose a related activity that reinforces the goal. Invite families to observe and participate in these activities so that you can model for them appropriate use of educational TV, quality children's book reading, and related activities.

♦ *Promote selective viewing at home.* Encourage families to view educational programming together. This can become a "special family time" with opportunities for interactions between adults and their children.

♦ *Create a video library.* Build a collection of educational videos that can be used by childcare professionals and families. Orga-

Sroka, Betancourt, & Ozaeta

nize these around themes, such as cooperation, self-esteem, human diversity, early math, and early reading. Themed tapes can help you introduce more abstract concepts that may otherwise be difficult to explain, such as ethnic diversity.

◆ *Lend the tapes and books to families.* Encourage family members to borrow these tapes and use them for viewing at home. Include suggestions for simple activities that take advantage of everyday teachable moments (for example, neighborhood walks, household activities, shopping, or fieldtrips). Make available to families books related to the themes of your tapes.

◆ *Encourage reading in all languages.* Inquire about the languages and dialects spoken in the children's homes. To the extent possible, provide books and reading experiences that reflect the languages with which your children are familiar. Encourage families to read at home with their children in the language with which they are most comfortable.

These are only a few of the many strategies that can forge a link between childcare programs and children's homes through the use of educational TV, children's books, and related activities. These strategies can provide childcare professionals and families with innovative and creative tools to enhance children's experiences by stimulating their creativity and fostering a love of reading.

## Future Plans

Research indicates that while families express an interest in becoming more involved in their children's education, they are often unable to do so, reportedly because of time or language barriers. Nevertheless, we believe family members can become active participants in their children's education if given the opportunity and support to do so. The *Sesame Street* PEP materials for families are intended to link families with their children's early education program. Additional materials will be designed to extend the reach of *Sesame Street* PEP. The outcome will be a *Sesame Street* PEP for families built around materials that require little preparation time and are simple to use. As always, awareness of diversity of families' culture, language, reading ability, and learning styles will be essential considerations.

The Community Education Services Division of Children's Television Workshop is also forging new collaborative partnerships with organizations that share *Sesame Street* PEP's mission to reach families. Through the development of new partnerships and materials, the *Sesame Street* PEP program for families will assist more families, particularly those most in need, to share in their children's education and foster a love of reading within families.

As a final example of the effect of this program, one mother told us that prior to being introduced to *Sesame Street* PEP, she had never read a book to her children. She was encouraged by the training to begin reading with her children, even though reading English was difficult for her. She now reads and writes with them all the time, and they ask to be read to. She has a library card, and she and her children go to the library together and check out books. Other adults agreed that they were more motivated to read with their children even though reading in English is difficult for them. Some of them were relieved to find out that it was all right for them to read to their children in Spanish and that fostering a child's love of reading is important and valuable in all languages.

## References

Anderson, D.R., & Collins, P.A. (1988). *The impact on children's education: Television's influence on cognitive development* (Office of Research working paper no. 2). Washington, DC: U.S. Department of Education, Office of Educational Research and Improvement.

Britt, D. (1993). *Memorandum on revised mission statement of Children's Television Workshop*. New York: Children's Television Workshop.

Brown, D., & Bryant, J. (1990). Effects of television on family values and selected attitudes and behaviors. In J. Bryant (Ed.), *Television and the American family* (pp. 253–274). Hillsdale, NJ: Erlbaum.

Community Education Services Research Department. (1993a). Sesame Street PEP *New York City Demonstration Sites: Exit interview report.* Unpublished research report, Children's Television Workshop, New York.

Community Education Services Research Department. (1993b). Sesame Street PEP *New York City Demonstration Sites: Family survey report.* Unpublished research report, Children's Television Workshop, New York.

Community Education Services Research Department. (1993c). Sesame Street PEP *New York City Demonstration Sites: Report on implementation at P.S. 43.* Unpublished research report, Children's Television Workshop, New York.

Community Education Services Research Department. (1993d). Sesame Street PEP *New York Demonstration Sites: Results from research through March, 1993.* Unpublished research report, Children's Television Workshop, New York.

Community Education Services Research Department & RMC Research. (1993). Sesame Street PEP: *Executive summary of the national study on early implementation.* (Available from Community Education Services, Children's Television Workshop, New York.)

Dorr, A., Kovaric, P., & Doubleday, C. (1990). Age and content influences on children's perceptions of the realism of television families. *Journal of Broadcasting & Electronic Media, 34*(4), 377–397.

Fisch, S., & McCann, S.K. (1993). Making broadcast television participative: Eliciting mathematical behavior through *Square One TV. Educational Technology Research and Development, 41*(3), 103–109.

KRC Research & Consulting. (1993). *The proposed PBS Ready to Learn service: Perceptions, reactions, evaluations.* Report submitted to the Public Broadcasting System. New York: Author.

Rice, M., Huston, A.C., Truglio, R., & Wright, J. (1990). Words from *Sesame Street*: Learning vocabulary while viewing. *Developmental Psychology, 26*(3), 421–428.

Wright, J., & Huston, A.C. (1993). *Determinants of television viewing by target child in Period 1: Predictions of selected categories of viewing by family variables.* Early Window Project Report #3 submitted to the Children's Television Workshop. Lawrence, KS: Center for Research on the Influence of Television on Children.

# Chapter 15

# The Family Literacy Alliance: Using Public Television, Book-Based Series to Motivate At-Risk Populations

Twila C. Liggett

*Reading Rainbow and GPN/Nebraska Educational TV Network,*
*Lincoln, Nebraska*

Is there any value in using television as a springboard to family literacy outreach? Can TV really contribute positively to family literacy? The Family Literacy Alliance creators think so. They feel that television, a user-friendly medium, can be used to attract families to stories and books. And, if there is one function that TV does well, it tells stories. In fact, when TV producers discuss the creation of a particular program, they will often say to one another, "But what's the story here?" While the art of storytelling has been lost to many families, television, good television, can be a beginning to family interaction and literacy activities.

The Family Literacy Alliance began with funding from the Corporation for Public Broadcasting in 1990 as a collaboration of three Public Broadcasting System book-based series: *Reading Rainbow, Long Ago & Far Away*, and *Wonderworks*. The FLA was built on three major tenets:

(1) we would focus on emergent literacy activities, which we defined as the stage at which storytelling or language activities are developmentally appropriate in a family's literacy growth; (2) we would build relationships with organizations and community groups that were already working with families; and (3) all materials and activities would be developed cooperatively with the organizations or families with whom we were working.

In the lives of many of the at-risk families that the FLA hoped to reach, the notion that books or reading (or for that matter, any literacy-based activity) could be enjoyable was inconceivable. Yet as we began to work with isolated rural families, women and men in prison, Native American Centers, halfway houses, homeless shelters, and inner-city housing projects, we found that book-based television helped make books and reading approachable, even desirable. In one example in Beatrice, Nebraska, even seemingly unwilling program participants became enthusiastic about reading. It was with some trepidation that Ann, the FLA coordinator in Nebraska, began to work with the job readiness program in Beatrice because she knew that the family literacy sessions were required and that participants were reluctant to attend. The director of the program had become very interested in FLA and had asked Ann to help them integrate the model into their course.

Located in a geographically isolated area, Beatrice has the highest welfare and illiteracy rates in Nebraska. The job readiness program (run by the state department of social services) provides 40 hours of instruction and assessment over 12 weeks with the goal of employment. In order to participate, however, applicants are required to attend ongoing family literacy activities, which address parenting and literacy issues.

At her previous sites, Ann had overwhelmingly positive reactions from adults who watched *Reading Rainbow* with their children. However, at the new Beatrice site, the initial *Reading Rainbow* viewing was greeted by the query, "Why are we watching a *kids'* show?" The director persisted in showing different episodes, providing books, and talking about related activities that parents could do with their children. One night after a parenting session, Mike, one of the fathers who had been quite resentful about participating, said he wanted to know how he could get the books and maybe a library card so that he could share the featured books with his child. Mike returned the following week with a glowing report about watching a *Reading Rainbow* video while looking at the books with Danny. From then on, Mike was an enthusiastic and outspoken supporter of sharing the joys of books and reading with his child.

## Program Beginnings

Because this project began with the producers of three public television series, the FLA targeted public TV stations (which are located throughout the United States and connected through a national association) as the key community agency. The initial group involved five public TV stations: WGBH, Boston (Massachusetts); WQED, Pittsburgh (Pennsylvania); GPN/Nebraska Educational TV Network; WNED, Buffalo (New York); and KNME, Albuquerque (New Mexico). This core group carefully developed a process that was formulated through actual work with participants, who were groups of people living in economically disadvantaged or geographically isolated situations. Most of them had not had the opportunity to enjoy books and reading because their lives were defined by survival issues—housing, food, and health care. But they all watched TV. So by starting in the most basic way of all—storytelling—through the TV medium with which they were intimately familiar, we predicted that our book-based series would lead to involvement in the books and reading.

The FLA process was originally conceived as the responsibility of public television outreach staff to establish relationships with community agencies who have identified family literacy as a goal. Public TV staff members would provide an overall model or plan as well as resources and concrete ideas to help these agencies integrate the project process into their ongoing activities. Eventually, the community agencies were to incorporate FLA into their regular program and require minimal support from the public TV station. By providing an adaptable framework, not a ready-made panacea, the FLA was successful in its attempt to develop a flexible process model.

## First-Year Evaluation

In 1992 RMC Research, a research firm based in New Hampshire that has extensive experience in educational and television analysis, conducted an evaluation of the FLA's pilot-year phase. RMC found that FLA's approach had increased and improved parent-child interaction for all ages of children, all types of community programs, and all types of populations. What was particularly important, RMC found, was that the FLA activities modeled positive, literacy-promoting interactions for parents and children. For example, in an unsolicited letter to the deputy superintendent at the Pittsburgh State Correctional Institution, a male inmate praised the WQED program coordinator and the FLA program. He wrote, "[You] have put into place a program which enable[s] parents and children to communicate in a nurturing...manner [which] fosters a healthy...relationship." He went on to request that the FLA be incorporated within the treatment component of the correctional institution.

RMC (1992) also found that this approach had stimulated an interest in stories, books, and reading among children and their families. A remark frequently made by community workers was, "I've seen children who have never read books before now, reading" (p. 39). Not surprisingly, RMC concluded that public television programming can create interest in reading by people who have been intimidated by books and libraries.

## Project Expansion

Once extensive pilot development and testing was completed, we addressed the issue of expanding to more stations and communities. We envisioned a version of a multiplier effect in which the 5 station coordinators would train 10 additional station coordinators, who in turn would help train 40 more and so forth, thus multiplying this approach. An important element of the expansion or dissemination of the prototype is a mentoring process that grew out of the pilot experience. During the pilot, the coordinators held regular telephone conference calls (and sometimes met in person) to share what worked and to brainstorm new approaches and ideas. The pilot phase coordinators felt that this system of support had been a major element in the success of the first stage. Thus, as the new stations were selected, they were also assigned to a "mentor" (coordinator) from the original group.

A special training workshop was also developed by the pilot project's team of coordinators. The intent of the workshop was, and is, to help the new coordinators understand that their role is as a facilitator, resource person, and learner—*not* as reading teacher or administrator in charge of good works. Other issues are also addressed in this training, including local fundraising and many examples of what worked.

As with far too many worthwhile endeavors, continuation funding for the project was sporadic and minimal. Even so, and with a much reduced budget, in 1992 the FLA selected (from over 100 applicants) 10 public TV stations as "model stations." Following the workshop, the model station coordinators began to identify their programs and sites for the FLA approach. The model station sites initially included a city library, a Native American reservation cultural center, several federal government–funded program sites, a homeless shelter, and a Salvation Army site. Earlier sites (including prisons and Even Start programs) from the pilot phase continued the FLA approach as part of their ongoing programs.

As the process matured and continued to evolve, we found that the truly exciting results were in the reports of changes in the lives of parents and children—not on a grandiose scale, but in a meaningful way. Model station coordinators and community leaders told us, "When parents [are] visibly having fun, you can see them adopting a different attitude towards their kids. They're more open" (RMC, 1993, p. 13).

In one success story, the Clark Street Developmental Learning School in Worcester, Massachusetts, thrived on the FLA program. Worcester has a population of more than 50 percent Hispanic students and qualifies for compensatory education in reading and math. Many of the students live in a housing project nearby. When the FLA was offered for a second time, all the parents originally enrolled signed up again. The principal reported that the parents would not be participating in school activities if it were not for FLA:

> We have one little guy in the first grade who was doing progressively worse each week until the FLA program came along. Since his mother began attending the program and paying more attention to him, his performance has dramatically improved. We know it's because of the FLA (from a monthly coordinator report).

The evaluation (RMC, 1993) of the ten model stations confirmed that a straightforward approach to a family literacy program can become the catalyst for making meaningful contributions in the lives of children and their parents. During the first two phases of the project, 15 stations were able to initiate 51 sites with an estimated 3100 families affected. Among the sites were 14 Even Start programs, 6 inner-city housing projects, 3 Head Start programs, 4 homeless shelters or halfway houses, 4 hospital or clinic waiting rooms, a female offender program, a male offender treatment program, two refugee centers, and other programs reaching African, Native, Asian, and Latino Americans as well as some nonminorities. There were also a large number of after-school programs and centers.

Not surprisingly, *Reading Rainbow* was the most used series because of its flexible program design, positive messages of diversity, multiple subject matter and appealing topics for all ages, segments on "real life" and "how to," and direct book connections. In addition, *Reading Rainbow* is broadcast Monday through Friday on most PBS stations.

The evaluators were struck by the enjoyment and positive feelings the participating families experienced during direct and simple activities we often take for granted, such as parents and children viewing *Reading Rainbow* while following along with a copy of the actual book. The most frequently used follow-up activities were arts and crafts projects that encouraged families to be involved together. The completion of something that could be taken home gave them a sense of accomplishment and pride. The enthusiastic participation of these families was remarkable because many of them had not had previous opportunities to be involved in parent-child activities.

Finally, the evaluators found that the theme that runs through the FLA project is the sense of empowerment felt by all those individuals involved. "This is a project which has to do with reaching out and touching the lives of others in small but important ways," one coordinator said. Emphasizing this point, another coordinator in the report concluded, "You need to have people understand that you are not going to make a big difference right now. It may take years to see that and the change" (RMC, 1993, p. 29).

## Loss of Funding for the FLA

In January 1994 we conducted a final training session for additional, interested PBS stations, which brought the total number of stations trained in the FLA model to 22. Regrettably, due to a shift in funding priorities, the FLA lost its funding from the Corporation for Public Broadcasting. Intense effort was made to find other financial support, but after six months with no prospects in sight, the project was unable to continue and was officially closed. One of the producing agencies of *Reading Rainbow*, GPN/Nebraska ETV Network, became the repository of project materials and records. It should be noted, however, that the ultimate goal was to see this model become integrated into the way public TV stations and their communities work with family literacy. The FLA was never envisioned as an institution in and of itself.

Even though the project has ceased to exist officially, there are still many stations using the FLA model of becoming partners with community-based organizations and schools to create family literacy programs. Indeed, our experience within schools, especially with Even Start, Head Start, and after-school care programs, showed that this approach could flourish in schools. This is especially true in those school settings where parent programs are in place, in the planning stage, or where teachers are given official support to reach out into their community. One example of such a setting is the Thompson School in Arlington, Massachusetts (near Boston). In 1992 this school incorporated the FLA approach into its compensatory reading time. The teachers of kindergarten through second grade students recruited parent participation on "parents night." Every two weeks, parents and children spent an hour together, watching quality TV programs, sharing books, and doing follow-up activities.

As the excitement of the parents and children grew, the teachers shared the creative results of the program activities on bulletin boards throughout the school. Soon other kids in the school were asking, "Can me and my Mom [and/or Dad] come too?" The FLA has become a permanent part of Thompson School's compensatory program.

## Implications for Teachers and Teaching

In his comprehensive analysis of TV research studies *Television and the American Child*, Comstock (1991) disputes the view that TV viewing is passive and cites research that indicates the opposite—there is a lot of mental activity while watching or "monitoring [which] implies attention to audio, visual, and social cues as to the desirability of paying attention to the screen" (p. 23). Not only did Leitner (1991) confirm this view, but in her doctoral study she concluded that "children's comfort and familiarity with television may enable them to interpret the program vicariously as a *direct* [italics added] experience" (p. 131).

Many teachers have been effectively using TV as a motivational tool in their classrooms. According to the Corporation for Public Broadcasting (1991), teachers have made *Reading Rainbow* the most used TV program in schools. The FLA approach, however, encompasses much more than TV use in the classroom. It presents a framework or model for working with parents or for schools to work cooperatively with other community agencies to help develop family literacy. In her unpublished paper, McMahon (1993) discusses the importance of home-school relationships that have been long recognized by major researchers in the field of reading. She quotes one conclusion made by Catherine Snow and Jeanne Chall: "Across all grades we studied, children made greater gains where their parents were in direct contact [with schools], regardless of whether the contacts were initiated by parents or teachers" (p. 5).

Recognition of home-school programs is also reflected in the priority that Even Start and now Head Start place on outreach to and involvement of parents, as mentioned in Chapter 11. More and more schools are considering their responsibility to involve parents in their children's learning—especially parents who otherwise view schools with suspicion or outright hostility.

It is important to note that what FLA has been careful to establish is a philosophical stance that we do not know it all. We do know that we can work with parents and community groups to develop activities and parent involvement programs that encompass their concerns, perspectives, and needs with their help and input. What we are able to provide is a wonderful, free resource: quality TV programming that is highly motivational. What we can develop together is a program involving children with their parents in literacy activities. In one example of such a program in Boston at the Cambodian Mutual Assistance Association (a nonprofit educational center for Cambodian refugees offering ESL and GED classes, daycare for preschoolers, and other services), the fact that their children were acclimating more quickly to a new country was embarrassing to the mothers involved in the ESL class. That is, until the day that they and the center's director thought of the idea of the mothers' teaching their children a childhood rhyme in their native Khmai while discussing how to translate "Frog and Toad Are Friends," a *Long Ago & Far Away* program. A special bond was created, and eventually four of the mothers translated the story into Khmai, complete with illustrations. They then shared the outcome with the kindergarten class, which included some of their children. The classroom visit was "joyful" according to the center's director, and most important, the mothers felt confident by feeling that they could contribute to their children's education.

If your school serves an at-risk population and you are interested in pursuing this approach, the first step might be to contact your local public TV station's outreach or instructional department or director. If they are already involved in the FLA program, they will most certainly be eager to establish a school-based site. Be prepared to explain how there is already an existing parent program at your school or how one can be developed. If, however, your PBS is not familiar with the FLA, the following outline will help you start your own program.

### Starting a FLA Program at Your School

*1. Determine the status of your population and school and home involvement.* As already noted, is there a large at-risk population? Are there any groups or individuals that you can cooperate with, for example, an active parent volunteer program? Try to enlist at least one more teacher if at all possible. Most important, is your school administrator supportive?

*2. Determine whether the following FLA objectives are appropriate for your community or school:* to increase parent-child interest in language, stories, and reading; to model positive parent-child interactions; to increase parent involvement in the educational life of their children; to establish a regular program that supports literacy development (at home); to increase language skills of non-native speakers of English; to model replicable activities that enhance parent-child interactions (at home) and to model selective, quality TV viewing.

*3. Outline some ideas that you think will attract parents.* Although it is important to be able to present some initial activities, be sure to personally invite several parents to participate in developing a plan they find valuable. At that first meeting, it might help to show a *Reading Rainbow* program that you think will appeal to the parents. Demonstrate how you will have the actual books for parents and children to look through while viewing the program. (Most school libraries have the videotapes and books. If not, check with your local public library.)

Describe or demonstrate the possibility of linking arts and crafts projects to a specific program. Related arts and crafts have been among the most successful activities used by FLA coordinators. Other successful FLA activities include an event in which parents were shown how to check books out of the public library and were given their own library cards. One coordinator developed a mobile *Reading Rainbow* book bag library for parents and children to take books out for a month at a time. Each bag contained one *Reading Rainbow* tape, the related feature and review books, additional related books, and an activity guide.

*4. Develop an overall plan for a semester (at minimum).* In whatever plan you develop, be sure that, at minimum, it includes a goal of positive family interactions, access to a TV and VCR as well as books, arts and crafts supplies, and snacks. In our experience, we found that providing snacks attracted parents. Be open to and flexible about parent concerns and involvement. Ideally, each different group of parents and their involvement in planning will result in slightly different programs, approaches, and related activities. Think about keeping records of your successes so that you can use actual examples to promote or fundraise for your program. A good example of an activity that has been very successful is based on the *Reading Rainbow* episode, "Through Moon and Stars and Night Skies." Prior to the viewing, children and their families shared a meal, and the video was introduced. (The book and episode recount stories of how families can be formed through adoption.) After the viewing and with encouragement by the leaders, the children and parents enthusiastically talked about their own families: How many children? How old? Where did their aunts, uncles, or grandparents live? and so forth. Then, art materials were supplied—primarily collage materials—and the parents and children were encouraged to cooperatively make a family portrait, which resulted in a great deal of discussion between parents and children. In fact, issues such as absentee family members or divorce came up and in most instances engendered a nonthreatening but meaningful discussion. In follow-up sessions, other family members were invited to attend. In one situation, some of the grand-parents invited the group to hold future meetings at the senior center.

Obviously, most teachers' background and training equip them to work with parents in developing creative programs that will motivate parent-child involvement in literacy-based interactions and activities. Teachers also have classroom resources and experiences that can be expanded into parent involvement programs and activities.

Teachers, like many other busy professionals, may have time and budget limitations. First, find out if the school library or media center director, art specialist, or cafeteria personnel can help support your program. Of course, the parents who are involved in the program should be encouraged to help organize and plan the sessions. Next, check with community groups; we found that there were many people from the community who were willing to volunteer help to the FLA effort. We also

*A father and his children use their literacy skills to work on a project together.*

found that local businesses were willing to donate small amounts of money for us to purchase videos, books, snacks, and art supplies. In some communities, local sites received a small amount of funding from local fraternal groups.

## Recommended Reading

Because family literacy issues and theory have not been at the education forefront for very long, studies about TV and family literacy are in short supply. It might be useful to teachers and others, however, who are not acquainted with the study of the effects of TV, particularly in relation to children, to take some time to browse through the following texts. One of the most comprehensive books (referenced earlier) is *Television and the American Child* by George Comstock (1991). In an exhaustive review of the research conducted by behavioral scientists over the last 40 years, Comstock focuses on TV's effects on young children and adolescents. His assessment of commonly held beliefs in light of the most recent research and his opinion of conflicting research results are especially valuable. In *Television and Child Development*, Judith Van Evra (1990) integrates communication and developmental perspectives. By focusing on cognitive and social and emotional development, she helps the reader understand the "complex and significant interplay between other forces in a child's life and the television viewing experience" (p. xvii).

Other books worth reviewing include *Television and America's Children*, in which Edward Palmer (1988) talks about the untapped educational potential of the medium. In the process of calling for a solution to the continuing crisis in children's TV, Palmer discusses the failure of the commercial networks and points to the success of children's TV on the international scene. *Children's Understanding of Television* (Bryant & Anderson, 1983) is a compilation of research on children's attention to and comprehension of TV and an interesting companion to the Comstock book. The contributors are academic researchers, so the writing is formal, but for those who are interested in primary research, the book may be a useful resource. *Images of Life on Children's Television* (Barcus, 1983) delves into the issues of TV's portrayal of sex roles, racial minorities, and families. Due to its publication date, some of the "politically correct" language may be missing, but the reality is that the problems Barcus identifies have remained the same and in some cases have worsened. The lack of positive roles for African, Asian, or Hispanic Americans is only one of the current, disheartening examples. It is important to understand the scope of these problems and their subtleties when using TV as a tool. *Teaching Television* by Dorothy and Jerome Singer and Diana Zuckerman (1981) is, despite its publication date, still a valuable resource as a guide to helping children view TV critically. Not only do the authors point out problems, but they also offer actual ideas and exercises for parents and children that can help encourage communication between them.

## A Look Toward the Future

The FLA goal is to help all families have fulfilling, worthwhile literacy opportunities. At-risk populations are often weary of one-time, do-gooder events. A long-term, permanent program with top-level support is the only helpful and meaningful approach. If you are interested in initiating a family literacy program, above all, do not make assumptions about parents' concerns and needs until you have met with and listened to them. Even though the FLA created a guide, it studiously avoided a set group of activities or approaches with its participants. A major element of the FLA's success is the individualization of each application to the specific participants at each site; a path must adapt in concert with each new group of parents. Last of all, this is not the solution to all the school community's problems. It is not likely that the FLA approach will drastically change participants' lives; however, it just might help them change their attitude toward reading and books.

### References

Barcus, F.E. (1983). *Images of life on children's television: Sex-roles, minorities and families.* New York: Praeger.
Bryant, J., & Anderson, D.R. (Eds.). (1983). *Children's understanding of television: Research on attention and comprehension.* New York: Academic.
Comstock, G., with Paik, H. (1991). *Television and the American child.* New York: Academic.
Corporation for Public Broadcasting. (1991). *Summary report: Study of school uses of television and video, 1990–1991 school year.* Washington, DC.
Leitner, R.K. (1991). *Comparing the effects on reading comprehension of educational video, direct experience and print.* Unpublished doctoral dissertation, University of San Francisco, CA.
McMahon, A. (1993). *Children at risk: The need for systematic change in home/school relationships.* Unpublished paper, University of Massachusetts at Boston, Boston, MA.
Palmer, E.L. (1988). *Television and America's children: A crisis of neglect.* New York: Oxford University Press.
RMC Research Corporation. (1992, June). *Family Literacy Alliance evaluation [of the pilot phase].* Final report. Portsmouth, NH: Author.
RMC Research Corporation. (1993, August). *Family Literacy Alliance evaluation of ten model PBS stations.* Final report. Portsmouth, NH: Author.
Singer, D.G., Singer, J.L., & Zuckerman, D.M. (1981). *Teaching television: How to use TV to your child's advantage.* New York: Dial.
Van Evra, J. (1990). *Television and child development.* Hillsdale, NJ: Erlbaum.

# Part Three

◆◆◆

## Developing New Practices: Research and Perspectives

The purpose of this section is to provide information from varying perspectives for practitioners to develop new initiatives in the family literacy field and to learn to fully incorporate different cultural and ethnic backgrounds in programs to suit family needs. In the first chapter, Colin Harrison addresses family literacy practices in the United Kingdom. Although this book deals with family literacy mainly from the U.S. point of view, we felt it important to discuss the issue from another national perspective. Harrison's chapter aims to do three things: to talk about what the term *family literacy* means in the United Kingdom; to give information on umbrella organizations that have attempted to widen the availability of information about literacy work, especially literacy partnerships; and to give some examples of family literacy practices in the United Kingdom. This chapter reinforces the fact that family literacy has worldwide relevance and that all perspectives should be considered when developing new programs.

The authors in the remaining chapters in this section discuss their observations of literacy events that occur in the routine of daily family life and the effects of different types of family literacy on children's developing concepts about literacy. The authors make no deliberate or explicit connection to the school curriculum or to school- or community-based goals; rather, they focus on how families use literacy to mediate their social and community lives. Unfortunately, families that are from minority or multicultural backgrounds or those that are considered disadvantaged are too often viewed in their deficits and dilemmas rather than in the richness of their heritage and experiences. Educators emphasize how parents can learn from schools about family literacy activities but give little attention to how schools might learn from parents. Families can of course learn a great deal about literacy development from the school, but it is also true that teachers need to learn more about how parents and children share literacy on a daily basis and to explore how such events can serve school learning. The focus of this section is on what can be learned from and about families. This information should be used to help design appropriate new programs to suit the needs of families from diverse backgrounds.

Linda Baker, Robert Serpell, and Susan Sonnenschein describe opportunities for literacy-related learning in the homes of urban preschoolers. Their chapter begins with a brief discussion of five dimensions of early literacy development on which a child's home experiences can have a significant influence. From their study of prekindergarten children and their families, the authors document the home experiences through which these aspects of early literacy are nurtured across several different sociocultural groups. Findings help us understand the contexts in which children from various backgrounds experience literacy as they make the transition into formal schooling. How this type of information might be used as a resource for the cooperation of parents and teachers in furthering children's literacy development is discussed.

Diane H. Tracey investigates the practice of children reading aloud to their parents at home. She provides information regarding what is known about this practice and offers practical suggestions to educators interested in helping parents with their children's oral reading. Tracey also presents the findings of her own research on the topic, and she focuses on the implication of all the research for practitioners.

In the next chapter, Daniel Madigan describes the various forms of written and oral literacy that occurred in the lives of adults from an inner-city setting he studied. These adults are family members of children with whom he had worked to explore children's critical uses of literacy. Madigan takes a close look at three different cases, one in which, for example, a grandmother used her knowledge of the purposes for reading and writing to influence her grandson, who was having difficulty with these processes in elementary school.

The last chapter in this section, by Vivian L. Gadsden, suggests that parents' participation in literacy programs depends on how they perceive literacy and literate individuals. Gadsden describes the perceptions of African American and Puerto Rican parents participating in a series of literacy workshops in a Head Start program and contends that learners' images are fundamental openings to working with families in literacy programs. In terms of implications for practice, this study promotes the idea that parents and other caregivers should be collaborators in the development of literacy programs—in the evolution of images through planned activities that generate discourse, engage parents in the development of ideas and approaches, and build on their strengths.

# Family Literacy Practices in the United Kingdom—An International Perspective

**Colin Harrison**
*University of Nottingham, Nottingham, England*

In *Reading for Fun*, Dina Thorpe (1988, pp. 1–7) opens with a series of vignettes describing a family reading group meeting. The sense of what such meetings are—how they are conducted and what effect they have—gradually emerges through the words of the librarian, parents, and children who attend.

> Child: It's a library and you go into it and there are quite a few tables laid out with books, quite a few different, all new.
>
> Child: It's somewhere where you can talk to people about books and hear people talk about books, and people show you interesting books.
>
> Parent: I showed one to Mary and then she read it and then I found another one in the series and she read that one as well.
>
> Parent: Perhaps the cover of some of them took his eye that he might not have picked if he was only looking at the spine of the book on the shelf.
>
> Parent: He picks out his books a bit more, not by the picture on the cover. He goes into it a bit deeper.
>
> Child: There's some...grub and some drink.
>
> Child: I like the biscuits.
>
> Parent: It's more social than anything else.

Librarian: Parents seem to sort through the books quite a lot. The fact that the parents go, that they go with the children, encourages them.

Child: It is better if my Mum comes, because usually while I am looking at one pile, my Mum looks at another pile and finds some books.

Parent: I liked the three of you saying briefly what some of the books were about. I think that was a good idea, because you can't always tell what a book is going to be like.

Child: You explained books, if you liked them, to people—made people laugh if they liked them. If you wanted to make them laugh you read them the funny bits.

Child: You can take as many books as you like, you can read as many books as you like, and after you've chosen your books in a little while, people sit down and talk about some more books, about how they like them and everything, and then after that you are allowed to check in your books, and maybe collect a few more books, and then you can go home.

It is clear from this range of comments that the meetings meant different things to different participants—and, indeed, that literacy, reading, and books are viewed in a wide variety of ways. In the United Kingdom, as in other countries, the issue of what we mean by *literacy* is not trivial. Definitions can empower some groups and disempower others, and many reading professionals share Auerbach's (1989) view, explained in her Chapter 2 in this volume, that the ways in which we use the term literacy carry certain assumptions.

Consider this statement: "Poor standards of literacy lead to unemployment, which leads to poverty, which in turn leads directly to crime." These words were spoken by Norman Tebbitt, Secretary of State for Employment under Margaret Thatcher and a former chair of the Conservative Party. Some people would accept these words as an obvious truth, but to many of those working in the literacy field in the United Kingdom, the statement is inflammatory, misleading, and false. To imply that teachers are responsible for rising crime, which many commentators felt Tebbitt wished to assert, seems simplistic as well as harsh, but there are other assumptions in the statement that also need to be explored. Does improving literacy levels lead to fuller employment? This is by no means certain, although it seems that for many politicians, literacy is a commodity valued primarily because it contributes to the economy. But if everyone in the United Kingdom were literate, it is still likely that unemployment would be serious if the economy were weak. And is literacy the sole responsibility of the schools, as is often suggested by politicians and others? In the United Kingdom, many groups have attempted to treat literacy in a way that acknowledges this perception but also recognizes that some definitions of literacy tend to disregard the significance of individuals, undervalue linguistic and cultural diversity, and ignore the role of the family.

What we are talking about here is a difference of perspective, a difference that can sometimes lead to misunderstanding as well as to distinct ways of approaching the design and implementation of literacy teaching in schools and in literacy projects conducted outside of the classroom. The conflict is between a definition of literacy that falls within the boundaries of what is sometimes called a "deficit model" and those that follow more closely what I will call a "wealth model," similar to the strengths model explained earlier in Chapter 12. Of course, the term *deficit model* is pejorative; it is used most frequently by those who prefer the wealth model to emphasize what they find unacceptable in the other perspective. Because the deficit model stresses that illiteracy is dangerous to society in that it leads to unemployment, poverty, and crime, those who hold this view advocate for government involvement in and general funding for intervention programs. The wealth model, by contrast, argues that every family strives to develop the literacy of its members, often in harsh economic and social contexts. It suggests that deficit models undervalue the literacy skills that every family has, skills that are often crucial to survival but are not noted or valued in assessments of literacy levels in populations. Literacy projects built on wealth models attempt to approach the issue of literacy development from within the family rather than through intervention from without, as Auerbach stressed. They do this by recognizing the importance of the literacies already present and seeking to build on them.

In the United Kingdom literacy workers face an ethical dilemma when seeking to attract financing to develop their programs. The dilemma comes from the fact that government and industry are much more likely to fund projects that work for the deficit model and stress the economic and social dangers of illiteracy and the hope that literacy initiatives will avert or diminish the possibility of social and economic collapse. Major, well-funded projects tend, therefore, to be ones that are based, broadly speaking, on the deficit model. By contrast, wealth model projects tend to be small, operate at the local level, begin with individuals working with families, and go on to involve at most small groups of people. In essence, the dilemma is this: if you wish to attract major funding for a project, you are more likely to be successful if your proposal is written in the discourse of a deficit model, even if your preference is for a wealth model.

Another interesting aspect of family literacy in the United Kingdom is that the term itself is not widely used. Perhaps this is so because there are so few high-profile literacy projects, and the only major one is funded by the Adult Literacy and Basic Skills Unit. Because ALBSU is associated primarily with adult basic education, the terms *family literacy* and *adult literacy* have come to be closely linked in some people's minds, so the term family literacy is particularly connected with this organization. The unit has been given substantial funding from central government to develop a range of family literacy programs, all of which stress an intergenerational model of family literacy with great emphasis on parents and children learning to read together.

Another group that has brought some attention to the family literacy issue—if not to the term itself—is the National Literacy Association, which grew out of an attempt to bring together literacy organizations, politicians, trade unionists, community representatives, writers, parents, and teachers to promote literacy. In a national conference organized by the association in 1992, Sheila Wolfendale made a helpful contribution to discussions of the family's role in literacy acquisition by listing a series of central assumptions that she felt should underpin all research on parental involvement in the development of children's literacy. The list merits fuller discussion than is possible here, but I shall simply present it as an example of an attempt to give central attention to the part played by the parents (or other caregivers) in family literacy activity.

- All parents care about their children's welfare and well-being.
- Parents want to do what they believe to be in their child's best interest.
- Parents want to cooperate.
- Parents will respond to invitations to participate in school if they can see the benefit to their children.
- Parents are the primary educators of their children and are experts on their children.
- Parents' and teachers' skills complement each other.
- Parents often have vital information and insights concerning their children.
- All parents have the right to be involved in and can make a contribution to their children's education.
- Parents should be involved in decision making, not simply receiving information.
- Parents can be involved effectively in teaching their children.

All this relates directly to what we know about how literacy develops. In Scotland, for example, parents, grandparents, and other caregivers tend to teach children to read. Margaret Clark (1976), who documented the literacy activities in families in which the children learned to read before going to school, wrote, "While half the [Scottish] parents felt the children were helped daily, many stressed that this help was casual rather than systematic, and that it was part of their daily life rather than something separate" (p. 53). In other words, in Scotland, family literacy is part of the culture. The result is that reading standards in Scotland are higher than those in England and Wales, and some reading tests even use separate Scottish norms to compensate for this.

Unfortunately for those of us in the rest of the United Kingdom, we are not able simply to document organized family literacy initiatives in Scotland and learn from them. After all, when family literacy is part of the culture, it is unlikely to be the focus of development programs. Clearly, the existence of effective literacy practices is not always reflected in funded and researched family literacy initiatives, and to consider funded programs only is to miss at least part of the point—it is like attempting to describe how a culture keeps itself healthy by studying only its hospital system and not looking at how its people live. In this chapter, therefore, when I describe some family literacy initiatives that have received funding, it is always with the understanding that these are only a part of family literacy. Family literacy is about all the literacy activities that occur in families, and family literacy projects are best viewed as augmenting what is already there rather than as filling a vacuum.

## Parents and Reading: Two School-Initiated Programs

Hewison's research into reading attainment in the London area (reported in Hewison & Tizard, 1980) demonstrated that parental help with reading was a better predictor of a child's reading success than was intelligence, and that this effect was sustained across socioeconomic groups and was independent of the home language. The Haringey project (Schofield, 1979) was an intervention project aimed at establishing whether the effect Hewison noted could be achieved through systematically encouraging parents to listen to their children reading. Researchers set up three experimental groups at each of two project schools in Haringey, a working-class area of north London. Parents of children in the intervention classes were encouraged to listen to their children read at least two or three times per week, and researchers visited each home to explain and monitor this process. One control group experienced no special program, while another received remedial assistance in school four times weekly. The researchers reported that the home-intervention program was associated with significant gains in reading attainment in both project schools. The control group made the expected chronological gains in standardized reading tests, but the home-reading group gained significantly more, and success was recorded across the whole range of reading attainment in this group. Equally encouraging was the fact that parents in the home involvement group welcomed the advice they were offered, and even if they had had very little education themselves, they proved to be excellent in a collaborative role. The home involvement group included parents who might have been described as "illiterate" in other contexts, along with parents who were not fluent speakers of English. This project received a good deal of publicity, especially within teachers' organizations, and it has been widely copied (Bastiani & Bailey, 1992). For a more complete account of it, see Bloom's (1987) *Partnerships with Parents in Reading.*

The House of Fiction is another well-known school-based initiative. This group was an informal association of teachers from nine primary schools in Nottinghamshire who chose to meet to share practice and experience. They came together, like other groups of teachers, not because of any national or local policy, but because they wished to support one another in involving parents in teaching children to read. They recorded their ideas in a small book, *Building a House of Fiction* (House of Fiction Group, 1989), which has become widely known in England.

The House of Fiction teachers had the dual goals of developing partnerships with parents and of creating a project that did not use a published reading scheme or basal program. Instead, they wanted to use what is called in the United Kingdom the "real books" approach. This approach calls for individualized instruction and, as in "whole language," a plentiful supply of children's literature and picture books. The emphasis is on building meaning from and creating enjoyment in reading rather than on moving to the next book in a series, and the House of Fiction teachers felt that partnership with and support from parents was essential for the approach to be successful. As Marcia Puckey, one of the teachers involved in the project, made clear, it was the group's view that parents have to be fully involved from the outset in all aspects of the developing reading processes of their children (House of Fiction Group, 1989). Her school distributed a booklet illustrating how parents can help develop children's literacy at home, and the booklet was promoted and discussed with parents.

*Parents should be fully involved from the onset in all aspects of their child's literacy development.*

Children in the project, who were all about four or five years old and were attending six different schools, were given books to take home each evening—not just one, but often three or four—and "comment books" in which parents were kept informed by the teachers as to why and how their child had selected their books. Parents could also use these books to correspond with the teachers. Meetings with large groups of parents were avoided. Instead, every parent was interviewed individually by his or her child's teacher at a convenient time. More than 50 parents came regularly into Puckey's school to assist by hearing children read and to augment the home involvement program in other ways. Such an approach is very demanding in terms of time and commitment for both parents and teachers, but for Marcia Puckey and her colleagues the partnership has been enormously important. The results in terms of the children's enthusiasm for and success in reading make the efforts worthwhile.

## Nonschool-Initiated Programs

With the publication of more research on the benefits of parental involvement in their children's development of literacy and the documented success of programs such as Haringey and the House of Fiction, other projects encouraging parents to share books with their children sprang up all over the United Kingdom. Many of these were associated with the concept of "paired reading." Paired reading is a procedure that uses nonprofessional tutors, and it has been fully described and carefully evaluated by Keith Topping, the person with whom the concept is most closely associated (see, for example, Topping & Linsay, 1992). Although the process is often used with pairs of adults, unrelated children and adults, or older and younger children, it is particularly helpful for parents whose literacy skills are not highly developed and who are uncertain about how to help their children. In paired reading, both tutor and tutee read aloud simultaneously from the same book, with the tutor gradually taking a less active role as the tutee becomes more confident. This instructional method, depicted in the flow chart in the figure on page 231, has become prominent in the United Kingdom as part of the parent involvement program encouraged by many schools, but it is also used increasingly in nonschool projects.

Two nonschool initiatives that have become well known in the United Kingdom are the Family Reading Groups project (Beverton et al., 1991; Obrist, 1978; United Kingdom Reading Association, 1993) of the United Kingdom Reading Association, IRA's national affiliate in the United Kingdom, and the Children's Book Foundation's Bookstart project (Children's Book Foundation, 1993). Both projects place great emphasis on the role of parents and other caregivers in helping children develop a love of reading through sharing books within the family.

The first family reading groups were set up 15 years ago, following a decision by the UKRA Research Committee to undertake some action research at the grass-roots level in the area of initial literacy development. Research in Bedfordshire (Obrist, 1978) highlighted problems in two areas: lack of books in many homes and lack of liaison between home and school. In response, Cecilia Obrist for UKRA and Christine Wright, a young people's librarian, initiated a series of monthly early-evening meetings for parents and children at which library books were displayed and discussed. At first, talks on children's literature were delivered by library staff, but as the nature of the meetings became more familiar, a review form was devised on which parents and children each wrote (or dictated) a review of books they were reading. At the end of the meeting, children selected library books to take home. Family reading groups had one central aim: to share with children the enjoyment of books and stories.

The first pilot groups met in a single school in Bedfordshire, but as the initiative became more widely known, parents, teachers, school librarians, and public librarians sponsored new groups. Meetings took

# An Outline of Paired Reading

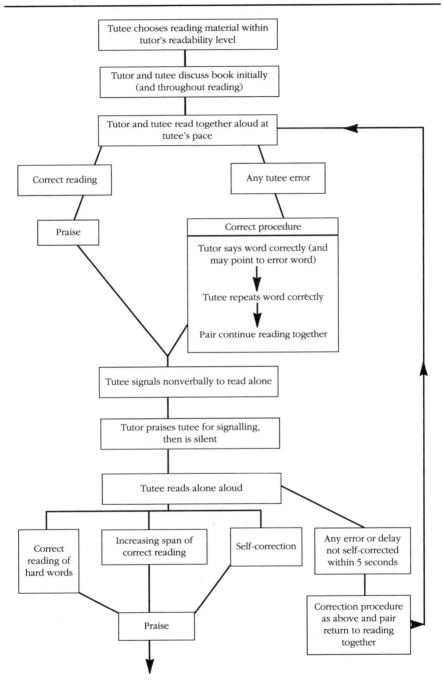

From Topping and Linsay (1992), *Research Papers in Education,* 7(3), p. 200. Reprinted with permission.

place in homes, libraries, or schools. Groups focusing on preschool children were formed, but most family reading groups involved children up to age 12. Because a supply of books for borrowing was essential, meetings generally included the participation of a librarian. Many of the parents who attended family reading groups were not members of local libraries, and library staff were especially pleased to bring awareness of library services to this audience.

In 1988 UKRA received funds from the Department of Education to explore the operation of family reading groups and evaluate their effectiveness. As part of the evaluation conducted by Beverton and colleagues (1991), it was decided to set up a number of new groups and to monitor the effectiveness of these as well as of the existing ones, in order to be able to report more fully on conditions for initiating them and sustaining their success. At first, most groups had been located in the south of England in relatively affluent rural areas, and the new groups were set up in the northwest, in less affluent areas around the urban center of Manchester. Of the seven new groups that were established, three had large memberships (80 percent or more) drawn from the Indian subcontinent, and, in these communities most fathers knew English but home-bound mothers did not. Most of the new groups were run by teachers or librarians, but two were run by parents with occasional input from literacy professionals.

In their report, Beverton and colleagues noted that the new groups were a success. Parents who were not confident in English had their children act as interpreters. Meetings in the school with the highest proportion of minority parents became so popular that weekly sessions were held, and fathers took time off work or adjusted their working hours to attend and to drive the home-bound mothers—who usually do not drive—to the program site. Those with new babies or preschoolers often brought these younger children along. Some mothers began to learn English, and a bilingual community worker gave assistance to those who wished to learn how to read stories in English to their children. Whole-group discussion was not widespread in this group, but families exchanged experiences in small groups, calling upon the assistance of teachers, librarians, or the community worker as necessary.

In fact, it seemed that everyone who participated in the groups—both the established ones and the new—benefited. The children's voluntary reading became more frequent, their listening and speaking skills improved, their vocabularies increased, and their knowledge of books and genres grew. Their confidence in their opinions increased, too, although naturally this took a little time. (In the first meetings, children's contributions to discussions made up 20 percent of the discourse; a year later, this had increased to 80 percent.) But parents gained as well: they reported that their knowledge of children's literature had been extended, their understanding of their children's needs had deepened, and they felt happier and more confident in dealing with teachers and school administrators. In addition, the teachers valued this informal contact with parents and students, and both parents and teachers reported that they gained from working with and learning from librarians.

The UKRA produced a film on how to run family reading groups, and it has followed up the research report with a booklet of guidelines summarizing what was discovered and giving detailed advice on how to set up and maintain a new group (United Kingdom Reading Association, 1993). The following is a list of factors that Beverton and colleagues (1991) reported were crucial in developing and sustaining successful family reading groups:

◆ Parents need to be involved as leaders, not simply as participants.

◆ A friendly atmosphere should be established through such things as book-related games.

◆ Discussion should be focused on books, and everyone's comments and questions should be valued.

◆ Leaders should be comfortable in facilitating discussion and must have a genuine love of books, but they do not have to have a professional background in children's literature, reading, or education.

◆ Librarians' knowledge and published book lists should be tapped for information about books.

◆ Parents should be encouraged to learn about their own and their children's literacy development.

◆ Recruitment efforts should be active, and all participants should attend regularly.

Bookstart, unlike the other initiatives described here, is aimed specifically at the parents of very young children. The Children's Book Foundation, a charity that receives support from trade publishers, worked with children's librarians from Birmingham's Library Services department to launch the project. Now, all over the United Kingdom, the packages of promotional material, health care information, and free samples of baby products that are given to new parents are supplemented with a package explaining and encouraging parental involvement in the development of their child's language and reading. Parents are given a letter (in English or another language, if the latter is more appropriate to the parents' needs), a book, a poetry card, an invitation to join the local library, book lists, a poster, a bookmark, information about local bookstores, and a questionnaire. A subsequent questionnaire assesses changes in book use and purchase.

At the heart of the Bookstart project is the belief that early support of literacy within families will benefit children and that the sharing of books in families will encourage a positive attitude toward reading. At the very least, the project has helped avoid the situation in which some children begin school without ever having held a book (see Wade and Moore, 1993, for an evaluation of Bookstart).

## What Do We Mean by Partnership?

Each of the projects and initiatives I have described in this chapter is based on partnerships among any number of parents, teachers, librarians, community workers, publishers, representatives of charities, children, or academics. It seems appropriate to conclude, as I began, by reflecting on the discourse of literacy, but this time by considering the use of the term *partnership*. A partnership can be a shared and equal relationship; it can also be an arrangement within which there is a senior and a junior participant. If there has been a change in the use of this term in the United Kingdom in relation to reading, it perhaps revolves around the recognition by reading professionals that it is no longer acceptable to regard parents as junior partners in the business of their children's education. Today teachers acknowledge that the role of parents is crucial, and many actively support each parent's unique and valuable contribution to the partnership of developing his or her child's literacy. Perhaps we still have a little way to go before we realize that, when it comes to family literacy, in many important respects those of us who work in education are really the junior partners.

### References

Auerbach, E.R. (1989). Toward a socio-contextual approach to family literacy. *Harvard Educational Review, 59,* 165–181.

Bastiani, J., & Bailey, G. (1992). *Directory of home-school initiatives in the U.K.* London: Royal Society for the Encouragement of Arts, Manufactures, and Commerce.

Beverton, S., Hunter-Carsch, M., Stuart, A., & Obrist, C. (1991). *Family Reading Groups project report.* Ormskirk, UK: United Kingdom Reading Association.

Bloom, W. (1987). *Partnership with parents in reading.* Sevenoaks, UK: Hodder & Stoughton.

Children's Book Foundation. (1993). *Bookstart: An introduction.* London: Book Trust.

Clark, M.M. (1976). *Young fluent readers.* London: Heinemann.

Hewison, J., & Tizard, J. (1980). Parental involvement in reading attainment. *British Journal of Educational Psychology, 50,* 209–215.

House of Fiction Group. (1989). *Building a house of fiction*. Sheffield, UK: National Association for the Teaching of English.

Obrist, C. (1978). *How to run family reading groups*. Ormskirk, UK: United Kingdom Reading Association.

Schofield, W. (1979). *Haringey reading project* (Final Report to the Department of Education and Science).

Thorpe, D. (1988). *Reading for fun*. Cranfield, UK: Cranfield Press.

Topping, K., & Linsay, G.A. (1992). Paired reading: A review of the literature. *Research Papers in Education, 7*(3), 199–246.

United Kingdom Reading Association. (1993). *Running family reading groups: Guidelines for teachers*. Widnes, UK: Author.

Wade, B., & Moore, M. (1993). *Bookstart* (Book Trust Rep. 2). London: Book Trust.

# Chapter 17

# Opportunities for Literacy Learning in the Homes of Urban Preschoolers

**Linda Baker, Robert Serpell, and Susan Sonnenschein**
*National Reading Research Center and University of Maryland,*
*College Park, Maryland*

Researchers and educators have identified many characteristics of the home environment that are associated with literacy development, as mentioned in Parts One and Two of this volume. However, we do not yet have a detailed understanding of how children's everyday activities contribute to literacy development. In this chapter we describe the first phase of an ongoing longitudinal study, the Early Childhood Project, that addresses this issue by exploring the contexts in which young urban children from various sociocultural groups become literate. The framework for the project draws on several contemporary perspectives. We share Bronfenbrenner's (1979) view that human development occurs in a context of overlapping and interdependent systems of social and cultural organization. To understand any aspect of development, including literacy development, it is important to examine each of the relevant contexts and their interrelations (for example, home, school, and community), including the beliefs and values of the adults responsible for structuring the environments (Serpell, 1993; Sonnenschein, Brody, & Munsterman, in press). Our research is also guided by the view that when children are reared in a literate society, they are exposed from infancy onward to cultural practices that provide opportunities for learning about reading and writing (Morrow, 1989; Sulzby & Teale, 1991). This learning occurs in a social context as the child gradually acquires competence through interaction with others who are literate (Vygotsky, 1978).

The opportunities to which children are exposed have the potential to influence several complementary dimensions of early literacy development. These include the development of (1) knowledge about print; (2) knowledge about the structure of narrative; (3) phonological awareness (knowledge about the sounds of language); and (4) positive attitudes toward reading. Our study documents the home experiences through which these dimensions of early literacy are nurtured across several different sociocultural groups.

# Dimensions of Early Literacy

## Development of Knowledge About Print

Although all preschool children in U.S. society have at least some exposure to print during the course of their daily lives, the nature and extent of exposure varies considerably. Children who have frequent and varied positive experiences with print are more likely to acquire print-related knowledge that is conducive to literacy learning in the early school grades. They become aware of print in their environment, they come to understand the various functions of print and the meaning of its symbol system, and they develop an interest in the written word and a motivation to learn to read on their own.

The early experience of joint storybook reading, which has been discussed throughout this volume, stands out for its well-documented effects on knowledge about print as well as the other aspects of literacy development we are considering. Although storybook reading is widely regarded by educators as an important means by which parents prepare their children for school, an absence of storybook reading does not necessarily mean that children are growing up without exposure to literate practices. Other types of literacy events, such as reading the mail or looking up a television listing, provide children with opportunities to learn about the functions and uses of print. In our study we explore children's participation in various kinds of activities that have the potential to increase their knowledge about print.

## Development of Knowledge of Narrative Structure and Function

Home experiences that promote knowledge of narrative structure and function are relevant for literacy development, in part because most of the print materials children encounter in the early years of schooling consist of stories. Children understand material better when it is presented in a familiar structural and stylistic format. Reading stories to children will foster this familiarity, as will oral storytelling and conversation. Our study explores these various opportunities available to children for learning about narrative structure and function.

## Development of Phonological Awareness

Phonological awareness involves knowledge about and sensitivity to the sounds that comprise language (for example, phonemes). There is a well-established relationship between phonological awareness and reading achievement (Sulzby & Teale, 1991). Opportunities in the home for language play, singing, and rhyming are likely to be particularly valuable in fostering children's sensitivity to the sounds of their language, an important precursor to their learning spelling-sound correspondences. In our study we explore the availability of such opportunities.

## Development of Positive Attitudes Toward Reading

Many different kinds of experiences in the home can foster positive attitudes toward reading, along with an interest in reading and a motivation to learn to read. Joint storybook reading is once again an experience of particular importance. Parents who read with their children show by their behavior that they value reading and that it is a pleasurable activity. In addition, storybook reading gives children an opportunity to have a warm and supportive interaction with their parents.

The beliefs, values, attitudes, and expectations parents or other caregivers hold with respect to literacy are likely to have a strong effect on children's motivation to read, as mentioned earlier in this volume. The opportunities parents provide for literacy, such as taking their child to the library, implicitly reflect the value they place on literacy. Parents also convey explicit messages that affect a child's motivation to read, as when they express positive attitudes toward reading and encourage their children to read. In our study we explore the cultural meanings that inform the activities through which caregivers first introduce a child to literacy (Serpell et al., 1993).

Baker, Serpell, & Sonnenschein

# The Methods of the Early Childhood Project

## The Participants

A total of 41 prekindergarten children and their primary caregivers participated in the phase of the Early Childhood Project described here. The children were enrolled at six public elementary schools serving Baltimore, Maryland, neighborhoods with four contrasting demographic profiles, populated mainly by low-income African American families in two schools; low-income Euro-American families in two schools; a mix of low-income African and Euro-American families in one school; and a mix of middle-income African and Euro-American families in one school. Note that most families residing in the middle-income neighborhood are not as affluent as typical middle-income suburban families.

All the children in the project had at least one older sibling. Approximately half the families were headed by single parents; this figure was similar across neighborhood types. In all but one family, the caregiver who participated most actively in the project was the child's mother.

## How Information Was Collected from the Families

During an initial home visit, each child's primary caregiver was asked to keep either an oral or written diary documenting all the activities that the child engaged in during the course of one week (for example, going to the supermarket, doing homework, watching TV, and so on). The purpose of asking the caregiver to keep a diary was to give us a record of the everyday activities that the child engages in, with particular interest in those that may foster literacy. It is important to note, however, that the parents were not informed that our primary interest was in literacy, so their records were unlikely to be biased in this direction; they were simply told that we were interested in learning about *all* the experiences children have at home. The diary information was used during a second home visit, in conjunction with follow-up questioning, to complete an "ecological inventory" of household literacy opportunities.

A structured portion of the ecological inventory explored children's participation in specific activities in the following areas: games and play; mealtime activities; interaction with TV, video, and music; recurrent outings; and reading, writing, and drawing. The parents were asked to indicate the frequency of their child's participation in each activity as well as the principal coparticipants. For example, within the area of game and play activities, the parent rated pretend play, play with board games, singing, oral storytelling, and play with educational toys. The specific activities selected for inclusion in the inventory were seen as potentially significant influences on the development of knowledge and competencies associated with early reading, as discussed earlier (see Baker et al., 1994, for further detail).

## An Illustrative Excerpt from a Diary

The diaries, parent interviews, and structured portions of the ecological inventory are rich sources of information that reveal the diversity of literacy-relevant resources and opportunities available to children. There was considerable variation in the style, content, and length of the diaries, but we were pleasantly surprised by the willingness and even enthusiasm with which most parents approached this task. The following excerpt from one of the diaries illustrates the information they provided. The writer is a low-income African American mother who described her four-year-old son's afternoon and evening on a particular day.

> 12:00 James and I went to the job bank at unemployment and had lunch from a venders cart. He wanted to know how they got the stoves and ice boxes on the trucks. We had hot dogs and sodas.
>
> 2:00 Playtime James drew two pictures one of his family the other a bunch of worms.
>
> 2:30 Michael and Peter home after the two older brothers do homework they all play together school, cars, simon says...
>
> 6:00 James and Michael played store together they used a toy cash register. James is able to push several numbers he just can't get the hang of the money yet...

The excerpt reveals much about the child's everyday experiences that have the potential for fostering literacy. For example, James engages in various pretend-play activities where print is involved, which provide both reasons and opportunities to discover that literacy has practical value. He is also beginning to use symbolic representations through his drawing and his play with the cash register, a cognitive process that will be essential for mastering the formal symbol system of written language.

# Children's Experiences with Literacy-Fostering Potential

How do the children's home experiences relate to the four dimensions of early literacy development introduced earlier? We use two different sources of information to answer this question: (1) the frequencies of engagement in specific activities reported in the ecological inventory in response to direct questioning; and (2) the activities spontaneously reported in the diaries, classified according to the purposes of literacy they suggest. Table 1 presents the mean frequency ratings provided by caregivers for selected activities in the ecological inventory. The first column shows the mean rating for all participants, the second and third columns allow for comparison of families in the middle-income neighborhood with families in the four low-income neighborhoods; and the fourth and fifth columns allow for comparison of families in the two homogeneous Euro-American low-income neighborhoods with those in the two homogeneous African American low-income neighborhoods. Table 2 shows the percentages of caregivers who spontaneously reported in their diaries that their child participated at least once during the week in various kinds of print-related activities—those undertaken for entertainment or the cultivation of literacy skills or as part of a daily routine. (For a more detailed presentation of the data collected in this study, see Baker et al., 1994.)

## Experiences Related to Development of Knowledge About Print

Most of the children in our sample were involved with print in their environment on a regular basis, and they had many different kinds of opportunities to learn about print. Because of the diversity of experiences related to this dimension of early literacy development, we have organized our discussion according to specific kinds of activities.

*Participation in daily routines.* Much of the children's everyday contact with print comes about through participation in daily routines, as reflected both in diary data and ecological inventory data. About 60 percent of the parents in each sociocultural group spontaneously reported activities in their diaries that reflect encounters with print through daily routines, such as assisting with food preparation and shopping (see Table 2). The ecological inventory also showed that the majority of children participate in food preparation on a regular basis, on average almost once a week (see Table 1). This gives them opportunities to interact with print on food product labels, to attend to adults reading recipes or package directions, or to assist in measurement. In addition, children are taken shopping almost as frequently (see Table 1). Most stores, but especially grocery stores, are rich sources of environmental print. A low-income Euro-American mother wrote about her daughter's ability to recognize product labels at the store that enabled her to help her mother pick out the "right" cheese and cereal. A middle-income African American father revealed sensitivity to the benefits a child can derive from participation in such everyday activities: "Shopping is also a time for more awareness of the practical application of arithmetic and language arts."

## Table 1
## Frequency of Children's Participation in Selected Activities Reported by Parents in the Ecological Inventory

| | Overall Mean (n=41) | Income Level | | Ethnicity (low inc) | |
|---|---|---|---|---|---|
| | | Low (n=31) | Middle (n=10) | EurAm (n=13) | AfAm (n=10) |
| Food preparation | 1.85 | 1.74 | 2.20 | 2.15 | 1.50 |
| Shopping | 1.71 | 1.81 | 1.40 | 2.08 | 1.40 |
| Storybook reading | 2.39 | 2.26 | 2.80 | 2.46 | 2.20 |
| Pretend play | 2.35 | 2.20 | 2.80 | 2.15 | 2.44 |
| Educational toys | 1.51 | 1.41 | 1.80 | 1.17 | 2.00 |
| Oral storytelling | 1.50 | 1.47 | 1.60 | 1.46 | 2.00 |
| Meal conversation | 2.32 | 2.45 | 1.90 | 2.54 | 2.50 |
| Singing | 2.44 | 2.48 | 2.30 | 2.54 | 2.90 |

Note: Figures are based on mean frequency ratings; 0 (never), 1 (rarely—less than once a week), 2 (occasionally—at least once a week), and 3 (often—every day or almost every day).
The income-level comparisons include the full sample; the low-income ethnicity comparisons include only those families living in homogeneous neighborhoods.
EurAm = European American; AfAm = African American

## Table 2
## Percentages of Parents Spontaneously Reporting Children's Print-Related Experiences in Various Domains at Least Once in the Diaries

| | Income Level | | Ethnicity (low inc) | |
|---|---|---|---|---|
| | Low (n=31) | Middle (n=10) | EurAm (n=13) | AfAm (n=10) |
| 1. Entertainment | | | | |
| a. joint book reading | 59 | 67 | 67 | 50 |
| b. independent reading | 34 | 78 | 42 | 30 |
| c. play involving print | 41 | 67 | 42 | 30 |
| 2. Cultivation of literacy skills | | | | |
| a. homework | 48 | 44 | 42 | 60 |
| b. practice | 41 | 11 | 25 | 50 |
| 3. Daily routines | 59 | 67 | 58 | 60 |

*Joint storybook reading.* Storybook reading also provides an opportunity for children to learn about print. Most parents in each sociocultural group reported that their children had storybooks read to them at least once a week (see Table 1). Nevertheless, reading is not a *daily* activity in many of these homes. When we considered whether the parents reported that their children interacted with any type of book on a daily basis, we found income-related differences: 90 percent of the middle-income parents reported daily book reading activity, while 52 percent of the low-income parents did so. Thus, our findings indicate, in contrast to some other studies, that most of the low-income children do have opportunities to learn about print through joint storybook reading, although these opportunities do not occur as frequently as for middle-income children.

*Visits to the library.* The library is perhaps the most print-rich environment available to a child. Sociocultural differences were found in the percentages of parents who reported visits to the library at least once a month: 90 percent of the middle-income families reported that their child visited the library, whereas 43 percent of the low-income families did so.

*Independent use of print as a source of entertainment.* The child's self-initiated or independent use of print as a source of entertainment was much more frequently reflected in the diaries of middle-income parents than low-income parents (see Table 2). To illustrate, one middle-income Euro-American child had a "quiet time" every day in his room, during which he "usually reads books or plays action figures." Another child from the same community went to his room and got some books, which he and his younger sister "pretended to read to each other." And a low-income African American child "read books she has to her dolls." Kerry's spontaneous storybook sharing, shown in the photograph, also reflects this type of behavior.

Not all uses of literacy as a source of entertainment involve book reading, however. The following diary excerpt from a low-income Euro-American mother reveals her child's orientation to environmental print and her efforts to learn about it:

> Then I decided we would take a nap. Unfortunately, Meghan decided she didn't want to. But while we were laying down, she was looking at my shirt. She was having me tell her the letters on it. She was having me tell her what they were and she was saying them as she was pointing to them. I would say them, then she would say them. And she went back and said the ones she knew.

Similarly, a middle-income Euro-American child "has a good time spelling every cereal box. He draws on the chalkboard with the cereal box [in his hand] to copy letters."

*Four-year-old Kerry "reads" to her two-year-old cousin, Jimmy, during a holiday in her home.*

Children also had opportunities to explore literate practices through play. Pretend play was a common recurrent activity for a substantial number of the children across all sociocultural groups, though it appears to be most common among middle-income children (see Tables 1 and 2). Through pretend play children construct their understandings of the physical and social world, including literate practices. Approximately 25 percent of the parents in each sociocultural group indicated in their diaries that their children played school. One low-income Euro-American child "acted like she was a teacher reading to the class," and another "played school with her friend, taking turns writing on the chalkboard." In this context, too, literate behavior serves as a source of entertainment. Other relevant play activities included play with toys designed with an explicit educational focus.

Parents' descriptions of their children's early efforts to engage in literacy activities often reflected amusement but also suggest awareness of the value of such behaviors. A low-income African American mother wrote,

Him and daddy will read a book. He likes to listen to you when you read to him and then he likes to tell you the words you told him, so that makes it likes he's reading the book to you, but he's just memorizing the words.

And a middle-income Euro-American mother wrote that her son particularly likes Spot books: "He likes to lift the flags. Also they are short and words are big, so he memorizes them very easily and pretends—or actually thinks—he's reading."

*School-related activities and explicit instruction.* Because all the children participating in the study were enrolled in prekindergarten, they had many opportunities for learning about print through their experiences at school. Approximately half of the parents reported activities in their diaries that involved homework (see Table 2). All the prekindergarten teachers assigned homework of some sort, though it varied in its academic content. As described by a low-income African American mother,

The type of homework Natasha has to do right now she has to review her alphabet, she has to count from 1 to 30 which she can do that, she has to identify different pictures in her homework.

Additional opportunities for learning about print were provided by parents who engaged in explicit instruction in literacy skills of their own accord, not simply because work was sent home from school. There were sociocultural differences in the extent to which parents reported such activities, with more low-income families of both ethnicities reporting them than middle-income families (see Table 2). Parents frequently reported working with their children in identifying letters of the alphabet, teaching their children to write their names, and working with flashcards. A low-income African American mother described several instances of literacy activity for the sake of learning literacy in one of her diary entries: "After dinner it was time for Bible study, Raymond studied his work, practiced writing his name, practiced reading, and practiced saying his numbers from 1 to 40." Another mother from the same sociocultural group reported explicit literacy instruction in each day's diary entry. For example, on one day she wrote that she was "teaching her [daughter] how to spell and to identify the letters in her name using paper and pencils and flashcards."

## Experiences Related to Development of Knowledge of Narrative Structure and Function

Opportunities for acquiring knowledge of narrative structure and function arise from many everyday experiences. Storybook reading, which we have already discussed, is an activity of major importance. Here we consider two other activities: oral storytelling and mealtime conversation.

Heath (1983) has reported in her ethnographic study that children of low-income families are often exposed to elaborate narratives in the course of their everyday life, and she suggested that this experience nurtures a high level of familiarity with the structural organization of stories. We tried to learn more about this aspect of children's everyday experience in our ecological inventory by asking parents to report the frequency with which children engage in oral storytelling. Oral storytelling reportedly occurred less than once a week on average, but it may be that parents simply did not think to mention everyday narratives when asked about storytelling because they assumed we were asking about an activity engaged in purely for entertainment.

Mealtime conversation also provides an opportunity for children to acquire knowledge about narratives, as family members recount their day's activities. Here, though, the context is less likely to be perceived by parents as entertainment oriented. We found that mealtime conversation occurs with high frequency across all sociocultural groups (see Table 1), thus giving children an experience that is of well-documented value in learning about language and communication.

## Experiences Related to Development of Phonological Awareness

Virtually all children had frequent experiences that had the potential for fostering phonological awareness. Most of the children in each sociocultural group sang on a regular basis (see Table 1) and also listened to music frequently. Because songs typically include rhymes, these experiences provide an opportunity for children to become attuned to the sounds of words. As discussed earlier, such experiences are important because phonological awareness contributes to reading success. There were many spontaneous reports in the diaries dealing with singing, including references to children practicing songs they learned in school, teaching songs to siblings, and singing along with songs on TV shows. For example, a low-income African American mother wrote, "She sits there and listen to the music on the radio and whatever on the radio, she'll sit there and sing the song if she knows the song."

The diaries also included references to other activities involving rhymes. Several parents reported reading books with rhymes; a low-income Euro-American mother wrote, "I read him a book called *Nursery Rhymes,*" and a middle-income Euro-American mother wrote that her son "read" a Baa Black Sheep book to her and "went through a period of really being into nursery rhymes." In addition, many of the parents noted that their children were learning poems in school and had to practice reciting them at home.

## Experiences Related to Development of Positive Attitudes Toward Reading

Although the ecological inventory did not include any specific questions about children's attitudes toward reading, it showed the extent to which parents provided opportunities for children to learn to value reading. Thus, as discussed earlier, most children had opportunities to engage in storybook reading at least weekly, although the middle-income children were more likely to have daily interactions with books and to visit the library more often. Other researchers have found that joint storybook reading is related to later interest in independent reading and that library use is a strong predictor of motivation to read.

The diaries gave us rich insights into parents' beliefs and expectations about children's reading. Some parents explicitly wrote about their child's current attitude toward reading. For example, a middle-income African American father wrote, "Her mother reads to all of the children. We have a set of stories and the children enjoy reading time very much." Other parents expressed a desire to foster a positive attitude toward reading. A low-income Euro-American mother reported that she reads to her child every night before bed and tries to make it exciting: "Why make reading boring? It stops a person from liking it." Another mother from the same sociocultural group said she read to her children at bedtime in part to show that she herself reads and that she wants her children to read for themselves, for their own enjoyment. Also, a low-income African American mother at least implicitly recognizes that she serves as a role model: "I was reading a book, so he went and got a book to read. He's reading the book, but he's using his own words."

Sociocultural differences in attitudes toward reading may already be emerging among the children in the study. Recall that children in the middle-income homes were much more likely to use literacy as a source of entertainment than those in low-income homes. Perhaps the middle-income children have already had sufficient positive experiences with books by the time they are four years old that they are intrinsically motivated to use books to entertain themselves. This clearly seems to be true of Kerry, the middle-income suburban child in the earlier photograph. However, it is also possible that a greater availability of materials contributes to this sociocultural difference.

# Conclusions and Implications for Teachers and Schools

Our study has shown that there is quite a bit of variation in the everyday experiences of urban prekindergarten children that may be important for later literacy development. Because we will be studying the same children over a number of years and collecting measures of their early literacy, we will be able to explore this issue. In addition, information we have been gathering from parents and teachers regarding their views about children's literacy learning and their roles in the process, as well as our ongoing analysis of how the children interact with others during literate activities, will further enrich our understanding of the contexts of early literacy development.

## Cultural Variations in Parental Understandings of Literacy Acquisition

Our study revealed, consistent with other research, that there are sociocultural differences in the ways families prepare their children for literacy. Middle-income parents' reports indicated that their children are more likely to use literacy as a source of entertainment and have more book reading experiences on a daily basis than low-income children. Low-income parents reported more frequent literate activities undertaken for the purpose of learning literacy than did middle-income parents. It may be that middle-income parents prefer to provide their children with opportunities that enable them to construct their own understandings of literacy through literacy materials for independent use. Low-income parents, in contrast, may feel they need to provide more structured opportunities for their children that involve direct instruction and practice. One reason for this may be that these parents, based on their own experiences, view the acquisition of literacy as a rather difficult and unrewarding task.

If indeed middle-income families tend to adopt a more playful approach to the early socialization of literacy than low-income families, there are several possible reasons why this difference in approach may arise. First, middle-income parents may feel more secure in the area of literacy because (1) they are more highly literate; (2) their social reference group expects children to become literate early and effortlessly; or (3) they themselves have no memories of difficulty with learning to read. Second, middle-income parents may be more committed to play as a general source of learning. This view appears to be a middle-class cultural theme of late 20th-century in the United States, partly informed by theories of child development. Third, middle-income parents may be

Baker, Serpell, & Sonnenschein

more protective of young children's right to play and to be spared from chores and other arduous tasks. This view also appears to be a middle-class cultural theme, partly informed by the prevalence of labor-saving domestic appliances and by concerns with preparing children for white-collar jobs. Fourth, it is likely that middle-income parents have been exposed to the "playway" method of teaching literacy and may have become convinced that it is more effective than didactic alternatives. This view could develop through their own socialization, through conversations with other parents of slightly older children, or through reading materials such as child development books, advice columns for parents, or instructional materials aimed at teachers.

What are the possible consequences of middle-class parents' more playful approach to the socialization of literacy? We know that play is a powerful context for helping children extend emerging skills and that it is intrinsically motivating; we also know that highly structured didactic methods may generate negative emotions and rigid learning strategies. With this knowledge we may well expect that parents who favor the playful approach will generally nurture earlier development of literacy in children. On the other hand, it is also possible that the specific literacy-related knowledge middle-class children acquire through their experiences will help them master more easily the particular kinds of literacy tasks they encounter at school.

## Implications of These Cultural Variations for Teachers' Interactions with Families

In line with our own findings, Goldenberg, Reese, and Gallimore (1992) observed that low-income Hispanic parents tried to help their children by emphasizing reading readiness skills such as letter identification and spelling-sound correspondences. The authors argued that although this practice is not consistent with the meaning emphasis common in classrooms today, it should still be encouraged because (1) it is more effective and adaptive to encourage parental involvement that is consistent with existing beliefs about how children learn to read than to try to change parents' views; and (2) these skills also contribute to reading development.

Teachers of preschool and kindergarten children may be in a good position to foster among low-income parents a greater awareness of the informal opportunities for promoting literacy through daily activities and routine household tasks. This approach should reduce the likelihood of children developing a premature conception of reading as arduous that could arise if parents focus exclusively on readiness skills. It may also help to reassure parents whose own literacy is quite limited and whose memories of school include failure experiences that they are fully competent to perform a vital motivational role in their child's early encounters with print. They can perform this role by focusing on literacy's potential for pleasure and by rewarding signs of the child's emergent competence. Many parents may not be aware of the significance of early literacy behaviors and may dismiss them as cute but irrelevant. For example, a child's early attempts to "read" a storybook with which he or she is highly familiar, but which he or she is holding upside down, is a valid construction on the part of the child of what it means to read. The extent to which parents encourage, support, and value such behaviors is likely to play a major role in stimulating children's desire to participate in literate activities.

It is important to recognize, however, that the direction of influence is not unidirectional—from parent to child—but rather bidirectional; that is, children's behaviors influence those of their parents, which in turn influence future behaviors of the children. For example, a child who is read to very frequently as a toddler may develop a strong interest in reading. This interest is conveyed to the parents, who in turn provide extensive materials for the child to read. The availability of materials further enhances the child's knowledge about print and promotes the child's motivation for independent reading. Another parent may also start out reading to his or her child frequently, but the child by temperament may be restless and unwilling to sit still long enough for a complete story to be read. The parent in response will not read to the child as often, and the child will likely develop other interests. Such individual differences may occur even within the same family. One of the recurrent themes of recent crosscultural research is that there are many different routes to successful developmental outcomes. Teachers may be more helpful to parents by suggesting multiple resources and techniques than by seeking to define a single, ideal pattern of parenting.

## Potential Benefits to Teachers in Using Our Methods to Understand Children's Everyday Experiences

We believe the approach we have taken to documenting children's everyday experiences can be useful to teachers who wish to learn more about the home experiences of the children in their classes. Interviews with teachers of the children participating in our study revealed that they saw a need for knowledge about experiences available to the children at home. Our procedure affords an opportunity for teachers to learn what literacy-related resources and opportunities are available to the child at home and in the community. Understanding the range and nature of these experiences will enable teachers to design activities and social interaction structures that are consonant with the children's home experiences. Greater gains can be made in literacy learning when there is a match between the cultures of home and school (Baker et al., in press; Thompson, Mixon, & Serpell, in press). Documentation of the home experiences of young children is an important prerequisite to building connections between home and school, especially among socioculturally diverse populations. Teachers can use this information to begin a dialogue with parents about ways to establish an open interchange of experiences.

## Notes

The original research described in this chapter was supported in part by the National Reading Research Center, University of Georgia and University of Maryland, under the Educational Research and Development Centers Program (PR/AWARD No. 117A20007) as administered by the Office of Educational Research and Improvement, U.S. Department of Education. The findings and opinions do not necessarily reflect the position or policies of the National Reading Research Center, the Office of Educational Research and Improvement, or the U.S. Department of Education.

The research in this chapter represents a collaborative effort, and we deeply appreciate the contributions of our other colleagues on the research team: Hibist Astatke, Marie Dorsey, Sylvia Fernandez-Fein, Victoria Goddard-Truitt, Linda Gorham, Susan Hill, Tunde Morakinyo, Kim Munsterman, and Deborah Scher.

## References

Baker, L., Allen, J.B., Shockley, B., Pellegrini, A.D., Galda, L., & Stahl, S. (in press). Connecting school and home: Constructing partnerships to foster reading development. In L. Baker, P. Afflerbach, & D. Reinking (Eds.), *Developing engaged readers in school and home communities*. Hillsdale, NJ: Erlbaum.

Baker, L., Sonnenschein, S., Serpell, R., Fernandez-Fein, S., & Scher, D. (1994). *Contexts of emergent literacy: Everyday home experiences of urban prekindergarten children*. (Research Rep.) Athens, GA: National Reading Research Center, University of Georgia and University of Maryland.

Bronfenbrenner, U. (1979). *The ecology of human development*. Cambridge, MA: Harvard University Press.

Goldenberg, C., Reese, L., & Gallimore, R. (1992). Effects of literacy materials from school on Latino children's home experiences and early reading achievement. *American Journal of Education, 100,* 497–536.

Heath, S.B. (1983). *Ways with words*. Cambridge, UK: Cambridge University Press.

Morrow, L.M. (1989). *Literacy development in the early years*. Englewood Cliffs, NJ: Prentice-Hall.

Serpell, R. (1993). *The significance of schooling: Life-journeys in an African society*. Cambridge, UK: Cambridge University Press.

Serpell, R., Baker, L., Sonnenschein, S., & Hill, S. (1993, June). *Contexts for the early appropriation of literacy: Caregiver meanings of recurrent activities*. Paper presented at the symposium on learning and development in cultural context, American Psychological Society, Chicago, IL.

Sonnenschein, S., Brody, G., & Munsterman, K. (in press). The influence of family beliefs and practices on children's early reading development. In L. Baker, P. Afflerbach, & D. Reinking (Eds.), *Developing engaged readers in school and home communities*. Hillsdale, NJ: Erlbaum.

Sulzby, E., & Teale, W. (1991). Emergent literacy. In R. Barr, M.L. Kamil, P. Mosenthal, & P.D. Pearson (Eds.), *Handbook of reading research* (Vol. 2, pp. 727–758). White Plains, NY: Longman.

Thompson, R., Mixon, G., & Serpell, R. (in press). Engaging minority youth in reading: Focus on the urban learner. In L. Baker, P. Afflerbach, & D. Reinking (Eds.), *Developing engaged readers in school and home commmunities*. Hillsdale, NJ: Erlbaum.

Vygotsky, L.S. (1978). *Mind in society: The development of higher psychological processes*. Cambridge, MA: MIT Press.

# Chapter 18

# Children Practicing Reading at Home: What We Know About How Parents Help

**Diane H. Tracey**
*Kean College of New Jersey, Union, New Jersey*

Recently, I showed a class of undergraduate education students two videotapes of children reading aloud to their mothers at home. The first tape showed an accelerated reader reading aloud to her mother, and the second showed an at-risk reader reading with her mother. A segment of each of the transcripts is presented here. The first tape begins with the accelerated reader, Jennifer, and her mother sitting comfortably on their living room sofa. Jennifer's mother has her arm draped warmly around her daughter's shoulders. The atmosphere appears relaxed and pleasant. Jennifer picks up a book called *Five Minutes' Peace* by Jill Murphey that she has been reading to her mother and begins to read, with beautiful expression, in a clear and confident voice.

> Jennifer reads: Mrs. Large ran a deep, hot bath. She emptied half of a bottle of bubble bath into the water, plunked on her shower cap, and got in. She poured herself a cup of tea and laid back with her eyes closed. It was heaven.
>
> Mother says: Oooh, that does look good. Like when you go under, when you first get into the bath and you go underneath. Oooh.
>
> Jennifer reads: "Can I play you my tune?" asked Lester. Mrs. Large opened one eye. "Must you?" she asked. "I've been practicing," says Lester, "Can I, please, just for one minute?" "Go on then,"

253

sighed Mrs. Large. So Lester played. He played "Twinkle, Twinkle, Little Star" three and a half times. In came Laura. "Can I read you a page from my reading book?" she asked, "No, Laura," said Mrs. Large. "Go on, all of you, off down the stairs." "You let Lester play his tune," said Laura. "I heard. You like him better than me. That's not fair." "Oh, don't be silly, Laura," said Mrs. Large. "Go on, then, just one page." So Laura read. She read four and a half pages of *Little Red Riding Hood*.

Jennifer says: She keeps saying one and it turns into four.

Mother says: Umm. Do you think that ever happens around here?

Jennifer says: Umm.

Mother says: (laugh) I think so, too.

Jennifer says: Like, may I please have one glass of apple juice? One turns into three more.

In contrast to this relaxed and pleasant experience that demonstrates how a parent extends the text and personalizes it to Jennifer's life, the transcript of the at-risk reader, Michelle, begins with Michelle and her mother seated awkwardly on the side of the bed without anything to support their backs. Michelle's mother sits with her arms folded to herself as Michelle begins to read a book she has been practicing recently. The general atmosphere is uncomfortable and somewhat tense. Michelle begins reading *The Messy Monster* by Michael Pellowski in a halting, word-by-word monotone.

Michelle reads: Picnics are fun to, fun. Do you like picnics? Sam Skunk and his friends like picnics. They had a good picnic place. The picnic place had a, I mean big trees. It had nice grass. It was by a lake. What a good place to picnic. Sam Skunk liked it there in the

Michelle says: Ma?

Mother says: shade

Michelle reads: in the shade of the trees. He liked to sit eating apples. Mandy Mouse liked the picnic place, the picnic place, too. She liked the nice grass. Mandy liked to sit on the grass and eat popcorn. Brown Bear liked the big trees. He sat on the trees and eat honey. Bears like to, bears like to picnic on honey. Sue Squirrel liked to sit in the treetops. She sat and read the, the newspaper. She ate the nuts. "What a good place to picnic," Sue said. Bob Bunny liked the lake. It was a good place to picnic. Bob had carrots and jars

Mother says: carrots

Michelle reads: and juice by the lake. "Picnicking was fun, is fun," said Sam Skunk. "One day I will go on a picnic." Sam went to the picnic place. "Oh, no," said Sam. What did Sam see? The picnic place was not nice. It was all messy. The mess was not little.

It was big. It was messy by the trees, by the grass, by the, was, by the grass, was messy. It was messy by the lake. What a mess there were, where, were. Noddy shell

Mother says: nutshells

Michelle reads: Nutshells, apple cores, and carrot tops.... Sam thought about the mess he, about the mess. He thought and thought. What about his friends? No, Sam had good friends. They would not do such a thing. "There is too much mess through here," thought Sam. A mouse could not make it. A squirrel or a bunny could not make it. Even a bear is not big enough, big

Mother says: enough

Michelle reads: enough to make so much mess. But someone had made the mess. Who, who, who, who, who, was big enough to make a monster mess, a monstrous mess? "What a messy,

Mother says: a mystery

Michelle reads: mystery," said Sam. "I must find out who made this mess. I must solve this messy mystery." Sam want, wand,

Mother says: went

Michelle reads: went to see Mandy Mouse...

My students were astounded at the differences in what they saw. They wanted to know why the mother of the at-risk reader did not seem to care about helping her child, and why she was not more supportive during the reading. They wanted to know why this mother did not touch her daughter during the reading, while the mother of the accelerated reader had her arm laid casually around her daughter's shoulders during the entire reading session. More important, my students wanted to know if the parents acted the ways they did because of the differences in their children or if the children had different capabilities because of the ways their parents worked with them.

I felt that my students were asking good questions and questions to which I had not previously found answers in the professional research. This chapter attempts to answer some of my students' queries and others posed by me. What was it that these mothers were doing differently? What is the nature of the at-home oral reading experience for these children and for others? What do we know about how parents help children who are practicing reading at home?

## The Importance of Studying Children's At-Home Oral Reading

Despite the impressive amount of research that documents the powerful influence of parents and the home environment on children's literacy learning, few studies have examined the natural practice of children reading aloud to their parents at home (Durkin, 1966; Hannon, Jackson, & Weinberger, 1986; Lancy, Draper, & Boyce, 1989; Morrow, 1993). This is most surprising because investigation of the topic seems necessary for several reasons, the most obvious being that it is a practice extensively recommended by educators. According to a survey of 600 schools in the United States and approximately 3700 teachers, parent-child reading is the parent involvement technique most frequently recommended by teachers (Becker & Epstein, 1982), as Edwards also stressed in Chapter 4. Two-thirds of the surveyed teachers reported often asking parents to listen to their children read to them or suggesting parents read to their children. Yet, despite the frequency with which shared literacy experiences are recommended to parents, we know very little about how the practice of children reading to parents is actually implemented and what takes place during these encounters. For example, we do not know if poor readers reading to their parents is actually a practice that contributes positively to the child's overall literacy development or if it perhaps adds only frustrating, negative episodes to the child's experiences.

A second reason that further study of the practice of children reading aloud to parents is needed is that parents want to learn more about how to help their children with reading (Boehnlein & Hager, 1985; Moore, 1990). It has been found repeatedly that parents, especially those from disadvantaged backgrounds, want guidance in how to help their children with reading and writing at home (Moore, 1990). Yet, the only information we can currently offer parents is limited by the fact that it is grounded, almost exclusively, on school- and teacher-based models of education. Are parents to respond to their children's oral reading as teachers do? Investigations of the ways in which parents naturally assist children during children's at-home oral reading can allow researchers to identify parental helping strategies that are, and are not, supportive of children's literacy development. This information can then be shared with parents.

## What Is Known About How Parents Help?

### Should Parents Be Taught How to Help Their Children with Reading?

I have read much of the literature regarding children reading aloud to parents at home and found that the majority of the studies are ones in which experimental interventions with parents are evaluated. Studies of this type train parents to use specific instructional strategies designed to improve their child's reading ability. They report on how well parents are able to implement the instructional procedures and the degree to which the child's corresponding reading behavior changed. For example, some studies have trained parents to increase their wait time before correcting a child's reading error or to be more positive when correcting their child's reading errors (Henderson & Glynn, 1986; Love & Van Biervliet, 1984). Other programs have taught parents to praise their children's reading more often and to use meaning and context prompts rather than just supplying their child with the word (Thurston & Dasta, 1990; Wilks & Clarke, 1988).

Efforts to teach parents strategies to help their children with reading have been largely successful (for a review of programs see Topping & Wolfendale, 1985, and Topping, 1986). Most studies show that parents are able to learn and use the experimental strategies and that children's reading often improves as a result of the experimental intervention. While it is promising that parents are able to implement strategies taught to them, it is disheartening that the content of what parents are taught to do is based exclusively on studies of what successful teachers do, rather than on studies of what parents of successful readers do. Common sense dictates that programs should be available to guide parents in how to help their children with reading because, as noted earlier, many parents strongly desire such assistance. However, for programs to be most appropriate and effective, interventions must consider findings from studies in which parents of successful readers help their children read, rather than rely exclusively on studies of teachers and students reading at school. At present, too few programs meet this criterion.

## How Does Frequency of Practice Relate to Children's Reading Achievement?

With the strong positive relationship that has been reported between the frequency with which parents read to children and children's reading achievement (Anderson et al., 1985) it is surprising that mixed findings have been reported regarding the relationship between how often children read to their parents and children's reading achievement. For example, Francis (1975) and Hewison and Tizard (1980) reported positive relationships between how often children read aloud to their parents and children's reading achievement. In fact, Hewison and Tizard found that the frequency with which children read aloud to their parents was more closely related to children's reading achievement than was how often parents read aloud to their children. In contrast, my own work has shown a different pattern (Tracey & Young, 1994). In examining the self-reported practices of college-educated mothers of third grade at-risk and accelerated readers, I found that accelerated and at-risk readers did not differ in the frequency with which they read aloud to their parents during first grade, and that at the second and third grade levels *at-risk readers read aloud to their parents significantly more frequently than did their accelerated peers*. Thus, this work suggests that the simple issue of frequency of practice was not positively related to improved reading ability. One explanation for these findings is that, for the older, proficient readers, oral reading practice was being replaced by silent, independent reading. Meanwhile, the at-risk children continued reading aloud for practice. The finding that second and third grade at-risk readers were reading aloud to their parents more frequently than were second and third grade accelerated readers also underscores the perceived value that parents of poor readers place on this practice.

## How Does Children's Reading to Parents Compare to Their Reading to Teachers?

In one study, descriptions of children reading aloud to their parents were compared to descriptions of the same children reading aloud to

*Mother and child practice reading at home together.*

their teachers (Hannon, Jackson, & Weinberger, 1986). Among many observations it was found that parents were more likely to intervene during children's reading in response to reading errors, whereas teachers were more likely to intervene at other times. Also, it was found that parents were more likely to use criticism during children's oral reading than were teachers. Advantages to parent reading sessions were found in the fact that at-home reading lasted longer than school reading sessions and there were fewer external interruptions during reading. The researchers concluded that there was no support for the belief that working-class parents were inadequate to hear their children read, and that, in contrast, parental practices were mostly very similar to teachers' practices in hearing children read. While this study has added to our knowledge of the reading practices between parents and children, it has been criticized for its lack of authenticity because parents in the study were provided with a list of what to do and what not to do during reading (Francis, 1987).

## How Does a Child's Gender Affect His or Her Oral Reading at Home?

When examining sex differences, I was interested in how often boys versus girls read aloud to their parents as well as the differences between the conversations of boys reading aloud to their mothers versus girls reading aloud to their mothers (Tracey & Young, 1994). Interestingly, there were no differences with regard to sex for any of the factors measured. Specifically, neither boys nor girls read aloud to their mothers significantly more frequently than the other at the first, second, or third grade levels. With regard to the conversations between the children and their mothers during the children's oral reading, neither girls nor boys spoke more during the reading sessions, and mothers did not use error corrections, comments, or questions more frequently with boys or girls during their children's oral reading. Although no other studies were found, this study suggests that a child's sex is not a primary factor affecting either the frequency or the quality of children's at-home oral reading.

## How Does the Difficulty of the Text Affect Children's Oral Reading at Home?

In reviewing the literature on the practice of children reading aloud at home, only one study was located that addressed the issue of the effects of text difficulty on children's at-home oral reading (Tracey & Young, 1994). In this study, the oral reading experiences of at-risk and accelerated third graders were compared in two situations: first, when all children read third grade reading material (the grade-level condition) and second, when all children read material matched to their individual instructional level (the instructional-level condition). The conversations during the children's oral reading of these texts were then coded according to the factors described earlier (the total number of words not in the text spoken by the child, the number of error corrections and comments made by the mother, and the number of questions asked by the mother during the reading session). The results of the study indicated that both groups of readers were greatly affected by the difficulty of the text they read. For all children, the reading of difficult text was associated with more mother-child conversation, and during the reading of easy text there was less mother-child conversation. The following transcripts of an at-risk reader and her mother reading both instructional- and grade-level text (from *Holt Science*, 1986, third grade level, p. 221) illustrate the effect of text difficulty on the conversations of a mother-child pair during a child's oral reading.

> Noelle reads: What are these children looking at? You may have seen something like this at home or school. Do you know what it is?
>
> Mother says: I think you left out a word.
>
> Noelle reads: Oh, at *your* home or school.... When you finish this section, you should be able to list ways we can save electricity, describe how electricity is made, describe three ways of producing electricity without using up fuel. The picture above shows an electric meter. It measures how much energy is used in a building. Some of the electricity
>
> Mother says: Start that sentence again.
>
> Noelle reads: Some of the electric companies...
>
> Mother says: Uh huh. Let's start here with this word right here.
>
> Noelle reads: Someone from the electric company comes electric company reads the meter each month. The electric company send a bill to the people in the building. Electricity costs money. People, if people use a lot of electricity they get big bills. We should not waste electricity. That is why we should turn off radios, televisions, and lights when no one is using them.
>
> Electricity is made by mostly by burning fuel. Fuel is something that can be burned. Coal, gas, and oil are fuels. When fuel is burned, burns, it produces heat.
>
> Mother says: Good job.

In contrast to the previous reading of an at-risk mother-child pair reading an easy text (instructional level), a segment of the same mother-child pair reading a harder text (fourth grade level from *Holt Science*, 1986, p. 329) is presented here:

Mother says: Let's read that from the beginning.

Noelle reads: Insect poisons, insect poisons that farmers spray on their crops also pollute the air. Some of these poisons kill, kill harmless animals as well as insects. They may also harm people.

Mother says: Pretty close.

Noelle reads: Activity. How do oil spills affect environment? Gather these materials: motor oil, mineral oil...

Mother says: Good.

Noelle reads: feather, water, brush, and newspaper. Spread the newspaper over your desk. Look at the bird feather. Notice its appearance and weight. Coat the feather with motor oil. What did the effect of the motor oil have on the bird feather?

Mother says: What do you think will happen when you put motor oil?

Noelle says: It's gonna get heavier.

Mother says: Umm humm. What else could happen? Two things.

Noelle says: It's going to become black and you won't be able to see it.

Mother says: Well, what happens if it also becomes heavier it also gets, it, it, it gets sticky so that, you know, the feathers aren't loose, they'll...and bunch up and get all squishy and bunch up. It also takes the waterproofing out of the feathers. You wouldn't know that, but it does.

Noelle reads: How would this affect the life of a bird?

Mother says: No, How would this affect a live bird?

Noelle says: It would coat the bird and [uninterpretable] fly over a stream it .would just [uninterpretable] into the pond.

Mother says: Right. Do you think it would be able to fly again? If it got into the stream, got motor oil all over it, could it go up? It would be too heavy, wouldn't it?

Noelle says: It'd go down.

Mother says: Yeah. It couldn't fly again, that's for sure.

Noelle says: Unless some nice group of humans came along and like washed the bird off.

Mother says: Right. Okay. Now,...

Implications of the finding that the use of difficult text during children's at-home oral reading is associated with greater parent-child conversations during reading for both at-risk and accelerated readers are discussed at the end of this chapter.

## How Does a Child's Reading Ability Affect Children's At-Home Oral Reading Practice?

Two studies were found that examined the effects of children's reading ability on their at-home oral reading experiences. In the first study kindergarten and first grade children were divided into two groups: early fluent readers (good readers) and late nonfluent readers (poor readers) (Lancy, Draper, & Boyce, 1989). According to the authors' analysis of the interactions, the parents of the good readers adopted what the authors called an "overall underlying expansionist strategy" (p. 95). This strategy of parental support and intervention entailed much scaffolding in response to children's reading and was characterized by parents' high degree of sensitivity to avoid any frustration for their child during reading. In contrast, parents of the poor readers used "reductionist" strategies when their children read. In these exchanges the children were taught to use only a very limited array of cues, for example, an almost exclusive reliance on decoding cues. In another instance of a reductionist strategy, the authors cited a mother who repeatedly covered the pictures when her child read so that her child did not "cheat" when learning to read. In addition to the finding of the use of reductionist strategies by parents of poor readers, the researchers also reported that the interactions between the poor readers and their parents were characterized by a high degree of frustration for the child and the frequent use by the parent of criticism, which was sometimes harsh.

My work also examined the effects of reading ability on the quality of children's read-aloud experiences at home (Tracey & Young, 1994). The data on the differences between the helping behaviors of mothers of accelerated readers and mothers of at-risk readers were examined in relation to the difficulty of the text read. When reading a text matched to their child's instructional level, mothers of accelerated readers used significantly more questions and comments than did mothers of at-risk readers, and accelerated readers spoke more than did at-risk readers. Mothers of at-risk readers did not employ any strategies more frequently than did mothers of good readers on instructional-level materials. When the two groups were compared on the reading of third grade–level text (which was easy for the accelerated readers and difficult for the at-risk readers), significant differences between the at-risk and accelerated groups were found only in the use of error corrections, with mothers of at-risk readers using significantly more error corrections than did mothers of accelerated readers. Thus, both of the investigations of the effect of reading ability on the quality of children's at-home reading experience suggest that important qualitative differences exist between the at-home practice reading of at-risk versus accelerated readers, and both studies suggest similar patterns of interaction for each group of readers. The transcripts following illustrate the differences in the conversations during an accelerated reader's oral reading versus that of an at-risk reader. The first transcript in which an accelerated reader reads from *Holt Science* (grade six, 1986, p. 306) with her mother, illustrates the ways in which mothers of good readers interact with their children during the reading of instructional-level text. It is an interaction marked by the frequent use of a mother's comments and questions and a child's frequent use of conversational language during reading.

Rebecca reads: Let's not forget solar energy. Engineers and architects are finding ways to use solar heat. Solar cells for making electricity are except, are expensive. But scientists feel they are close to making them very cheaply. The roofs of buildings then could be huge solar batteries. Biologists have found a new way to grow vegetables and grains without soil. They grow them in trays that contain special chemicals dissolved in water. This method of growing plants is called hydroponics.

Mother says: Umm hmm.

Rebecca reads: Hydroponics can be used where the soil is poor. The deserts, for example, have poor soil. Or hydroponics can be used indoors in climates that permit, permit little growth. With, with, with used indoors

Mother says: Artificial light

Rebecca reads: With artificial light, the floors of tall city buildings could be farms of the future. Then food would not have to be grown thousands of miles from where it is used.

Mother says: Do you know where else hydroponics is used?

Rebecca says: Where?

Mother says: In space stations.

Rebecca: (laughs)

Mother says: Yeah, isn't that incredible? Because they don't have to transport soil, and why would you not want to have to bring soil on a spaceship?

Rebecca says: Because it's just going to float in the air.

Mother says: Well, not necessarily float but think about, well, you've never carried a bag of soil have you?

Rebecca says: No.

Mother says: Can you make a guess at how heavy you think it might be?

Rebecca says: 80 pounds.

Mother says: Well, a bag, it depends on if you get a 5-pound bag. Do you think soil, a lot of soil, would be heavy or light?

Rebecca says: Heavy.

Mother says: Mucho heavy. So there's no way they're going to want to transport soil in a spacecraft if they have to use all this fuel to get the heavy spacecraft with all the soil off the launchpad. But, hydroponics. All they have to do is have water. And there's a lot of ways they can recycle water and use it for this. You know, you saw hydroponics. At Disneyworld. Remember, we took those boats?

Rebecca says: No.

Mother says: Yeah. We, it was, what was it? Forest, rain, not rain forest. We took boats and they took us through. And it told you about how, how food is produced, how it's grown, and then at the end of it they had all this, all the plants were growing from the ceiling. Remember? They had them on things on the ceiling. You do.

In contrast, the following transcript segment illustrates what the reading experience is like for an at-risk reader, Scott (who reads from *Holt Science*, grade three, 1986, p. 9). In this transcript it is important to note that the mother chose to correct each and every deviation from the text that the child made, even though several of the child's "errors" did not affect the meaning of the passage.

Scott reads: A strong, healthy dog is in the backyard.

Mother says: Is in

Scott reads: in this backyard. It is easy to tell that a dog is a living thing. A dog can move by itself. The swimming

Mother says: No. The

Scott reads: swing in the picture can also move. But it cannot move by itself. A swing is a nonliving thing. You know what? Do you know why animals must eat young animals.

Mother says: No. The end of that sentence. "Do you know why animals must eat?" It's a question.

Scott says: Okay.

Scott reads: You

Mother says: No.

Scott reads: Your, young animals need food to grow and stay...

Mother says: And to

Scott reads: and to stay alive. Grown animals need food, too. Does a swing need food? Does a swing grow? The answer to the questions...

Mother says: These questions

Scott reads: these questions are no. Now, ask questions about other things in the picture on page eight. If the answers are yes, the living, these are living things. Living things.

Mother says: These are living things. Period.

## Implications for Practitioners

One of the first issues addressed in this chapter was that of the frequency with which children read aloud at home. Based on a review of the literature available on this topic, it appears that not only is at-home oral reading a frequently recommended practice, but it is a frequently implemented practice as well (Becker & Epstein, 1982; Epstein & Becker, 1982; Tracey & Young, 1994). Although the results from my work in this area should only be generalized to communities of similar socioeconomic profiles, the finding that children from middle- and upper-middle class families are indeed reading aloud to parents at home frequently is important information for the many practitioners who work in such areas. I would encourage educators from such communities to keep in mind the likelihood that many of their young students are engaged in frequent at-home oral reading sessions with their parents. This information can be used when planning opportunities for parent involvement or classroom extension assignments. For educators working in less advantaged districts, I am not aware of any studies that have specifically examined the frequency with which children from low-SES backgrounds read aloud to their parents or other caregivers. I do, however, believe that this information is critically important to obtain and hope to collect such data in the future. Meanwhile, I hope that educators from low-SES districts continue to encourage children to read aloud to their parents at home. Particularly for adults of limited literacy ability, having children read aloud to them may be one way in which literature can be shared within the family in a positive way.

Another issue examined in the reviewed literature is the relationship between how often children read aloud at home and children's reading ability. While several studies reported strong positive relationships between the frequency with which children read aloud at home and children's reading ability, my work indicated that all children read aloud for similar time periods in first grade and that as children became better readers, they read aloud to their parents less frequently. Presumably, oral reading to parents is replaced by silent, independent reading as children improve in ability. In considering these opposite findings, I am struck by how commonsensical each finding is, independent of the other: for example, it makes sense that the more that children read aloud, the better readers they will become; it also makes sense that as children become better readers they will read aloud less frequently. While I am unable to state conclusively why the studies present such inconsistent findings on this issue, I speculate that the findings are relative to the ages of the children studied. In all likelihood, for younger beginning readers frequent oral reading is associated with improved reading performance. As children become more mature, however, the better readers will begin to read independently, in place of reading aloud to their parents.

I believe the most important practical implication of the relationship between the frequency of at-home oral reading and children's reading ability is the finding that older, poor readers read aloud more frequently to their parents than do older, better readers. The finding that third grade at-risk readers read aloud to their parents or other caregivers more than twice as much as their accelerated peers indicates two very important points. First, it validates the belief that both parents and teachers consider at-home oral reading practice to facilitate reading improvement. If parents and teachers did not highly value such a practice it is unlikely that we would see it occurring with such frequency. Second, the finding underscores the importance of the quality of these at-home reading sessions for the at-risk reader. I believe that if we, as educators, are encouraging at-home oral reading practice and if our recommendations are being implemented, as the data suggest they are, then we are obligated to consider the quality of these at-home reading experiences for children, particularly for at-risk readers.

The results of the studies examined on this topic suggest that important differences do exist between the ways in which mothers of at-risk and accelerated readers help their children during their oral reading at home. More important, the differences between the helping behaviors of mothers of at-risk readers and mothers of accelerated readers are observable even when the text read has been individually matched to the child's ability level. Practitioners can use the knowledge that mothers of accelerated readers ask more questions and make more comments during children's oral reading than do mothers of at-risk readers to help parents of at-risk readers improve their coaching style. Adopting what Lancy, Draper, and Boyce (1989) have called an expansionist strategy may help parents of at-risk readers become more effective. Practitioners can help parents learn scaffolding techniques and increase awareness of their child's frustration level. Similarly, at-risk readers can be encouraged to engage in more conversation during their reading sessions, as do their accelerated peers.

With regard to the difficulty of reading material, based on strong evidence, educators can feel confident that difficult reading material is associated with more commenting and questioning from parents, and more language use from children having both above and below average reading skill (Tracey & Young, 1994). The use of difficult text is also associated with more frequent error correction interventions by parents of at-risk children, which may lead to negative reading experiences for this group. Teachers who choose to send home difficult texts for at-home oral reading to promote increased conversations between parents and children should consider alerting parents of at-risk readers to avoid overcorrecting during the reading session. Simply telling the child the correct word or words will allow the parents and children to experience the benefits associated with reading a harder text (in other words, increased parental and child conversation) while minimizing the negative effect associated with overcorrecting.

The study of children reading to parents at home is a relatively new area of investigation within the field of family literacy, which has opportunities for meaningful understanding of the ways in which parents and children influence each other during children's literacy development. This area of study also holds great promise for collaborative efforts between researchers and practitioners, which can lead to real-life improvements for many children's at-home literacy experiences.

## References

Anderson, R.C., Hiebert, E.H., Scott, J.A., & Wilkinson, I. (1985). *Becoming a nation of readers: The report of the Commission on Reading*. Washington, DC: The National Institute of Education.

Becker, H.J., & Epstein, J.L. (1982). Parent involvement: A survey of teacher practices. *The Elementary School Journal, 83*, 85–102.

Boehnlein, M.M., & Hager, B.H. (1985). *Children, parents, and reading: An annotated bibliography*. Newark, DE: International Reading Association.

Durkin, D. (1966). *Children who read early*. New York: Teachers College Press.

Epstein, J.L., & Becker, H.J. (1982). Teachers' reported practices of parent involvement: Problems and possibilities. *The Elementary School Journal, 83*, 102–113.

Francis, H. (1975). *Language in childhood*. London: Paul Elek.

Francis, H. (1987). Hearing beginning readers read: Problems of relating practice to theory in interpretation and evaluation. *British Educational Research Journal, 13*(3), 215–225.

Hannon, P., Jackson, A., & Weinberger, J. (1986). Parents' and teachers' strategies in hearing young children read. *Research Papers in Education, 1*, 6–25.

Henderson, W., & Glynn, T. (1986). A feedback procedure for teacher trainees working with parent tutors of reading. *Educational Psychology, 6*, 159–177.

Hewison, J., & Tizard, J. (1980). Parental involvement and reading attainment. *British Journal of Educational Psychology, 50*, 209–215.

Lancy, D.F., Draper, K.D., & Boyce, G. (1989). Parental influence on children's acquisition of reading. *Contemporary Issues in Reading, 4*(1), 83–93.

Love, J., & Van Biervliet, A. (1984). Training parents to be home reading tutors: Generalization of children's reading skills from home to school. *The Exceptional Child, 31*(2), 114–126.

Moore, E.K. (1990). *Increasing parental involvement as a means of improving our nation's schools*. Washington, DC. (ED 325 232)

Morrow, L.M. (1993). *Literacy development in the early years: Helping children learn to read and write* (2nd ed.). Englewood Cliffs, NJ: Prentice-Hall.

Thurston, L.P., & Dasta, K. (1990). An analysis of in-home parent tutoring procedures at home and in school and on parents' tutoring behaviors. *Remedial and Special Education, 11*(4), 41–51.

Topping, K.J. (1986). *Parents as educators*. London: Croom Helm.

Topping, K.J., & Wolfendale, S. (1985). *Parental involvement in children's reading.* London: Croom Helm.

Tracey, D.H., & Young, J.W. (1994). Mother-child interactions during children's oral reading at home. In D. Leu & C. Kinzer (Eds.), *Multidimensional aspects of literacy research, theory, and practice* (Forty-third yearbook of the National Reading Conference (pp. 342–350). Chicago, IL: National Reading Conference.

Wilks, R.T., & Clarke, V.A. (1988). Training versus non-training of mothers as home reading tutors. *Perceptual and Motor Skills, 67,* 135–142.

## Children's Books

*Holt Science.* (1986). New York: Holt, Rinehart and Winston.

Murphey, J. (1986). *Five minutes' peace.* New York: Putnam.

Pellowski, M.J. (1986). *The messy monster.* New York: Troll.

# Chapter 19

# Shared Lives and Shared Stories: Exploring Critical Literacy Connections Among Family Members

Daniel Madigan
*Bowling Green State University, Bowling Green, Ohio*

*In the small conference room, crowded with eight- and nine-year-old children and their proud parents, he looked out of place. He was about 20 years old, dressed in suit and tie, with a serious smile. As he worked his way across the room toward me, I wondered: In what way is this man interested in our forum about children as authors? He extended his hand and said, "I'm Craig. My brother wrote the poem...."*

*Jackie, the secretary, peeked curiously through the classroom door and noticed, I imagine, the chaos of third and fourth grade students moving about and sharing stories they had written. Both Vicki, my colleague, and I had talked to Jackie in passing as she asked teachers if they had anything for her to run off on the duplicating machine. But this time it was different. "Hello," Jackie said. "Do you mind if I come in and listen to the children for awhile?"*

*I wondered where Paul was. He had missed the train that arrived two hours ago in Ann Arbor, and when I called his home in Detroit, the person who answered said he was on his way by car with his grandmother. Then, a taxi cab pulled along side the curb where I waited, and out stepped an elderly, stately woman whom Paul was following. The woman spoke first, "Hi, I'm Aimee, Paul's grandmother. You must be Dan?"*

And thus begins my story about how I was first introduced to Craig, Jackie, and Aimee. Little did I know at the time that these adults would play a critical role in influencing my thinking about the importance of strengthening literacy links between home and school.

Later that morning as Craig and I talked more, I discovered that he was the brother of nine-year-old Robert—a child who had recently written a poem about growing up in Detroit. Craig, a manager at a deli where he worked 10-hour shifts, had taken time off to see his brother and other children from our class perform readings at The University of Michigan—a day to celebrate child authors from an African American community. Craig too was an author. Since he was 13 years old, he had written poems that reflected the social complexities of his life as a young black male growing up in an inner-city environment. Yet until he shared some of them with me, his poems had remained hidden from public view.

I first heard about Jackie through my colleague, Vicki. Jackie was hired by the school to do various clerical tasks for a large teacher pool. Vicki had mentioned that Jackie had a child about to attend our school and that she was curious about what really happened in a writing classroom. As the year progressed, Jackie appeared more often at Vicki's classroom door. One day, she mentioned to me that she had always wanted to write an autobiography, but did not know where to begin.

While Aimee and I continued to stand and talk, I found out that she had been instrumental in her grandson's upbringing since his birth and often had to intervene in Paul's education so that he would not miss out on learning opportunities. Aimee knew what a lack of education could do to a person: reared in the southern United States, Aimee "made it" through school with limited knowledge about reading and writing. At 58 years old, Aimee often imagined writing possibilities for herself.

At my first meeting with these adults, they appeared to be merely concerned family members interested in the educational welfare of child family members. But in each case, as I began to inquire about the importance of literacy for the children in their family, they began to share with me the importance of literacy in their own lives. And as I listened closely to their stories of how they valued writing at home and in their neighborhood, I began to see a fascinating parallel to the preferred writing practices of the children I taught, who shared the homes and neighborhoods with these adults. Suddenly, the student writing I had witnessed in this community school took on new meanings as I began to envision possibilities for forging links between home and school.

## Visualizing Literacy Links Between Home and School

In 1989 I was invited to Parkman Elementary School by Vicki, a third and fourth grade language arts teacher who had lived and taught in the Detroit, Michigan, school system for 30 years. I had been a secondary English teacher for 13 years, but at the time of the invitation I was Vicki's classmate in a graduate literacy class. As Vicki and I shared experiences in our literacy course, we found we that we had much in common. We both loved teaching, and we both had a profound interest in literacy. Soon, despite my limited experience in working with small children, we decided to collaborate and develop a language arts program based on reading and writing workshops for the children that Vicki taught daily. It would not be easy, she said, but she desperately needed help, and I was spellbound by her commitment to the children of the community where she lived and worked. Once a week, I, along with another colleague, was invited to participate as a co-teacher in Vicki's classroom of 35 children. There were few teacher aides in the school and none in our class, a few out-of-date textbooks, and a limited budget for trade books. In addition, the African American community in which the children lived had experienced severe unemployment as a result of the slowdown and closing of auto factories. Eventually, however, our project proved successful: we established new collaborations with city libraries, reading and writing workshops in a rearranged classroom, the Writer's Cafe, a student magazine called "On the Wall," and a video documentary about the children's neighborhood (Madigan, 1993), which the children used as a foundation for writing and critical discussions about their lives.

As our students became interested in writing and reading about the community in which they lived, we began to notice a unique way in which students viewed their writing. At the end of the first year of the program, Aimee's grandson Paul commented about "Enslaved," a story he published for his student magazine: "When something happens to me I can write about it…and that changes me…. I can get ideas from a partner…from the teacher. And sometimes I give the teacher ideas." Paul goes on to say that his writing, primarily about his family and the working-class neighborhood in which he lives, might influence others to see possibilities in their lives. Writing, intimated Paul, just might make a difference in the way life could be in the troubled city where he lived.

We began to understand Paul's literacy perspective, and that of his peers, as a way in which individuals used writing and reading as means through which they become agents of their own lives (Brodkey, 1992) and agents capable of social change (Freire & Macedo, 1987; Giroux, 1988; McLaren, 1989). In commenting on a story she wrote about the death of her cousin, Latoya said, "The more I talked to other people, discussion came out about people and their families, and it made me feel good that I helped them." For Latoya, Paul, and many others in our language arts classroom, writing became a way in which to view the world and as a means to take action to effect change in that world. As my discussions with parents and adult siblings of these children expanded, I also became aware that many adults from his neighborhood community shared similar views about writing. For example, at the reading performance that Craig attended to celebrate his brother's poetry, I met with several adults who talked about using writing as a way to shape their own lives, and perhaps the lives of others. These were literacy connections among family members that neither Vicki nor I had anticipated when we first developed our language arts program—connections that we could not dismiss if our program was to develop more fully. I decided to pursue these connections further.

Studies of family literacy are not new, as the authors in this work have shown. In the past, Taylor and Dorsey-Gaines (1988) explored the ways in which home settings provide dynamic literate environments where writing and reading are an integral part of the family life. Similarly, Heath's study (1983) of low-SES families from rural communities described the many functional ways that literacy was used by adults and their children. Recently, Moll (1992) studied ways in which parents can be viewed as literacy-rich resources that schools can draw on to enhance the literacy learning of children. As an extension to these studies, I have discovered that, like their children, many adults from the community in which I now work have struggled to find ways to use literacy for their own purposes. For example, in an earlier study (Madigan, 1992), I found that despite teachers who discouraged Craig to write, he did. His story revealed that historically his poetry, which describes himself situated in a community beset with crime, poverty, and violence, provided him with a way to become active in envisaging change for both himself and others. In time, other adult family members shared similar histories of critical literacy experiences. None of these adults were professional writers. In fact, almost all wrote as a clandestine activity, fearful, based on their experiences, that their writing would not be accepted by others.

For Vicki and me, such knowledge about the critical uses of literacy among adult family members and their children was insightful. With the opportunity, both groups wanted to be heard through their writing. We wondered how we might encourage the voices of these two familiar groups, children and adults, to interact in meaningful and purposeful ways. And, what might such an interaction mean for the language arts classroom we were continually developing? Eventually, we began to find ways to extend invitations to adult family members to celebrate their own literacy experiences in relation to the children with whom they shared communities.

## Adults and Children as Agents for Change

What follows are three case studies describing Craig, Jackie, and Aimee that reflect extended invitations to adults. These studies, or stories as I present them, represent a number of adults over the last four years who have in many different ways shared literacy experiences with the children in our classes. These case studies were extensive in that they involved multiple observations, interviews, and story sharings among adults and children over a year or more. Because of space limitations, I have written each case study as a partially constructed story that focuses on an adult and the children they wished to influence with their knowledge of literacy. These stories contain multiple and intersecting voices, which represent the complex interactions that occur in all stories. In addition, these passages describe story links between children and adults who share communities and interests. Such knowledge is useful for educators interested in pursuing collaborations that encourage literacy activities that are meaningful to all members of a shared community.

### An Invitation to a Poet—Craig and Jakeem's Story

In early conversations with me, Craig explained that his writing helped him to "get things out." But he also was emphatic that his poems might help others. He said,

> I would like to share with a lot of kids…to let them understand what it's like to be a young adult in Detroit—where a black male's life from the age of 16 to 26 is like little to none…. I want to write this down, to share this with kids…. I'm scared as hell.

For Vicki and me, it seemed natural to invite such a writer and activist to our class. Craig's brother and many other children in our class knew, as Craig did, that life was not easy for young men and women in the community that they shared. Besides, our children also wrote about their community. Perhaps Craig's poetry could help everyone, we reasoned. Eventually he was invited as a guest for an entire morning of poetry reading and discussion.

During Craig's presentation, in which he shared several poems with our students, I was amazed at the complex level of discussion that occurred in the class. In an attempt to capture such a moment, I have particularized the events of that day into an isolated story about Craig and one student, Jakeem, as they discuss a single stanza from Craig's poem "Society." As a guest teacher, Craig proves to be a valuable resource and more. As a student representative, Jakeem reveals the complex relationship that all readers and listeners bring to a discussion about a story they have heard. Further, both Craig and Jakeem celebrate writing as a transformative act and a reaffirmation of their commitment to a shared community. To capture the essence of the intersecting voices in this story, I have layered Jakeem's own story "Emergency" within the dialogue between Craig and Jakeem to represent how Jakeem's comments to Craig have been influenced by his past actions as a writer. Also, Jakeem's asides (noted in quotations throughout this section) serve to reflect similar responses that took place among the other children who participated in the event.

Upon arriving at our class, Craig carefully read his entire poem "Society." It was the last stanza of the poem that really ignited a discussion among the children:

I was once caring and loving,
concerned by travesties, mourning
the cruel death of others.
Now, after torture,
I am just as cruel and unfeeling.
As if nothing matters.
plain and simple,
I am jaded,
I am
society!

As the final words of the poem hung in the air of the room, Craig explained why he wrote his poem. He reflected on his teenage years when he was a member of the M & M gang. "Ever since I was a kid I tried to fit in.... I just felt different, and I wanted to lash out...get in the business. It wasn't the money. It was the point that I was doing something bad." Craig continued to talk about how the gangs and the violence started to scare him. "I got beat up one day, and I just said, 'Forget it, it's not for me.' And one of my friends got killed—no, a lot of my friends got killed."

As Craig paused, Jakeem commented about the poem: "I recognize what you meant when you said people die because of the poisons they deal." Indeed Jakeem does. In the not too distant past lies his own written story about such an issue:

> One day I stayed home from school because I was sick. My father was taking care of me. When my twin brother, Jason, came home from school my brother's friend, Roderick, wanted to see my older brother, John. My father wouldn't let Roderick come in because he knew he dealt crack, and my brother John had gotten in trouble with him the day before (from "Emergency").

As the discussion continued, Craig explained, "I write as a way of getting things off [my] mind that bother me." Jakeem's soft response to Craig was barely audible above the noise of the rest of the children: "Someone hurt his feelings—in his heart. It sounds like he got rid of his hurt by writing." Echoes of Jakeem's own story support his comment:

> On the day I was sick, Roderick came down to my house with his friend. This is how it happened. They were pulled over by the police. My big brother John was with them. The police found crack in the car, so the car was confiscated. So Roderick came down to my house to talk to my brother, John. But my father wouldn't let him in. He asked my father, "What's your problem?" "I don't have a problem," my father said. Roderick and his friend backed away from the house. Roderick started to shoot and hit the window, and hit the stereo. He shot the kitchen and hit the cupboard. Jason and I got down on the floor.

Acknowledging Jakeem, Craig alluded to his own poem and suggested that society is controlling. He explained, "We have to look past that system and change that system. When the system is no good we must confront it." Confrontation was a situation Jakeem was very familiar with. He responded, "Most people in society are hurting [other] people and don't care what they do." Jakeem's written story reinforces his own hurt:

> The second time they shot, they hit the door. My mother came home from work. She is a teacher. My father told her what happened and they call the police. They came right over. My mother called the police at 9:30 p.m., but they didn't get there until 10:00 p.m.

In the final moments of the class discussion, Craig considered his purpose for sharing his poem: "What I hope is that my writing will help people see the problem and recognize it in their own family." Jakeem's comment drew the discussion to a close: "I understand what you are saying. I have a brother who had a problem with drugs." The final paragraph of "Emergency" is a haunting reminder of his level of understanding:

> We stayed with my grandfather until Friday. When I came home, I was sick. My father got protection. Nothing had happened so far. I think of this scary memory all of the time. It's really scary to me.

To clarify the relevance of the relationship between Craig and the children, it is important to step back in time for a moment. Several weeks before Craig's class visit, Jakeem read his story "Emergency" to many of the same students who participated in the discussion of Craig's poem. In response to Jakeem's story as part of a class discussion, these students revealed their fears about violence in their community and talked about how they might find ways to solve such problems. When Craig visited our classroom and shared his poems, our students were already prepared to respond both intellectually and emotionally. This does not mean, however, that Craig's presentation was redundant. As a literacy-rich resource, Craig was invaluable. Our visiting poet reinforced several notions about writing and writers that we as teachers had been emphasizing with our sometimes resistant student writers, such as literacy as an integral part of everyone's life. Craig, for example, was a cook, but used writing, as many of our children did, for understanding his world. Also, Craig's presence allowed the children to view their own writing as important.

Craig was an adult writer who celebrated writing as a living experience, an integral part of his life and responsibilities as a community member. In that sense, he served as a bridge that connected the communities of neighborhood and school. His presence reinforced for our children that communities can and should work together to effect change that is both meaningful and purposeful for all its members. Such a notion has been particularly useful to Vicki and me as teachers who see the fragmentation of communities as extremely detrimental for the children we teach and who see schools as becoming increasingly insular from outside communities. Finally, Craig's visit reinforced our thinking about how to teach writing as purposeful for one's growth as a human being.

## The Emergence of an Adult Writer—Jackie's Story

As mentioned earlier, it was not economic reasons alone that brought Jackie back into a neighborhood elementary school. In an early interview, Jackie commented, "With my oldest daughter, I was working a lot when she was coming up. And now I understand that I should have given her all the time that I'm now giving my baby. It helps them when you listen to them." She had been moved to listen to the growing voice and literacy needs of her youngest child and was drawn to the school environment, which reinforced and added to her ideas about the importance of listening to children.

For Jackie, becoming involved in our writer's workshops seemed a natural progression in fulfilling her needs as a responsible mother. Consequently, Vicki and I invited her to spend time with our students whenever she experienced a break from her duties as a part-time school employee. But there was more behind her volunteer work than I had first imagined. As her daily interactions with the children moved forward during the year, I heard another reason for Jackie's visit to our class: "I want to do an autobiography for myself, and I've started a lot of times, but I seem to not want to get into it," she said during a casual conversation. I was confident that our class would provide a safe environment for her own writing. Jackie added, "This way, the kids can help me, and I can help them...eventually I'll get it written." Indeed, she did write and was able to contribute to our class in ways that neither Vicki nor I had imagined.

Like Craig's story, Jackie's reveals how both she and the children experienced one another's voices in unique and meaningful ways—as agents of change for themselves and one another. And like Craig's story, Jackie's is meant to be read in a dramatic fashion. In the following exchange, Jackie presents and discusses a story she had written called "My Sister and Me" with a group of children who were reviewing the story for possible inclusion in their student magazine publication. Included in this exchange and emphasized in italics are reflections voiced by Jackie, which are echoes of her descriptions of herself as a volunteer in the class and as a participant in shaping the lives of children. This historical voice helps make explicit the act of writing as transformative, as she and the children are altered in the process of the discussion.

Jackie began to read from her story "My Sister and Me" as a group of five children sat in anticipation:

> It was 1959. I was 11 months old and my mother was about to give birth to her second little girl in which my aunt named Darla. Darla was the largest in weight between the two of us. Even at a young age, she and I were just like day and night, and I mean day and night. She climbed trees and catched the boys. I would be making mud pies, and my sister would be the one to throw them.

As she paused in her reading, a discussion began that revealed how the children negotiated several meanings with the author.

> Child: Okay, and you should put how she got that name, Darla.
>
> Jackie: Well, that's sort of going off.
>
> Child: No, it's not, it's telling how she got that name.
>
> Jackie: Okay, I could take out that second sentence where it says, "Darla was the largest weight.
>
> Child: That should be a whole new sentence. You just can't fit a whole bunch into one place.
>
> Jackie: I really prefer not to add another paragraph.
>
> Child: If you wanted to add another paragraph, it's really your choice. Just put it down here where the sentence is short you can explain it, and draw an arrow…and put it up here.

For a moment, Jackie the reflective teacher paused, as if she heard her own voice from the past: *"I'm just there to really help them organize it, like maybe she should have broken the paragraph off right here. I'll say, okay start a new one. They'll say, okay, maybe we'll put this in the next line…. That way they'll feel comfortable with it…."*

Jackie must have sensed the irony of the discussion in progress, but she never let on. She continued to read her story.

> At the age of five all our relatives and even mom would dress my sister and I alike. We weren't twins, but we were the only two girls in our family. On Christmas we were dressed alike. Let's just say all holidays we looked like twins.

As Jackie read, one child looked bewildered. Her own interpretation of the story seemed to be in conflict with Jackie's meaning. The child interrupted, "When you said different as day and night…I wasn't really thinking about the color. I was thinking about an attitude." Jackie replied, "Of course, attitude played a large part. I was the more careful one and she was the risk taker…. We were different. But to the eyes of the people in the house we were alike and we were girls, so we should look alike."

Jackie smiled, perhaps remembering her own compromises with student writers over the course of the year. *"I don't ever want to change their stories…. I try to keep it as much of their words as possible. So we'll talk about it, and I'll say if we add 'and' or something…. We compromise."*

As Jackie prepared to read the final paragraph of her autobiography, she slowed down and let the words sink in.

> By the age of teenagers, my sister and I were totally different in sizes. I was the tall skinny kid and my sister was the short and chubby kid. We were so glad

not to be looking like twins forever. We would laugh at them days. My sister would say, "Remember them pink and purple dresses, we worn one Easter?" I would reply, "Them wasn't the ones. It was them mini skirts that were too little in the first place and weren't our color anyway."

After her reading Jackie was asked by the children to comment on the first paragraph of her story. "When you said 'even at a younger age you were different' what did you mean?" In answering, Jackie fashions a new story, oral in nature, but remarkably similar to her written story:

You realize I explained up here about the way we were different, in weight at birth. I was like five pounds, but at birth she was at seven or eight. So we were different even as babies. But when I say "day and night," I also should have explained a little more. It's because of the two girls I'm the darkest and she's the lightest. It seemed to not make any difference to the people that bought our clothes, though...there were some colors that neither one of us should have had on.

During this last exchange, one can see how Jackie expanded her story to include details she left out of the original story. It was a practice she had become familiar with as a facilitator of writing workshops with children. Her historical voice captures this relationship: *A lot of times they write things that they didn't mean. Okay, I say, so you meant this and this, and maybe they say yeah, and we write it in the story.*

Growth serves as a metaphor that describes the complexity of the relationship between Jackie and the children, as in Jackie's personal growth as she participated in this literacy event. And, as her story expanded in conversation, so too did her confidence as a storyteller and her ability to name her world for the purpose of a better understanding of her life and the lives of others. In addition, this metaphor signifies the growth of the children and Jackie together as they assumed responsibility as critical responders to one another's lives. Further, the children as individuals have benefited tremendously from Jackie's assistance and sharing. For instance, Jackie's participation allowed children to assume new roles as responsible teachers who created learning opportunities for one another, such as they did for Jackie. This kind of transformation, where the teacher becomes the student and the child assumes responsibility for the learning of others, celebrates the inventiveness and creativity of children and allows them to feel comfortable as participants and lifelong learners in the communities in which they live and learn.

As teachers, Vicki and I have benefited from these sessions in many ways. Both Craig and Jackie have taught us the value of opening our classroom doors to other adult writers and readers who have expressed

*Jackie volunteers her time to work with young writers.*

an interest in sharing ideas about writing and reading with children. Most recently we have been privileged to have several new adult guests participate in our language arts classroom: a mother and daughter who brought with them a wealth of experience as storytellers of African American tales, and a mother whose readings of Latino literature are rich and powerful and who has reinforced our multicultural literature curriculum. All these experiences have taught us that we need to listen for future opportunities. The continued presence of adult literacy learners in our classroom has added to the shaping of our language arts curriculum. Seldom are we surprised any more with the direction that these new learning opportunities might take us.

## Looking Beyond the Classroom—Aimee's Story

As Aimee and I talked during the year and shared in the excitement of her grandson's new-found interest in reading and writing, she confided in me that she had been influenced by the recognition Paul received for his writing in fourth grade. As a result, she had begun to view her own literacy, and especially writing, differently than she had before.

She commented, "We can use reading and writing to understand our-selves and others—to feel free to be part of what's going on around you. If you can't read and write well you don't understand and com-prehend too well."

Indeed, at 59 years old and for the first time in her life, Aimee began to use her own writing as a means to become more involved in the community in which she lived. Throughout the first year I came to know Aimee, I saw her transformation as a literacy learner (Madigan, 1992). She wrote a speech that she delivered to her church congrega-tion, and she wrote a poem that she read at her nephew's retirement party. It came as little surprise then when Aimee met with Vicki and me to explain how she was engaged in a letter writing campaign and extensive conversations with school officials about her grandson's ed-ucation. They wanted to put Paul—who a year earlier wrote and was honored for one of the best stories in his fourth grade class—in a spe-cial education class.

Unlike the intersecting voices of many heard in the two previous stories, Aimee's story is a reconstruction of her own multiple voices. In one voice (excerpted in this section), Aimee tells a story about her role in opposing a school system that wanted to redirect her grandson's ed-ucation. In another voice (identified by italics), Aimee reflects on her own past as a literacy learner. As background to the larger story that eventually evolves in this case study, one must consider that from the perspective of many educators, African American boys are dispropor-tionately represented in public school special education classes. And, of the number of children who have entered such programs in the past, 80 to 85 percent never returned to a mainstream classroom. This fact ap-pears to have greatly motivated Aimee's involvement in supporting both her grandson's and indirectly her own efforts to overcome struggles with literacy.

Aimee begins her story by speaking to me about how Paul's ability as a reader and writer was being questioned unfairly by his fifth grade teacher one year after he had proven himself a very capable writer in the class Vicki and I taught. Aimee said,

> It began in February during Black history week, when the children had per-formed readings from their book *Keep on Going*. When the recognition came back about how well they did and how their teacher from last year helped them, it upset one of Paul's teachers. She asked to see me. She said, "White teachers always want to label our boys, want to take over. You have to be careful of them."
>
> And right away I said, "I am not here to discuss black and white issues, I'm here to help Paul."

She said, "Yeah, but see Paul needs to be in a special education class."

I said, "Special ed? Explain to me what that's all about."

She said, "Well, it's when they can't learn. You see, children like Paul will never learn to do anything. He'll probably be selling dope on the street, and he won't even be able to get a job in an automobile factory because they now have computers, and he'd never be able to learn it."

It was easy for me to understand how Aimee could so readily identify with Paul. She often shared with others her own experiences as a literacy learner growing up in the southern United States: *"I struggled through school. I always wanted to learn, but I had a problem with reading and writing, and understanding.... I just knew I was not gonna be what someone had labeled me to be. My aunt said, 'You'll never graduate from high school. You're not going to be anything.' I would get called dumb, stupid.... I would go back over my writing to recheck it, to make sure it was right so I wouldn't get punished, rather than just pick up and start writing.*

As Aimee's story about her grandson continued, she revealed her willingness to act and become more involved in Paul's education.

I left her [Paul's teacher], because Paul was there in the presence of this conversation, and I knew this was not right. But on many occasions we had to talk because she was trying to force me to sign the papers for the child to go into special ed. Finally, I went back to her and asked if I could have permission to visit the special ed class at Paul's school.... I saw children that looked retarded, more or less, spaced out.... The teacher would be talking, and the children were not paying attention to what she was saying. And I knew Paul was not that type of person.

In the past, Aimee had told me that Paul's life as a child had never been easy: *"It was a struggle for Paul coming up. I don't want what happened to me to happen to Paul in the sense that nobody showed that they cared. If you don't have someone to show that they care, then you don't care."*

Like her description of her own past, Aimee's story about Paul took many complicated twists, as shown in the following part of our interview:

I have a cousin who works for the board of education, and she's taught for many years. I discussed the matter with her, and right away she said, "Oh no, not Paul! I find him to be very clever." I said, so do I.... She said, "No, never put Paul in special education."

But they tried to force me to sign a paper. The teacher and another psychologist from the school district came here [at work] several times. Just sign here, they said. Just sign here. One time the teacher and the psychologist went over to my daughter's house to get her to sign the papers because they found out I was not his legal guardian. But I had already instructed my daughter not to sign anything.

The teacher then became hysterical. It was almost like, "You were stupid to follow what someone else is telling you about Paul. I've been a teacher for 20 years, and I know what I'm talking about. I'm a black woman, and I know what our boys need."

As I listened to Aimee's story, her explanation of her custodial relationship with Paul continued to echo in the background: *"I identify with Paul. His mom was always there to punish him. When he'd ask questions she would say, 'Get out of here, I done told you that once! You're stupid, you should know it.' That's when I started to keep Paul at my house."* Angered over the direction that the conversation with Paul's teacher was taking, Aimee responded.

Finally, I said, "I can't trust what you're saying. He presented his story on stage, and you're going to tell me that this is a child that can't learn?" He was tested by one of the doctors that works for the board of education and he said, "No way this child should be in a special ed class. He can learn!" I gave him Paul's school history.... Paul missed two-thirds of the time [referring to Paul's absence from school during first, second, and third grade]. The days he was there he was late. And if you miss breakfast, you don't learn. Your head is not clear.

In summarizing the events of her story, Aimee concluded,

After this incident was over, this same teacher made a statement to me about the teacher Paul was going to have the next year. She knew the teacher very well. I knew right away that he couldn't go there. So I gave him money for the bus so he could go to a school next to my house. It was a better school. I said he lived at my address.

In earlier discussions about how she has come to understand the meaning of literacy in her own life, Aimee reflected, "I'm not so much afraid of being wrong like I used to be—if it's not right who cares? I go back and try to get it right if I can. It's not so important to satisfy anybody else anyway. I'm not that little girl anymore. We can learn from mistakes, and this is what I try to pass on to my grandson Paul."

As Craig said in a post interview, "If you just open one eye, or one person gets the hint, then you've done a lot." Such was the case with Aimee. She learned the value of literacy when she first saw her grandson receive recognition for his written story "Enslaved." Soon after that experience, Aimee began to write for herself for the first time in her life. Empowered through writing, Aimee, like Jackie, expanded her opportunities as a literacy learner. In the process of Aimee's growth as a critical literacy learner, Paul and many other children from our class have benefited. Paul is now a ninth grade student who is progressing well in his studies. He will continue to need help with his reading and writing because of his poor educational background during his first three years of school, but his confidence as a learner continues to grow daily. And as a result of our experience with Aimee and Paul, Vicki and I have become more attentive to students in our class who struggle with reading and writing. Consequently, we have provided new support systems to assist these students by, for example, incorporating a cross-age tutoring program in our language arts classroom. Fifth graders, who were our former students, visit our writing workshops once a week and assist our third and fourth grade language arts students with their writing. Such opportunities benefit all the students who participate in this program, but particularly those younger children who struggle with writing as a way of expressing themselves.

I am particularly grateful to Aimee for showing me that the urge to use writing in purposeful ways is not uncommon among individuals. Such knowledge has encouraged me to be creative and more imaginative in the language arts classes that I teach.

## Implications

Where do we go from here? Vicki and I have had to constantly re-focus on the needs of students in relation to the communities in which they live. This does not mean only developing links between home and school; we have expanded our classroom to include adults who are part of well-established community organizations and who, like our students, rely on critical uses for reading and writing to achieve social change in their communities. And how do we continue to bridge these communities? Some of the methods for achieving these relationships have already been discussed following the three case studies described earlier, but we have only begun to explore the possibilities of such relationships. We know, for instance, that organizations exist throughout the children's neighborhood in which adult members concern themselves with the same issues that concern our students. Two of these organizations are explained here:

1. Block clubs are grass-roots organizations that function as the eyes and ears of the neighborhood. Members patrol neighborhood streets and report possible crimes to police; they help build and renovate homes for those less fortunate; and they assist other community members in many ways.

2. Church organizations hold political rallies to support critical issues that affect the members. They also extend their network of social services to other members of their church and offer Saturday literacy classes for children and night literacy classes for adults.

These organizations provide places where relationships between children and adults can grow, as both groups use reading and writing as a way to achieve an understanding of their own lives and as a vehicle for social change. Also, such relationships allow individuals to achieve membership and purpose in their communities. Most recently, one child from our class, who was influenced by the efforts of block club members and their goal (achieved through a writing campaign) to curb violence during "Devil's Night," wrote her own concerns in a letter that was printed in the city's largest daily newspaper. Like the adults she emulated, she saw a purpose for writing that was meaningful to herself and others. We envision many more collaborations in the future as we continue to look and listen for opportunities to present themselves.

## Reflections on the Future

Adika sits patiently crafting a new play, *Choices*. It is a play about how to choose between good and evil—a play that reflects the persistent tensions among human beings who are caught up in a city that appears to have gone crazy—a play that reflects the life of her daughter.

Although this excerpt from an article published in a Detroit, Michigan, newspaper (Tobin, 1993) is about a woman I have never met, it seems especially fitting for this discussion. Adika's story parallels the lives of Aimee, Craig, and Jackie. She is not a professional writer by trade; she writes in her spare time and is a 42-year-old grandmother who at one time wanted to pursue writing as a career. Instead, Adika has taken on the responsibility of rearing her six grandchildren, and college is on hold. For Adika, *Choices* is an appropriate name for a play that has been written for the main purpose of telling others in her neighborhood community about available choices in their lives—about how others can take charge of their lives in a harsh city.

Like the stories of Craig, Jackie, and Aimee, Adika's story also reflects a tradition of adult writers in our community where the purpose for writing is more important than the final written product. Similar to the children we have worked with, these adults have come to understand the importance of a literacy perspective that celebrates one's voice—a voice that might be able to effect change in a community that has long awaited productive change. Adika represents the kind of example that Vicki and I continue to look for. We would like to invite her to our classroom or perhaps ask her if a few of our children might meet with her to discuss such reasons for writing. Who knows what might happen from there? These are the kinds of connections between adults and children that I had not clearly thought about until an adult family member of a child we were working with said, "You know, I have done a little writing myself."

## References

Brodkey, L. (1992). Articulating poststructural theory in research on literacy. In R. Beach et al. (Eds.), *Multidisciplinary perspectives on literacy research* (pp. 293–318). Urbana, IL: National Conference on Research in English.

Freire, P., & Macedo, D. (1987). *Reading the word and the world*. Boston, MA: Bergin and Garvey.

Giroux, H. (1988). Literacy and the pedagogy of voice and political empowerment. *Educational Theory, 38*, 61–75.

Heath, S.B. (1983). *Ways with words*. Cambridge, UK: Cambridge University Press.

Madigan, D. (1992). Family Uses of Literacy: A critical voice. In C. Kinzer et al. (Eds.), *Literacy research, theory, and practice: Views from many perspectives* (pp. 87–99). Chicago, IL: The National Reading Conference.

Madigan, D. (1993). *Shaping communities through reading, writing, and conversation*. A video documentary produced in collaboration with The Office of Instructional Media, Bowling Green State University, Bowling Green, OH.

McLaren, P. (1989). *Life in schools: An introduction to critical pedagogy in the foundations of education*. White Plains, NY: Longman.

Moll, L. (1992). Literacy research in community and classrooms: A sociocultural approach. In R. Beach et al. (Eds.), *Multidisciplinary perspectives on literacy research* (pp. 211–244). Urbana, IL: National Conference on Research in English.

Taylor, D., & Dorsey-Gaines, C. (1988). *Growing up literate: Learning from inner-city families*. Portsmouth, NH: Heinemann.

Tobin, J. (1993, September 26). 'Mama' once again. *The Detroit Free Press*, pp. 1c–2c.

# Chapter 20

# Representations of Literacy: Parents' Images in Two Cultural Communities

### Vivian L. Gadsden
*University of Pennsylvania, Philadelphia, Pennsylvania*

> When I think about reading and writing, well, I think about getting a decent job, not being poor, being able to make it and help my children make it.... I do a lot to help my children; I buy books and I try to help [the children] read and do their school work. When they're little like [my children], it's important to help them.... I would like to get more schooling for myself, to...improve myself, you know. But, if you work, and I do hard work, where are you goin' to get the time? If you don't work, as a black man you don't feel good about yourself, 'cause you can't support your family, and you may want to help your children and learn things and help them learn, but you are so down that you may not always do it. Education means a lot, it means a lot for all black children, and my family means everything to me!

This quotation is from a young African American male, who is employed, has young children, is experiencing difficulties making ends meet, and values education. It seems that literacy, family, culture, and race are important issues to him. Implicit in the quotation is the speaker's concern about the issues of literacy and schooling; it appears that he is committed to ensuring the education and well-being of his family and also seeks to understand better how to improve his children's academic performance and life chances. The quotation highlights the strengths and dilemmas that many families have. The quotation implies a life of difficulty for the father but also suggests that there is opportunity for the practitioner to engage the father about his literacy needs, expectations, and the ability of the educational program to support literacy learning within his family.

What the quotation does not tell us is what experiences enable the speaker to construct goals, beliefs, and meanings about literacy—what his images are of literacy and a literate person or what frameworks he uses to represent his images. These images may emanate from home experiences, school background, current employment needs, children's schooling, observations of revered individuals, or some other source. Nor does this quotation inform us about what the type and quality of literacy experiences and interactions are in the household, how to help the parent, how to provide this family with assistance, or where and how the issues of culture, race, and social relationships play into learning within the family. Yet, very often it is only this type of limited information that is available to practitioners who must develop approaches to help parents and respond to the literacy needs of families. Neither practitioners nor researchers find that they can access the data needed to address effectively the varied needs of learners and to explore the different backgrounds, histories, and experiences of their families. Here, I do not attempt to respond to this task specifically but aim to contribute to discourses on family and culture as contexts and as texts about the life experiences, literate abilities, and literacy needs of parents, children, and other individuals who constitute the "family" part of family literacy. To do so, I focus on the literacy perceptions and activities of African American and Puerto Rican parents who participated in a literacy program.

I have collected hundreds of quotations from my work that could have introduced this chapter. However, the speaker's demographic background is consistent with that of many parents for whom literacy programs are designed and who enroll in many of the literacy programs in which I have worked. His situation seems typical of other African American and Puerto Rican families living in low-income homes, yet it differs potentially from the experiences, literacy needs, and expectations of other families within his cultural or social group. In this quotation and many others that are a part of the texts of families' lives, parents provide representations of their life experiences as learners and images of a literate person. These images tell us what they expect of themselves and of their children, what they hope to achieve for themselves and their children as a result of literacy learning, and what the barriers are to that learning.

# Ideas About Family Literacy

As mentioned in earlier chapters in this volume, since the 1960s literacy research has consistently highlighted the importance of parent participation in children's early literacy experiences (Powell, 1991; Strickland & Morrow, 1989). Much of this work focused primarily on reading readiness in young children, that is, moving children from infancy to formal instruction in school. Recent research and practice in family literacy expands this work on children within school contexts and examines the role of parents in supporting their children's literacy learning both in and outside of school (Sulzby & Edwards, 1994). Bearing several different labels (for example, parent-child literacy, parent-child book reading, and parent-child interactions), this work, which is widely referred to as family and intergenerational literacy, calls attention to how parents use literacy for themselves and to assist their children. As earlier chapters describe, considerable attention in this area focuses on the effect of practices such as shared reading, availability of print materials, and reading aloud on children's literacy development (Leichter, 1984; Teale & Sulzby, 1986).

## Parent-Child Book Reading

Shared book reading activities have been the focus of research and practice in parent-child literacy over the past 20 years. Although recent family literacy efforts expand on this work, these activities continue as the basis for discussion in the field, in part because family literacy programs disproportionately focus on literacy relationships between parents and young children. Research studies from the 1980s to the present reflect the variety of new ideas about literacy and how parent-child book reading and literature are used in the home. For example, Doake (1981) observed that when parents and children participated in shared reading, children assumed more of the reading responsibility, reenacting what their parents had read to them. In a study of children from mixed ethnic backgrounds and low-income homes, Sulzby (1988) found that the children whose daycare teachers read books to them repeatedly used the same emergent reading behaviors as children from middle- to upper middle–income homes. Morrow (1992) identified several areas in which minority children's literacy improved through the uses of literature. Book reading, book sharing, and the use of literature in teaching reading are central components in literacy practices between parents and children.

Storybook reading is not a uniquely middle-class or mainstream phenomenon, but there seems to be a kind of value assigned to certain routine speech associated with storybook reading—a specific form of speech event. Snow & Goldfield (1983) suggested that parents who were read to as children know how to read to their children; parents who have not been read to may experience difficulty in constructing or re-creating the social routine. The story routine includes a parent engaging in a series of labeling questions such as, "What's that?" and interacting with the young child as though parent and child are participating in a two-way discussion. The parent and child are thought to be engaging together in the routine for which the parent can shift the responsibility of reading eventually to the child. Several research studies have been developed to examine the process (scaffolding) by which children assume this responsibility for print and the interaction that occurs between parents and children during the literacy event (Pappas, 1987; Pellegrini et al., in press).

## Other Literacy Program Efforts

Much of what is known about current notions about family literacy appears to be an outgrowth of reports about program models, many of which are described in this volume. In addition, parent-child reading curricula and on-site school programs have been developed by researchers and practitioners such as Edwards (1990), Paratore (1992), Strickland and Morrow (1989), and others in this book. Although recent emphasis in parent-child programs focuses on book reading, approaches used in studies over the past 20 years and the resulting programs have varied, ranging from direct reading instruction for parents to preparing parents to mentor their own children. Some programs in the 1970s in the United States were designed to assist parents in constructing reading games and to promote their children's beginning reading, such as Vukelich's (1978) Project PROP (Preschool Readiness Outreach Program). Others emphasized parent-child book reading as with the "Get Set" program in Philadelphia, Pennsylvania (Swift, 1970). Several programs encouraged parents to become more involved in their children's reading in school, such as Crosset's (1972) PPR (Parent Participation in Reading program). Raim (1980) in a study with low-income Latino parents developed a "reading club," which was designed to demonstrate for parents how to construct instructional devices appropriate for their children. Several other approaches have been used with varying degrees of success. Sittig (1982) provided parents with packets of ideas that they could use at home. Clegg (1973) developed individually planned learning games for low-income African American parents to increase their children's reading achievement in school. What these programs have in common is that they used a variety of strategies and provided parents with targeted assistance rather than direct instruction.

## Context of Our Study

What the programs just mentioned found was that parents have specific reasons for engaging in literacy activities and that participation and persistence may depend in large measure on how well programs integrate and build on these purposes and goals. Despite the expansion of work in family literacy, we still have many questions, some of which the authors have attempted to answer in this volume: How do parents perceive the usefulness and value of literacy in their daily lives and the lives of their children? What are parents, children, and other family members' images of literacy, literate behavior, and literate individuals, and how are these images connected to their cultural and social lives? How do the domains of literacy, family, and culture intersect, and what are parents' perceptions of the uses of literacy and the barriers to access? These questions are at the heart of a study that I and a research team conducted for two years.

The study, developed around a series of literacy workshops called the Parent-Child Learning Project (PCLP), examined literacy practices and activities within African American and Puerto Rican families in the U.S. government's Head Start program. The objective of the study was to understand how beliefs, practices, and uses of literacy are constructed and used within families and what the literacy needs are of low-income families. Much of what we learned tells us about cultural, social, and familial issues in relationship to literacy and the perceptions and valuing of literacy that are derived from this relationship.

## Contextual and Practical Issues in the Project Development

Family literacy often encompasses a variety of activities and programs, as mentioned. A primary feature of the study and program for parents in PCLP was the expectation that through their participation parents would develop additional ways to influence, assess, and take responsibility for fostering their children's learning. The research team recognized the limitations of the project; we understood that we could engage parents more easily than their children and other family members at the outset of the project. We defined our project as focusing on parents in the hope that in the evolution of the study we would be able to study intensively how families develop as systems of learning and how literacy is integrated into that system.

Participants in PCLP were 25 Head Start parents, who were mostly mothers. Participants ranged from 21 to 45 years in age and had completed an average of 9 years of schooling. Each parent had an average of three children, who ranged in age from 6 months to 21 years. In more than 65 percent of the families, there was a father or male provider. The typical family configuration consisted of two parents or other caregivers, two to three children, and often a grandparent. Approximately 25 percent of the families included other relatives (such as sisters, brothers, uncles, and aunts) or provided transitional residences for friends seeking employment.

Parents met with the research team in weekly two- to three-hour workshops focused on parenting and literacy issues. During these meetings, parents participated in discussions about the purposes of literacy, identified literacy questions and issues that arose in their family, and described literacy activities. Each week, parents completed written assignments, which they and the research team compiled to create a newsletter and a workbook, which was used in the workshop. The newsletters and workbook were distributed to both PCLP and non-PCLP participants at Head Start. Relevant issues, identified by parents and from the literature, became discussion topics. Parents were supported in learning approaches to assisting their children with early and emergent literacy activities, completing adult or parent tasks such as letter writing, identifying municipal resources, and developing communication skills. Parents who needed and wanted intensive literacy assistance were tutored individually throughout the project or referred to family or adult literacy programs in the following year.

In addition to the workshops, the research team conducted in-depth interviews with a representative group of eight parents in their homes. Initial interviews were audiotaped and conducted during two hours by two persons on the research team, one of whom served as a recorder; follow-up interviews were conducted by one person. The primary instrument was a family household protocol developed by PCLP staff, which contained seven sections with five to ten questions each. Protocol items focused on parent-child literacy behaviors and interests, parents' attitudes toward literacy, and their beliefs about and expectations of literacy (whether and how literacy would change their lives or the lives of their children).

The project was based in a Head Start program serving approximately 400 African American and Hispanic families in five sites in a large urban area. The composition of the program reflected the neighborhood, which contains large numbers of unemployed adults. PCLP was one of several programs competing for the time of the Head Start parents and staff. The Head Start program was developed around a multicultural philosophy of teaching and learning. With the exception of two administrators and one teacher, all the teachers and staff in the program were Latino or African American. Children whose primary language is Spanish were allowed to use their native or primary language and moved gradually into English. It was not uncommon in the early part of the Head Start year to hear children using Spanish only; however, by midpoint in their participation, the children began to use both English and Spanish consistently in their interaction with teachers and other children.

## Description of the Project

Research studies (Epstein, 1992) suggest that when participants are part of the decision-making process of a program that is intended "to help them," the program becomes more effective and the effect more durable. Parents bring to a program a wealth of knowledge that is seldom used and that provides crucial information for researchers to link the program to the real lives and experiences of the participants. With this as a fundamental basis of our efforts, we held eight meetings over two months with Head Start staff and parents to identify major issues facing parents and to outline the program prior to its implementation. The staff of the project was interested in providing parents with multiple reading strategies to use with their children and offering information about selecting appropriate books for their children. The purpose of the project was to investigate what literacy meant to the family as well as what the relationship was between home and school that affected literacy development for parents and children. Specifically, the study focused on (1) the ways in which parents integrate literacy learning into their own lives and transfer their attitudes and beliefs about literacy and schools to their children, and (2) the significance of cultural factors that affect literacy learning within homes and families.

The approach for the workshops was grounded in a sociocontextual view of literacy (Auerbach, 1989), within which intervention strategies derived from studies on reading and metacognition were embedded. The project was designed as a series of opportunities for staff and parents to explore the multiple uses for literacy, identify their own uses and purposes for literacy, increase knowledge of literacy strategies and resources, and use these resources regularly and effectively.

The project consisted of 16 workshop sessions. A lending library was created at the project sites, and a mobile library of 25 to 50 children's books was available at each meeting. Later in the program, parents obtained a library card, which they used to borrow books biweekly. Other materials used included journals and storybooks created by the children and parents or developed collaboratively between the parents and the research team. Parents took books home to read to their children and returned to the next session with an analysis of their experience. Parents described their assessment of (1) whether the book would be interesting to their child, (2) why the book appeared interesting to them, (3) parents' ability to read and explain the text, (4) book reading and questioning strategies, (5) children's reactions to the stories and their responses to the text, (6) instruments and tools used to give meaning to the text, and (7) obstacles and incentives to book reading activities (for example, interruptions by family members, children's losing interest, and parents' ability to explain or use strategies effectively). We found that parents had developed strategies for reading, some of which they strongly believed were effective. However, in some cases these strategies were inappropriate for the child's developmental stage or the reading ability of the parents, but in others they were well-developed approaches that promoted children's exposure to literacy.

The session was divided into two parts and structured around a combination of parents' expressed needs and interests and of current approaches to adult literacy. For the first part of the session, parents were asked to demonstrate the book reading, interactional, and modeling behaviors (for example, talking and listening) that had occurred during the week between themselves and their children as they engaged in reading and storytelling. Other parents and the research team used these demonstrations as a lead-in to discussion—the second part of the session—and to the presentation of new concepts. We began to explore a range of approaches that the parents already used or could use in the future to improve their own reading and to encourage their children to read. Parents spoke in Spanish and English.

We participated in a variety of activities during the project. Rather than relying entirely on commercial printed texts, parents and children developed storybooks about the experiences of the children, parents, and other family members. In their journals, children, parents, and staff wrote about emergent writing and shared stories about their lives. Some parents chose to write about their experiences as parents, while others used the writing as an opportunity to explore important issues in their lives. Parents were engaged in discussions about how literacy is used in various contexts and what their specific literacy goals are for their children and themselves. In particular, the research team was interested in how literacy is used to generate interaction within families, how it might expand interaction, and how it may create problems within families.

## Representations and Images of Literacy Within the Families

The research team and I reviewed field notes and interview data to determine parents' knowledge and perceptions of literacy development in their children. Much of the discussion in the workshop sessions, focus group meetings that accompanied workshops, and the interviews centered on parents' evaluation of their children's literacy development as a cognitive and social process. In examining the data, several themes emerged, including the images of literacy and critical issues identified by parents.

### Literacy as a Social Process

> My baby she reads every day, but she don't know how to read. She's only four but she reads. She picks up a book every day. She be reading to her little brother (Sheila).

Like Sheila, a young African American mother, many parents in the project expressed pride that their children were engaged in some form of literacy development, although at the outset of the project few of the young parents saw their children's activities as such. Children's awareness of reading as a social process and social function is evidenced in Sheila's observation as a parent. She suggests through her comment that although her daughter does not yet have the cognitive skills to read a book, her daughter understands that reading has a sharing function and that illustrations in books contain many stories. Sheila stated that this observation led her to believe that her child also understood the meaning of a book—to tell a story.

Project workshops focused on issues in early literacy development. Several parents brought their children's work (work done before and during the parents' participation in PCLP) to demonstrate the ways in which their children had developed early reading and writing skills. The research team was able to build on the knowledge that parents brought to the workshops, help articulate issues concerning the children's literacy learning, and facilitate parents' uses of tools that are influential in their children's literacy learning and education in general. One parent who at the outset of the program indicated that she never used to sit down with her children stated, "It's funny the way they think. You think that because a kid is small...but it is amazing what they know and think."

Parent-child literacy for many of the parents was built on experiences families have around literacy learning in the home and community—those activities that help parents articulate implicit knowledge. In the process of talking with other parents about their children's literacy learning, parents reflected on their own educational history and how their educational development was influenced by their parents and the schools they had attended. They also focused on the role that contextual factors played in their literacy and educational development, which they in turn used in working with their children.

## Literacy as Parent Empowerment

> [My reason for being in this program is] to help my children with their homework, teach them their Spanish and stuff like that. Like sometimes I can help them with their work but sometimes I don't. Sometimes I have to go school the next day to ask the teacher (Maria).

What Maria, a 30-year-old mother of three, describes in this comment is one of the two primary reasons parents gave for wanting to improve their literacy: to help their children with schoolwork or what the parents anticipate children will need when they enter kindergarten. The other reason was to get a good job. When Maria entered the program, her literacy level was much lower than most parents. She was tutored individually by a PCLP staff person throughout the workshops. However, like many of the other parents, Maria tried to plan for her children's future, although she had little knowledge or information about how to ensure the success she wanted for them. She relied on the school to give her that information, and when the information was not forthcoming, she sought assistance from individuals within her community whom she trusted. Not only did the parents plan for their children's needs but they also prepared themselves for what they thought the needs of the children would be once they entered school. In other cases, parents already were using rich approaches to work with their children and communicate with schools. For all parents, it was important to be more influential in their children's lives and more effective in mediating issues related to schooling. Almost 75 percent of the parents in one workshop stated that by increasing their effect on their children's life and school experiences, they could reduce the possibility of their children dropping out of school, "hanging out on the corner," or becoming involved with crime.

Maria's comment points also to what the other parents perceived to be an obstacle for them to be successful in providing educational assistance. The language barrier for the Puerto Rican parents and the educational level of many of the parents in general were seen as problematic in securing the best possible education for their children; parents felt they experienced difficulties in communicating with schools and teachers. Many Puerto Rican parents described their reservations about the schools their children would attend once they left Head Start; they felt their children would lose much of their culture. In the Head Start and PCLP sites, the teachers spoke Spanish and English, and all Head Start sites stressed the importance of the home culture. However, in public schools, attention may not be paid to this issue necessarily. Parents stated that they felt it was important for their children to carry on their cultural tradition but also to learn about the American culture. For the African American parents, the issue of culture was embedded in the discussion of discrimination and racism, as I discuss in the next section.

## Literacy as Racial Experience

We live in a prejudiced society. Not everyone has the same opportunity to [become literate] and get educated. The scale is not balanced in that area (Gina).

This remark by a young African American woman articulates profoundly the struggle in which many families of color are engaged to gain access to literacy learning and education. Only in the past decade has the discourse about literacy taken into account the social and cultural contexts of learning. As I have argued (1992), this debate refocused the attention to how learners from different ethnic and racial backgrounds acquire literacy and has brought into the discussion issues of historical and social conditions in which the literacy learning process often occurs. Gina's observations were reinforced by all but two parents in the program. Parents were keenly aware that while they and their children had access to the school as an institution, they had little access to the school as an opportunity for learning and social mobility. Noting that "where a child lives matters in what happens to [his or her] literacy and education," parents made a causal connection between the appearance of the neighborhood where the children live and the "quality of learning and education that would go on in the [neighborhood] school." At the time of the study, several of the Puerto Rican parents were involved in a struggle with the school district to close the school that most of their children attended. The school had been "temporarily" housed in a dilapidated factory for more than 20 years. In a span of two weeks, several fires had broken out in the library, and parents feared for their children's safety. For the parents it was clear that if the incidents had occurred in an upscale part of the city, the incidents would not have been allowed to continue.

In mentioning the environment as a barrier to their children's success in literacy learning and education, parents did not point exclusively to their social living conditions which, in their opinion, influence access to educational success. Their overriding concern was the influence of their children's peers on their children. On several occasions, in different workshops, parents were very concerned about peer pressure and about the crime that poverty encourages. Many parents felt that their children's peers were potential barriers to educational success or literacy learning. While parents expressed hope that their children would do well in school, they had fears that peer pressure of some kind by "kids in the neighborhood" would undermine their efforts. The parents valued the possibilities that literacy provided, but their images were tied to issues of discrimination that affected the quality of their neighborhood, their lives, and their perceptions of opportunities available to their children.

## Literacy as Life Necessity

> Even a child, an infant, when it's born the first thing they give you, it's a bracelet on the child. You have to read to know whether it's a boy or a girl. You can't try to go by colors.... They don't use them anymore. [Asked if she encourages children to read and talk with her about the stories] Yeah, always. Even though I don't want to listen (Carmelina).

Carmelina's comments here center on the purpose of literacy in a changing world. These changes have been discussed by Wagner (1987), who points to the variable nature of literacy and the increasing need for approaches that assist learners in using literacy to meet their needs. Carmelina, a 23-year-old mother, was asked how important literacy was in her everyday life. She immediately thought about her children and how, at least metaphorically, literacy mediates the parent-child relationship and the parent's knowledge of the child. In the earlier excerpt, Carmelina describes her amazement in realizing that even in hospitals—places in which a patient may be rendered helpless—a person relies on print. By highlighting the fact that hospitals do not use colors anymore to distinguish boys from girls, Carmelina seems to be hinting at the increased importance of literacy and noting that the world rarely accommodates those who lack literacy. Implicit in her statement is the common theme in many of the parents' comments: literacy matters more for their children's futures than in their own lives.

While it is disappointing that Carmelina does not value literacy for herself, she is committed to promoting reading activities for her children. She did not simply put the educational needs of her child above her own desires. Her responses and lack of response suggest that she has not determined how literacy and education might be valuable at this juncture in her life. This may be the result of her own indecision but may be affected also by relationships within her family. Carmelina is expressing a commitment to her child's early literacy development that belies the myth that the "urban poor" do not become engaged in their children's schooling.

## Parents' Issues and Concerns

Several issues emerged from the workshop sessions as areas of primary concern to the parents. The most common themes were parents' goals for their children's schooling, concern about children's literacy in school, home literacy activities, use of resources, family support for education, and functional uses of literacy. The goals that parents identified as important are typical of those reported in several other studies—to ensure literacy for their children and to participate in their children's education (for example, Paratore, 1992). The literacy issues were reflected in discussions about parents' goals, concern about children's literacy in school, and purposes of literacy in the household. Despite the familiarity of these issues, parents' interest in assisting their children was not restricted to helping them read and write but also included a desire and need to offset potential problems that their children could face. Parents sought a forum to engage teachers and administrators in conversations about their children.

As mentioned in earlier chapters, some parents have an implicit distrust of schools and those that administer or teach in them. This distrust is demonstrated in several of the parents' comments: for example, they often described literacy's value in identifying specific problems facing their children—in part because of what many parents perceived as linguistic and cultural intolerance (see Ogbu, 1994; Erickson, 1987). The implication here is greater for Head Start as an educational setting than for literacy as an area of focus in the program. Parents in the Head Start site develop over a relatively short time a high level of comfort working with staff and participating in program activities. Their perception of the Head Start program was that staff made every effort to assist them, particularly parents who had limited oral fluency in English, and to integrate issues related to their families' cultures. This perception contributed to feelings of trust between the parents and staff. This trust was not transferred, seemingly, to their relationships or expected relationships with school programs in which their children enroll after Head Start. The distrust of schools seems to be linked with a fear that schooling requires a trade-off with the home and ethnic culture of the children. Many of the parents stated that they wanted their children to be able to reconcile the societal expectation of speaking English with the family's goal of maintaining the cultural heritage.

In discussing issues related to book reading and other literacy activities, parents were particularly interested in understanding and learning more about book sharing approaches to use with their children. They were intrigued with the ways in which book sharing can become a social activity for their Head Start children and the children's younger siblings and asked for realistic approaches to engaging children and sustaining their interest in book reading. Parents described the book and journal writing activities they did with their children as some of the most useful interactions. While some parents were initially skeptical about attributing any importance to their children's scribbling as literacy, more than 75 percent reported using approaches developed in the workshop sessions later with their children.

Parents demonstrated both understanding of different genres in children's literacy and appreciation for culturally relevant children's books. Almost 75 percent reported that both they and their children were most interested in and intrigued by materials that depicted positively life in their respective cultures. Both African American and Puerto Rican parents expressed preferences for small books that children could manipulate or books that helped them explore a particular problem with a child or that described other realistic situations in the home. The books often were used as a "trigger" to generate discussions about parenting issues, such as talking to children, setting rules, and disciplining children. Parents noted the authenticity of the pictures in the book, the richness of the language, and the relationships of respect among children and between children and older family members and a preference for materials that portrayed boys and girls in traditional roles. However, they were willing to accept the fact that girls could have careers, if it were possible to reconcile having a career with a family.

# Conclusion

Imagine that you are a young parent of two children. You completed 11 years of schooling, during which you acquired only basic reading and writing abilities. You are a person of color or white person, living for the third generation in urban poverty or in rural America. You think it may be possible for your children to have a better life; you wrestle with the push-pull of reality and hope. You believe a literate person is someone who has status, is employed, can contribute both monetarily and intellectually to his or her child's development, has a sense of purpose, can communicate in any setting, and knows what resources exist and how to access them. And, although you do not consider yourself in this position, you feel literacy is valuable. In many ways, these are the images and representations of the parents in PCLP.

The literacy goals the parents have for their children and for themselves, the investments they are willing to make for literacy development, and their willingness to participate in educational programs often are tempered by hardship and general lack of information. The concerns, views, and issues raised in workshops, focus group meetings, and in-depth interviews with parents in PCLP provide a way of exploring possible responses to the question of images. These images and their representation in the workshops and focus groups provide a way to understand the nature of literacy and literacy experiences within the family and the ways in which literacy functions within the context of the home. Although some parents appeared disillusioned with "the system," their belief in the possibility of opportunity is demonstrated in the ways they chose to represent their views about literacy for their children and themselves; their statements reflect belief in education as a means to social mobility and economic success. The issues of literacy, schooling, and education are intertwined for many of the parents who see themselves as fighting battles to ensure access to schools for their children and needing literacy to win a real or perceived battle.

The implications of this study are rooted in the role that parents can play as collaborators in the development of literacy programs—in the evolution of images through planned activities that generate discourse. Practitioners might think broadly about ways to engage parents in the development of ideas and approaches—to identify the strengths of parents and families. This requires that parents understand fully the purposes of the programs and are able to conceptualize the specific ways that a program may assist them. Many studies and programs are provided for the short term. Thus, schools and other community institutions must participate in the collaboration to ensure that progress made in learning literacy is sustained. These learning relationships must be reciprocal and result in helping parents unmask ways that literacy can increase their capacity as parents, family members, and learners.

## Note

This work was supported by funding from the National Center on Adult Literacy at the University of Pennsylvania, which is part of the Educational Research and Development Center Program (Grant No. R117Q00003) as administered by the Office of Educational Research and Improvement, U.S. Department of Education, in cooperation with the Departments of Labor and Health and Human Services. The opinions expressed here do not necessarily reflect the position or policies of the National Center on Adult Literacy, the Office of Educational Research and Improvement, or the U.S. Department of Education.

## References

Auerbach, E.R. (1989). Toward a socio-contextual approach to family literacy. *Harvard Educational Review, 59*, 165–187.

Clegg, B.E. (1973, April). *The effectiveness of learning games used by economically disadvantaged parents to increase the reading achievement of their children.* Paper presented at the annual meeting of the Educational Research Association, San Francisco, CA.

Crosset, R.J. (1972). *The extent and effect of parents' participating in their children's beginning reading program: An inner-city project* (ED 076 946).

Doake, D.B. (1981). *Book experience and emergent reading behaviour in preschool children.* Unpublished doctoral dissertation, University of Alberta, Canada.

Edwards, P. (1990). *Talking your way to literacy: A program to help non-reading parents prepare their children for reading.* Chicago, IL: Children's Press.

Epstein, J.L. (1992). School and family partnerships. In M. Alkin (Ed.), *Encyclopedia of Educational Research.* New York: Macmillan.

Erickson, F. (1987). Transformation and school success: The politics and culture of educational achievement. *Anthropology and Education Quarterly, 18*, 335–356.

Gadsden, V.L. (1992). Parents, children, and literacy: Linking literacy events across sociocultural contexts. *New directions in child and family research: Shaping Head Start in the 90s.* New York: National Council of Jewish Women and the Society of Research in Child Development.

Leichter, H.J. (1984). Families as environments for literacy. In H. Goelman, A. Oberg, & F. Smith (Eds.), *Awakening to Literacy* (pp. 38–50). Portsmouth, NH: Heinemann.

Morrow, L.M. (1992). The impact of a literature-based program on literacy achievement, use of literature, and attitudes of children from minority backgrounds. *Reading Research Quarterly, 27*, 251–273.

Ogbu, J.U. (1994). Minority adaptation and literacy in comparative perspective. In V.L. Gadsden & D.A. Wagner (Eds.), *Literacy among African American youth: Issues in learning, teaching, and schooling.* Cresskill, NJ: Hampton.

Pappas, C.C. (1987). Exploring the textual properties of "protoreading." In R. Steele & T. Threadgold (Eds.), *Language topics: Essays in honour of Michael Halliday* (Vol. 1, pp. 137–162). Amsterdam, NET: John Benjamins.

Paratore, J. (1992, December). *An investigation of the effects of an intergenerational approach to literacy on the literacy behaviors of adults and on the practice of family literacy.* Paper presented at the National Reading Conference, San Antonio, TX.

Pellegrini, A.D., Perlmutter, J.C., Galda, L., & Brody, G.H. (in press). Joint book reading between Black Head Start children and their mothers. *Child Development.*

Powell, D. (1991). *Strengthening parental contributions to school readiness and early school learning*. Paper prepared for the office of Educational Research and Improvement, Washington, DC.

Raim, J. (1980). Who learns when parents teach their children? *The Reading Teacher, 34,* 152–155.

Sittig, L.H. (1982). Involving parents and children in reading for fun. *The Reading Teacher, 36,* 166–168.

Snow, C.E., & Goldfield, B.A. (1983). Turn the page, please: Situation-specific language acquisition. *Journal of Child Language, 10,* 535–549.

Strickland, D.S., & Morrow, L.M. (Eds.). (1989). *Emerging literacy: Young children learn to read and write.* Newark, DE: International Reading Association.

Sulzby, E. (1988). A study of children's early reading development. In A.D. Pellegrini (Ed.), *Psychological Bases of Early Education* (pp. 39–75). New York: Wiley.

Sulzby, E., & Edwards, P.A. (1994). The role of parents in supporting literacy development of young children. In B. Spodek & O.N. Saracho (Eds.), *Yearbook in early childhood education: Volume 4, Early childhood language and literacy.* New York: Teachers College Press.

Swift, M.S. (1970). Training poverty mothers in communication skills. *The Reading Teacher, 23,* 360–367.

Teale, W.H., & Sulzby, E. (Eds.). (1986). *Emerging literacy: Writing and reading.* Norwood, NJ: Ablex.

Vukelich, C. (1978). Parents are teachers: A beginning reading program. *The Reading Teacher, 31,* 524–527.

Wagner, D.A. (1987). *The future of literacy in a changing world.* New York: Pergamon.

# Author Index

*Note*: An "f" following a page number indicates that the reference may be found in a figure; a "t" that it may be found in a table.

# Subject Index

*Note:* An "f" following a page number indicates that the reference may be found in a figure; a "t" that it may be found in a table.

## A

ABC RADIO, 186

ABT ASSOCIATES, 162

ADOLESCENT MOTHERS: background, 105–106; family literacy program for, 106–114; guided participation in literacy, 104–114; as literacy learners and teachers, 115–128

ADULT EDUCATION: integration of literacy program components with perspective on, 178, 179f; literacy program component, 175–176; successful strategies, 176

ADULT EDUCATION ACT, 158

ADULT LITERACY (TERM), 226

ADULT LITERACY AND BASIC SKILLS UNIT (ALBSU) (UK), 226

ADULT LITERACY CLASSES: appropriate settings, 47

ADULTS: as agents for change, 273–284, 284–285

ADULT WRITERS: case study, 276–280

ALVAREZ, RINALDO, 83

ATTITUDES TOWARD READING: positive, 238, 247

AUDIOTAPES: beginning home reading with, 100; preparing, 95

AUTHORS: child, 269–271

AUTHOR'S SPOT, 74

## B

BALILES, JEANNIE, 188

BARBARA BUSH FOUNDATION FOR FAMILY LITERACY, ix, 12, 34, 183, 184–195; background, 185–189; establishing, 187–188; lessons learned, 189–191; look forward, 195; mission statement, 188–189; program elements, 191–195; program outcomes, 190–191

*BARBARA BUSH'S FAMILY READING TIPS*, 186

BARKER, MS.: home-school literacy program, 91–94; letter to parents, 91–92, 92f

BLAME THE FAMILIES: hypothesis for illiteracy, 23

BLOCK CLUBS, 284, 285

BOOK READING: parent-child, 289–290. *See also* Reading

BOOKS: comment, 229; guidelines for introducing, 97, 98f; lending, 203; as reward, 152–153; selecting, 94–95; taking home, 152. *See also* Children's books

BOOKSTART (PROJECT), 230, 233–234

BUDDY READING: lesson plan for, 123, 125f; observation guide, 122, 122f

BUILDING BLOCKS (PROGRAM), 192

BUREAU OF INDIAN AFFAIRS, 183

BUSH, BARBARA, 188

## C

CALIFORNIA ADULT SKILLS ASSESSMENT SYSTEM, 189

CAMBODIAN MUTUAL ASSISTANCE ASSOCIATION, 213

CAREGIVERS: literacy activities for, 47–48, 48–49; literacy instruction for, 193–194; storybook reading program for, 60. *See also* Parents

CENTER-BASED FAMILY LITERACY PROGRAMS: components, 170, 171,

310

73–84; components, 75–79; getting started, 79–80; looking toward future, 84–85; materials for parents and caregivers, 75–78; parent-child activities, 78–79; parent responsibilities, 78–79; Parent Weekly Activities checklist, 76, 77f; success stories, 80–83, 82f, 83–84

FIRST GRADERS: helping, 143–154

FLA. *See* Family Literacy Alliance

FORD FOUNDATION, 168

FUNDING, 182; for FLA, 211–212

# G

GENDER: effects on oral reading at home, 259

GET SET (PROGRAM), 290

GOODLING, WILLIAM, 187

GPN/NEBRASKA ETV NETWORK, 208, 211

GROWING UP READING WORKSHOPS, 131

GUEST TEACHERS: case study, 273–276

GUIDED PARTICIPATION: of adolescent mothers in literacy, 104–114; four processes in, 107–108, 109

# H

HARINGEY PROJECT (UK), 227–228

HARVARD FAMILIES AND LITERACY STUDY, 15–16, 19, 20

HARVARD UNIVERSITY: Kennedy School of Government, 168

HEAD START (PROGRAM), 159; family literacy initiative, 183; family literacy study of families in, 291–294

HEARST FOUNDATIONS, 132

*HELPING YOUR CHILDREN BECOME READERS* BROCHURE, 131

*HIGHLIGHTS FOR CHILDREN* MAGAZINE, 70–71, 72, 74, 75, 78, 84

HIGH SCHOOLS: two-week family literacy unit, 118–126

HIGH SCHOOL STUDENTS: buddy reading observation guide for, 122

& f; Memories questionnaire for, 118, 119f; Predictable Book Hunt checklist for, 120, 121f; Question Typology worksheet for, 123, 124f. *See also* School(s)

HOME(S): bringing books, 152; factor in literacy acquisition, 19–20; of language-minority children, 15–16; literacy connections with school, 271–273; literacy learning opportunities, 236–252; reading-rich environment, 146–147

HOME-BASED FAMILY LITERACY PROGRAMS: components, 171, 172f

HOME CULTURE: development of, 25. *See also* Culture

HOME INSTRUCTION: Even Start, 160–161

HOME LANGUAGE: development of, 25. *See also* Language

HOME READING: beginning with audiotapes, 100; children's oral, 255–256, 259–261; children's oral practice, 261–264; children's practice, 253–268; shared, 87–103; storybook, 54–69

HOME-SCHOOL LITERACY PROGRAMS: assessing, 100–101; continuing, 101–102; for ESL students, 88–90; introducing procedures to children, 97–100; introducing to parents, 99–100; organizing materials for, 96–97; planning, 90–101; suggestions for getting started, 94–101. *See also specific programs*

HOMEWORK: literacy activity, 48

HOUSE OF FICTION, 228

# I

ILLITERACY: assumptions about, 14–22; blame the families hypothesis for, 23; intergenerational, 14–22

# T

TAPE RECORDERS: acquiring, 95–96

TEACHERS: benefits of Early Childhood Project methods to, 250–251; children's reading to, 258–259; comments about RUNNING START, 144; conversations about storybook reading with, 59; guest, 273–276; implications of FLA for, 212–217; implications of national evaluation of Even Start for, 163–165; implications of NCFL for, 171–182; interactions with families, 249–250; literacy learning course for, 60–61, 63–65, 65–66, 66–67; parent response to "Read to Your Child" directive, 55–56, 58–59; teenage parents as, 115–128; thoughts about storybook reading at home and school, 54–69

TEACHING: implications of FLA for, 212–217; parents how to help children read, 256–257. *See also* Instruction; Literacy instruction

TEBBITT, NORMAN, 224

TEENAGE PARENTS: as literacy learners and teachers, 115–128. *See also* Adolescent mothers

TELEVISION (TV): to motivate at-risk populations, 206–217; prerecording appropriate segments, 202; recommended reading about, 216–217; selective viewing, 201–202. *See also specific shows*

TEST OF ADULT BASIC EDUCATION, 189

TEXT DIFFICULTY: effects on children's oral reading at home, 259–261

THOMPSON SCHOOL (ARLINGTON, MA), 211–212

TOMLIN, LILY, 186

TRANSITION OF SCHOOL PRACTICES MODEL, 14

# U

UKRA. *See* United Kingdom Reading Association

UNITED KINGDOM: Adult Literacy and Basic Skills Unit, 226; family literacy practices in, 223–235; literacy definitions, 224; National Literacy Association, 226; non-school-initiated programs, 229–234; reading standards in, 227; real books approach, 228; school-initiated programs, 227–229

UNITED KINGDOM READING ASSOCIATION (UKRA): Family Reading Groups project, 230–233

UNIVERSITY OF MASSACHUSETTS AT BOSTON: English Family Literacy Project, 12–13

URBAN PRESCHOOLERS: opportunities for literacy learning in homes of, 236–252

U.S. DEPARTMENT OF EDUCATION: Even Start, 35, 155–166, 183; national diffusion network, 183

U.S. NATIONAL EDUCATION GOALS, ix

# V

VERY OWN WORDS (ACTIVITY), 76

VIDEO LIBRARY: creating, 202–203

VIDEOTAPES: lending, 203

VIRGINIA LITERACY FOUNDATION, 188

VISITING POETS: case study, 273–276

# W

WALES: reading standards in, 227

WEALTH MODEL: of literacy, 225

WEBSTER GROVES SCHOOL DISTRICT (MO), 163

WGBH (MA TV STATION), 208

WHEN BONDS ARE BROKEN: FAMILY LITERACY FOR INCARCERATED FATHERS AND THEIR CHILDREN, 189, 195

WNED (NY TV STATION), 208

WONDERWORKS FAMILY MOVIE (TV SHOW), 35, 206

WQED (NY TV STATION), 208

WRAP. *See* Family Writing and Reading Appreciation Program

WRAP TIME, 75

WRIGHT, CHRISTINE, 230

WRITERS: emergence of, 276–280

WRITER'S CAFE (REARRANGED CLASSROOM), 271

WRITING: beyond classroom, 280–284; community uses, 21

The Family Literacy Commission of the International Reading Association is charged with conducting research and creating professional development materials in the area of family literacy.

# Also available from IRA and the Family Literacy Commission...

*A Survey of Family Literacy in the United States*
Lesley Mandel Morrow, Diane H. Tracey, Caterina Marcone Maxwell, Editors

*A Survey of Family Literacy in the United States* traces the field's historical development and provides an overview of the current state of family literacy in the United States. This rich resource for teachers, parents, and policymakers includes discussions of more than 100 sources about family literacy. The descriptions in this volume offer guidance for anyone interested in obtaining specific information about particular family literacy programs as well as new initiatives. (IRA publication no. 131-622, US$14.00, US$9.00/IRA members)

*Parents and Literacy*

This offprint of the combined April 1995 issues of *The Reading Teacher* and *Journal of Reading* addresses the growing concerns of educators regarding family literacy. Twelve articles, presenting different perspectives on the issue of family literacy, challenge and encourage educators to review the current programs, rethink definitions and perceptions, and reformulate projects and practices in order to develop stronger home/school partnerships. Included is an annotated bibliography of books for families to read together compiled by Isabel Schon. (IRA publication no. 139-622, US$12.00, US$10.00/IRA members)

SPECIAL PURCHASE: The Family Literacy Package includes *Family Literacy Connections in Schools and Communities*, *A Survey of Family Literacy in the United States*, and *Parents and Literacy* for US$40.00, US$28.00/IRA members.

To order, call 1-800-336-READ, ext. 266 (outside Canada and the United States, call 302-731-1600, ext. 266), or send orders to the International Reading Association, 800 Barksdale Road, PO Box 8139, Newark, Delaware 19714-8139, United States.